Edwardian Monetary Affairs (1279-1344)

A Symposium held in Oxford, August 1976

edited by

N. J. Mayhew

British Archaeological Reports 36
1977

British Archaeological Reports

122, Banbury Road, Oxford OX2 7BP, England

B.A.R. 36, 1977: "Edwardian Monetary Affairs (1279-1344). A Symposium held in Oxford, August 1976"

ISBN 9780904531640 paperback

ISBN 9781407320120 e-book

DOI https://doi.org/10.30861/9780904531640

A catalogue record for this book is available from the British Library

This book is available at www.barpublishing.com

CONTENTS

LIST OF CONTRIBUTORS

M. M. Archibald,
Department of Coins and Medals, British Museum

J. F. Hadwin,
Guildford County College of Technology

T. H. Lloyd,
Department of Economic History, University College of Swansea

M. Mate,
Department of History, University of Oregon

N. J. Mayhew,
Heberden Coin Room, Ashmolean Museum

D. M. Metcalf,
Heberden Coin Room, Ashmolean Museum

N. J. Palmer,
Oxfordshire Archaeological Excavation Unit

M. C. Prestwich,
Department of Medieval History, St. Andrews

S. E. Rigold,
Inspectorate of Ancient Monuments and Historic Buildings

D. R. Walker,
British Archaeological Reports

ABBREVIATIONS

EcHR	Economic History Review
BNJ	British Numismatic Journal
NC	Numismatic Chronicle
NCirc	Numismatic Circular
BullInstHistRes	Bulletin of the Institute of Historical Research
EHR	English Historical Review
CH	Coin Hoards
RN	Revue numismatique
RBN	Revue belge de Numismatique
CCR	Calendar of Close Rolls
CPR	Calendar of Patent Rolls
CFR	Calendar of Fine Rolls
OHS	Oxford Historical Society

KEY TO PLATE I

THIRTEENTH AND FOURTEENTH-CENTURY COINS

1. AR Groat Edward I London mint
2. AR Penny Edward I London mint, class IIb
3. AR Penny Edward II London mint, class XIII
4. AR Penny Edward III London mint, class XVd
5. AR Penny Edward I Durham mint, Bishop Bek, class IVb
6. AR Penny Edward II Durham mint, Bishop Kellawe, class XIc
7. AR Penny Edward II Durham mint, Bishop Beaumont, class XIV
8. AR Halfpenny Edward I London mint, class III
9. AR Farthing Edward I London mint, class III
10. AR Cut Long Cross halfpenny, Henry III (Oxford find)
11. AR Penny Henry III, London mint, moneyer Davi, Long Cross, Va
12. AR Penny John (reads Henricus), London mint, moneyer Abel, Short Cross, Vc
13. AR Sterling Jean I of Brabant, Brussels mint, Chautard 88
14. AR Sterling Gui de Dampierre, Alost mint, Chautard 8
15. AR Sterling Gui de Collemede, bishop of Cambrai, Cambrai mint, Chautard 216
16. AU Florin of Florence
17. Base metal jetton, Edward I, cf. Fox class VIIb. Reverse: Arms of John Langton?
18. Pewter token of type represented in the Winetavern Street, Dublin find

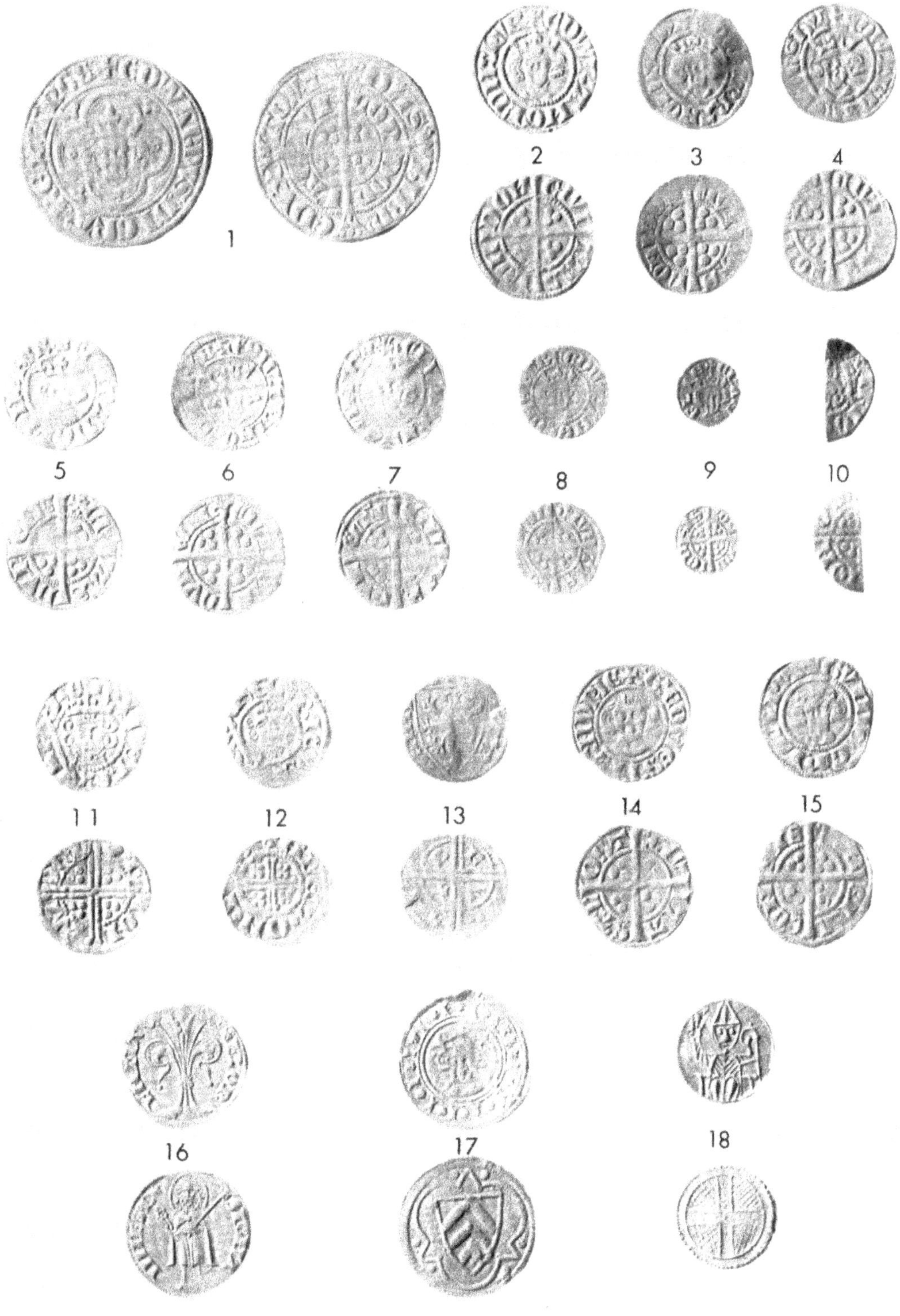
1
2
3
4
5
6
7
8
9
10
11
12
13
14
15
16
17
18

FOREWORD

The papers in this volume result from a Symposium on Edwardian monetary affairs held at the Heberden Coin Room in Oxford during August 1976. The meeting was designed to bring together medieval historians and numismatists, in the belief that they had much to learn from one another.

Although centred on the Edwardian coinage 1279-1344 the Symposium was not restricted to this period and these papers also consider the coinage of the early thirteenth century and monetary problems after the Black Death.

From an early stage in the planning of this meeting I have benefitted greatly from the advice of John Brand, the Director, and Peter Woodhead, the President, of the British Numismatic Society. In the Coin Room the help of my colleague Dr. Michael Metcalf has been indispensable throughout, while the Keeper, Dr. Colin Kraay, sanctioned the use of Coin Room facilities and funds, as well as offering his own whole-hearted support. Dr. Kraay also made arrangements with Wolfson College where we met when the Coin Room was closed, and ensured that the meeting was truly a symposium in the fullest sense of the word.

A SURVEY OF NUMISMATIC RESEARCH INTO THE PENNIES OF THE FIRST THREE EDWARDS (1279-1344) AND THEIR CONTINENTAL IMITATIONS

D. M. Metcalf

Nineteenth-century students were fully aware of the problem of distinguishing between the pennies of Edward I, Edward II, and Edward III, and they satisfied themselves with a solution which we now know to have been seriously mistaken and inadequate. The theory they accepted was that the king's name in the legend on the coin was a guide to its attribution: the coins of Edward I read EDW; those with the longer legend EDWARDVS were of Edward III or IV; and those with versions of the name of intermediate length - EDWA or EDWAR - belonged to Edward II. This idea reflected the wish to be able to assign individual coins to a particular king.

The classification based on the king's name was originated in the late seventeenth century by John Sharp, archbishop of York, and was accepted with few reservations or changes for more than a hundred years.[1] Sharp noted the absence of the French title and of DEI GRACIA on the coins of Edward I and II. "But it is not so easy", he went on, "to distinguish the first Edward's coins from the second's; for the weight, style, face, and reverse, are the same, only there is one difference observable in the coins, and that is in the putting of the name ... All that I dare affirm with confidence is, that all the coins where only the first three letters of the name are put, viz. EDW belong to the first Edward. My reasons for this are two: first, these coins are in much greater plenty than the other. I dare say, I have met with five of these for one of the other. Now, everybody knows that Edward the First coined more abundantly than his son, and therefore, in reason, that must be his of which there is most remaining."

A fuller analysis was made by Bartlet in 1778 using fresh observations which are still an important element in the correct solution as we know it today. The bishops of Durham, who enjoyed minting rights, placed on the coins they struck little secret-marks, and these provide an independent and incontrovertible means of dating the coins. Robert of Holy Island was succeeded in 1284 by Antony Bek, who held the see until 3 March 1311, and who used the cross moline from his arms. Richard Kellawe (1311-October 1316), instead of using a device from his arms,[2] added a pastoral staff as his distinguishing mark; and Lewis de Beaumont (1317-September 1333), whose arms were a lion rampant on a field semée of fleurs de lis, placed a lion and fleurs de lis on his coins. Richard of Bury (1333-45) used a small crown in the centre of the reverse; and Thomas Hatfield (1345-81) again adopted a pastoral staff, turned however to the right instead of to the left.[3] The marked coins of Durham are still a leading element in the dating of Edward pennies today, but our understanding of them is now more detailed, as far as the coins themselves are concerned, and has been complicated by considerations arising out of coins struck with no mark when the see was vacant or when the temporalities were in the hands of the king's receiver, in particular because of Edward I's quarrels with bishop Bek in 1302-03 and 1305-07, and during the vacancy of 1316-17.[4]

Ruding, in his Annals of the Coinage (3rd edition, 1840), gave an extensive account of what was known from mint records and other documentary sources about the currency, as well as summarizing earlier numismatic research.

When Edward Hawkins, of the British Museum, wrote his Silver Coins of England (1841) he summed up the general opinion as follows: "By a careful comparison of the types and workmanship of the coins of the several bishops with those of the kings, Mr. Bartlet deduced rules to ascertain the reigns in which each of the royal coins were struck. An accurate examination of a great number of these coins, found at Tutbury in 1832, confirms Mr. Bartlet's views, and the conclusion drawn is, that all the coins upon which only EDW. appear belong to Edward I, that those upon which the whole name EDWARDVS appears belong the Edward III, and that all the intermediate modes of writing the name are of Edward II." Thus Hawkins and other students made disappointingly little use of the new material available to them, and only saw it as confirming the earlier view.

Sainthill challenged this view in 1851, drawing attention to some light-weight coins reading EDW which he attributed to Edward III. Cuff and Bergne joined in a little debate, conducted in the pages of Olla Podrida.[5] The Edwardian pence had been struck at a standard of about 22 1/4 grains (1.44 g),[6] but the monetary problems of Edward III's reign led to successive reductions to to 20 1/4 gr. in 1344, 20 gr. in 1346, and 18 gr. in 1351. John Evans, writing in 1871, made use of the weight-standards to test the validity of Hawkins' scheme.[7]

When Edward Burns published his great work, The Coinage of Scotland, in 1887 he found it necessary to include an Addendum of some 35 pages on the English coinage of the first three Edwards which, as he says, constituted the main currency of Scotland for at least seventy or eighty years. This fact was known from a series of hoards from the latter part of the thirteenth and the first half of the fourteenth century, in almost all of which English coins predominated. Burns tells how a very large hoard of English, Scottish, and foreign sterlings found at Montrave, Fifeshire, in May 1877 was put into his hands for purposes of study. The English portion alone comprised nearly 9,000 coins of Edward I, II, and III. What Burns says next sounds thoroughly modern, and is different in spirit from the observations of his predecessors. In effect, he described one of the routine procedures followed by numismatists today. "In proceeding to classify the English portion I began by placing together those coins which had a common style of head and lettering, and this irrespective of the particular mints to which the several varieties belonged. In this way the several pieces naturally disposed themselves into distinct groups and classes, each group and class being distinguished by its own special characteristics." He goes on to define and illustrate a series of 53 varieties, arranged into a chronological sequence on the evidence not only of minute differences of style and lettering, but also of mules (such as a coin from the

Dumfries hoard with the obverse as variety 6 but the reverse as variety 5), and of hoards (for example the Northampton hoard of 1873, containing only varieties 1-5, and none with the mark of bishop Bek of Durham, therefore presumably earlier than ca. 1284.[8]).

Edward pennies were minted from time to time at a dozen different mints - London, Canterbury, Durham, Bury St Edmunds, Bristol, Chester, Exeter, Lincoln, Newcastle, Berwick-on-Tweed, Kingston-upon-Hull, and two mints at York, one royal, one episcopal. The Abbot of Reading minted ca. 1338-43.[9] But with a few interesting exceptions, as for example some coins of Bury by the moneyer Robert de Hadley,[10] the dies from which the provincial coins were struck were all made in London. They were suitably engraved with the name of the city or borough where they were to be used - Civitas Eboraci, Villa Bristollie, and so on - and were sent out to the various mints in batches as required. The style of contemporary issues is therefore the same, whatever their mint. Burns recorded all his varieties 19 to 36, for example, from the four staple mints of London, Canterbury, Durham and Bury St Edmunds, while variety 37 occurs also at Bristol, Chester, Newcastle, York, and Hull. Variety 37, it is thus established, correlates with the great recoinage of 1300.

The coins of one variety are all in the same style, that is to say they are all recognizably alike to the discerning eye, because the dies from which they were struck - and scores or even hundreds of dies may have been used up in the production of one variety - were mass-produced from a small set of iron punches. The design was built up, using one punch for the king's face, one for the fringe of hair on the forehead, two for the curls of hair to left and right, another for the crown, and a few simple straight lines, crescents, and wedges for the lettering.[11] Thus two coins may be struck from different dies, and yet may have the same face, indeed all the same details, with only the smallest differences in their alignment, because they originate from the same punches. It is usual to call the workmen who made dies by this method die-sinkers rather than die-cutters; little artistry was required. The punches in time wore out or were replaced, either as a group or piece-meal, and the identification of individual punches can be an extremely convincing method of arranging the varieties into their correct order on points of detail.

Burns' classification suffered the unkind fate of neglect.[12] It was then eclipsed, from 1909 onwards, by an outstandingly thorough and successful monograph of 135 pages on the same subject, published in instalments in the British Numismatic Journal by the brothers H. B. Earle Fox and J. S. (Shirley-) Fox.[13] Their detailed researches, based on a clear understanding of the way dies were made and supplied, and on a step-by-step correlation of numismatic and documentary evidence, led them to essentially the same scheme as Burns had established, but they used a different system of numbering, which placed the pence struck from 1279 to 1343 into Groups I-XV. Several of the groups are subdivided, as for example Group IV, a,b,c,d, and e. The characteristics by which each group can be recognized are clearly defined, and there is nothing arcane about the system. Provided that a coin is not worn or weakly struck in some crucial area, anyone with care and patience and a little practice can determine its correct place in the scheme. (The fact that one would often rather run a mile than make the effort is neither here nor there). Those who have subjected themselves to the discipline of handling many hundreds or even thousands of Edward pennies can identify one in a second or two. The Fox brothers, in discussing Group IIId, which is an anomalous early group minted only at the four northern mints of York, Durham, Chester, and Newcastle in 1280-81, say that "although it is difficult to explain wherein IIId differs from the southern coins, with a little practice specimens may be picked out of a heap of pennies without reference to the reverse."

The groups are identificatory in their nature, and that is all they are intended to be. They are not related to the length of time for which any particular variety was struck: Groups I, II, and III all fall within the period 1279-81, whereas Group VIII, for example, lasted from about 1294 to 1300. Nor are they related to the quantities of pence that were minted.

The same general principles apply to the categories of Edward pennies, halfpennies, and farthings minted at Berwick-on-Tweed from 1296 to 1318 and from 1333 onwards, for which dies were made locally, and which numismatis s have therefore had to study separately. The standard classification is by Blunt.[14]

The Fox brothers' classification stands today essentially as they left it more than sixty years ago, a monument to their considerable talents for thoroughness and for getting the facts right, There seemed to be little more to be said, until the subject was revitalized by Tatler and Stewart in 1962 in a paper which established a concordance between the Burns and Fox classifications, and republished the Montrave hoard. Tatler had already written a correction concerning the transition from Groups I to II.[15] With Stewart he discussed two further defects in the Fox scheme: the Fox sub-divisions of Group IV into a,b,c had been widely found impracticable;[16] and a fresh attempt to classify Group X c-f had been found necessary when Dolley and Tatler reported on the Whittonstall hoard (discovered in 1958).[17] Some more similar changes have since been made, by Woodhead and Stewart and by Miss Archibald.[18] Since about 1960, then, a small group of active students and collectors, closely in touch with each other, and with a meeting-ground in the British Numismatic Society, in the British Museum, and in the salon of A.H. Baldwin, Ltd., have subjected the Edwardian series to intense critical scrutiny, and as new hoards have come to light, they have published them meticulously. But at almost every point the Fox brothers were right, and each new hoard of the last sixty years has confirmed their acumen. Their work deserves to be read in the original, although there are also convenient up-to-date summaries incorporating the revisions that have since been made.[19]

A separate approach to the coinage of the first three Edwards, and one that is possibly of greater interest to economic historians than the classification of the coins themselves, was made by Arthur Hughes, C.G. Crump, and C. Johnson, who drew up tables of bullion coined year by year between 1272 and 1377, from the enrolled accounts of the Warden of the Mint, at the Public Record Office. Their paper was published in 1913,[20] but they had earlier made much of the information available to the Fox brothers, who had taken it into account in their work, and some of the figures had been included in their monograph. The accounts refer to the work of the London and Canterbury mints for the whole period, and to Bristol, Chester, Exeter, Newcastle, York and Hull for the year 1300 only. Thus nearly all the provincial mint records for the recoinage of 1279-81 are missing, and records for some of the mints, notably Durham and Bury, are lacking throughout. For London and Canterbury the figures show year by year how much of the bullion purchased was English and how much was foreign silver, and thus they give a valuable clue to international flows of currency. They also show unequivocally what very large total quantities of pence were struck. From November 1279 to Michaelmas 1281, for example, the Tower mint put out 72 million pence, 20 million halfpence, and 13 million farthings. Measured against the size of the population these figures raise insistent questions about the monetization of the economy, and one must emphasize that if pennies, as the largest available coin, were often gathered up in large quantities as a store of wealth, this was not true of the fractions, which were deliberately and very thoroughly excluded from most hoards. Stray finds have usually suffered more from burial in the soil than have hoard-coins, and most of the fractions one can see today are rather unattractive, pock-marked little objects.[21] We are therefore much less aware of the halfpennies and farthings than we are of the pennies, and need to be reminded of the output figures. The 33 million fractional coins mentioned above are not all. Whereas Canterbury in the same two-year period put out 14 million pence, with an establishment of 8 furnaces, Bristol and York each had 12 furnaces, and although bullion records have not survived, we know that they struck halfpence and farthings. So did the Lincoln mint; and Newcastle struck halfpence. The continuing need for small change from Michaelmas 1281 until the recoinage of Michaelmas 1299 was met by the issue year by year of, in total, another million pence from London and Canterbury. So for the twenty years 1279-99 we must envisage a total output, from all the mints, of something like 280 or 290 million coins, of which nearly 50 million were halfpence and farthings.[22]

From 1299 onwards (when considerable amounts of English silver were recoined) until the end of Fox Class XV, ca. 1335, a further 300-310 million coins were struck, including three-quarters of a million halfpence and a steady output of farthings at London running to nearly 18 millions.

The groats which Edward I attempted to introduce, but eventually abandoned, are not entered separately in the mint records. From the small number of known dies, one may assume that they were struck only in limited quantities.[23] They are remarkably handsome objects, in an expansive, Italianate style, and often they were gilded and mounted for use as jewellery. Although they receive attention in most text-books, and are sought after today, (one was offered for sale in October 1976 by Spink's for £4,000), their significance for monetary history is much less than that of the halfpennies and farthings.

English historians, as is well known, are uniquely fortunate in the amount of medieval documentation surviving to the present day. The opportunity to set side by side great numbers of coins of the first three Edwards, and a superb assemblage of mint-records, allows the numismatist to check his deductions from the coinage against contemporary written accounts in a way that is rarely possible in other parts of Europe, or in this country before the 1220s. For that and other reasons Edward pennies are the nursery slopes of medieval numismatics.

A notable example of their value as a training ground concerns the difficult question of how many coins on average were struck from a die before it was discarded. Medieval - and indeed ancient - numismatists are normally reduced to pure guesswork on this topic, but Stewart and Mate, in three articles of classic interest and wide relevance,[24] have demonstrated by carefully combining the numismatic and documentary evidence that an obverse die was used to strike, on yearly averages, anything from 24,000 to 70,000 coins, and that sets of dies were supplied in the ratio of two reverse dies to one obverse. We know exactly and in detail how many dies were supplied to the mints of London and Canterbury year by year from 1281 to 1327, and a good deal about the provincial mints as well. The average number of coins struck from an obverse die for Edward I's reign was 39,031, and for Edward II's reign, 28,187. In all, the records show the two main mints striking 420 million coins from 13,000 obverse and 26,000 reverse dies. No wonder if the coins have a mass-produced look.

Even with this magnificently detailed information, there are residual problems in trying to match the Fox varieties closely against the bullion records. The difficulties arise mainly because the groups do not coincide with the accounting periods.[25]

The real historical interest of the output figures, however, lies not in the Edwardian totals by themselves, but in a comparison with earlier periods. The figures adding up to about 280 or 290 million coins for the years 1279-99 and 300 or 310 million in 1299-1335 are not in any way exceptional. Throughout the thirteenth century England was awash with silver. In the immediately preceding Long Cross coinage of Henry III, from 1247 to 1279, 332 million pennies were struck at London and Canterbury alone, and the provincial mints, for which records are lacking, would boost this total to between 400 and 450 million pennies. Many of these were then cut with shears to make halfpennies and farthings, thus adding some further tens of millions to the total numbers of coins. For the Short Cross coinage from 1180 to 1247 the records are incomplete, but we know that London and Canterbury struck at least 160 million pennies between 1220 and 1247, i.e. in Classes VII and VIII, when the Short Cross coinage had already been in issue for the preceding forty years, with 16 mints operating.[26]

We have reason to think that in the time of Henry I the stock of bullion in England was utterly depleted, particularly up to c. 1125. Even as late as 1180 there was far less coinage than in the Short Cross period. A detailed estimate is possible of the original volume of output of Henry II's Cross-and-crosslets or Tealby coinage, struck from 1158 to 1180. Some 1285 surviving identifiable coins were meticulously checked for die-identity by D. F. Allen, who catalogued about 700 obverse dies, and almost exactly the same number of reverse dies. A method of statistical estimation developed by Lyon in connection with the corpus of coins of the Lincoln mint, and suitable where output per die is uneven, indicates an original total output equivalent to that from about 1,400 pairs of dies. If the average output of a die was the same as in the time of Edward I - and it seems unlikely that it was so high - the total Cross-and-crosslets coinage amounted to no more than 30 million coins. If the average output of a die was lower, the figure may have been nearer 20 millions. And whatever the total was, by 1180 a proportion of it is likely to have vanished away. As it is important that confidence should be placed in this estimate, the statistical details have been discussed in an Appendix (see below pp. 26-31). It is very clear that, leaving aside any short-term fluctuations, the volume of the English currency was rising like a rocket between 1180 and 1280. The figures indicate an astonishing fifteen- or twenty-fold increase in the quantities of coinage leaving the mint. There is a significant conflict of evidence here with the statistics from site-finds, admirably surveyed below by S. E. Rigold. His figures show that losses increased at a much more modest rate, three- or fourfold.[27] The facts are sufficiently clear to require explanation. Some of the Short Cross and Long Cross coinage may have very soon been officially exported and thus lost to the English currency. But similarly large amounts of bullion were again passing through the mints in the Edwardian recoinages. It may be, therefore, that at some point probably during the Short Cross coinage, the total issues began to exceed the amount for which there was an insistent day-to-day demand, and gradually an increasing proportion of the currency became available for use as a store of wealth, that is to say for private hoarding. The amounts of coinage passing from hand to hand, and therefore at risk to be casually lost, may have risen much more closely in line with the rise in prices; and this would perhaps help to explain the increased numbers of stray losses as between Long Cross and Edwardian pennies, at a time when mint-output was actually falling. Meanwhile the output figures remain the best indication of the number of coins in existence, if not actually "circulating".

One may well ponder these orders of magnitude, and a causal relationship (which has been discussed by P. D. A. Harvey)[28] between the growth of the money supply in the shires, and economic and social changes in the late twelfth and thirteenth centuries. The influx of new coinage in the 1180s was impressive enough, but with the issue of Classes V and VI, from 1205 to 1217, the volume of output rose to very roughly 100 million coins, so far as one can judge from hoard statistics published by Mme. Dumas and J. D. Brand.[29] So it seems that the currency was growing quite rapidly through the Short Cross period, but with the maximum rate of change, and probably the economically critical change, occurring between 1180 and 1220.[30] Prices doubled or trebled, the big landowners sought to protect their interests by direct cultivation of the demesne, and there was a general increase in money rents and wages. From very early in the fourteenth century the volume of the English currency was declining again, only a little less swiftly. When only the Edwardian output-statistics were available (that is, until 1971), it was easy to allow oneself to assume, influenced by the apparently very large totals, that the Edward pennies were a high-water mark. But the coinage of Edward I, although it was so plentiful, was already past the apogee.

The mints constituted, if not exactly a department of state, at least an important adjunct to royal government in a country as wealthy as thirteenth-century England. Their administrative structure and institutional history form a topic, of which Craig and Reddaway have made valuable studies as regards the Tower mint.[31] By studying the coins themselves in conjunction with the mint-records, we can reconstruct the working history of the mints, tracing their output year by year and identifying the varieties of penny by which that output was represented. What happened to the coins after they left the mints and passed into circulation is another matter altogether, and it has to be studied in other ways. For example, if the money supply influenced economic activity, it is not the yearly fluctuations in mint output that we should consult, but a quite different statistical series, namely the yearly fluctuations in the total number of coins, including foreign coins, circulating in England. There are, perhaps, three separate kinds of evidence, each with a contribution to make to the study of the currency: first, hoards; secondly, archaeological site-finds and other stray finds; and thirdly, documentary references which happen to throw light on the ways in which coins were used.

Hoards are the subject of an extensive literature, which is constantly being added to as new finds come to light. Each hoard-report generally appears as an article in the British Numismatic Journal, the Numismatic Chronicle, or elsewhere, and the interest of members of the British Numismatic Society in particular has served to maintain a very high standard of scholarship. Thompson's Inventory[32] provides a guide to the literature up to about 1955, but it is regrettably riddled with slips and errors, and it is essential to use both it and Dolley's more recent survey of 1968,[33] which corrects Thompson on innumerable details and reconsiders the whole body of information. Dolley lists 110 hoards from the period 1272 - c. 1350 from Great Britain, and a further 24 from Ireland. This may, however, give an exaggerated impression of the quantity of material available. Many of the hoards are too small to be of much statistical value, and many of the older finds, published before the Fox classification was available, and since dispersed without record, offer evidence of limited and uncertain accuracy. Of the British hoards, no fewer than 70 are from Scotland, while only 7 are from southern England,[34] and of those 7 only 2 were concealed before 1300. Thus the geographical distribution of the hoards is obviously very biassed by the unsettled conditions in Scotland and the north, and we actually have rather little direct evidence about the currency in the south of England, always the wealthier part of the country. The finds from the south tend to be smaller, and were perhaps put together in different circumstances. They tend to include more halfpennies and farthings.

The hoards tell us two things that we should otherwise have no way of knowing. First, they show that within at most one or two decades of their issue, the coins of different mints became almost perfectly intermingled in hoards from whatever part of Britain. The percentage composition of a series of hoards by mints has been tabulated,[35] and the overall impression is one of astonishingly little variation. In the late thirteenth century, it is true, the local provincial mint sometimes accounts for a few percentage points more than its expected share, but coins from all parts of the country - Bristol, Bury, Newcastle - are already present. In the 1320s and 1330s, London coins account for almost exactly 50% of the currency, Canterbury 25-30%, Bristol

2%, Bury 3-4% and so on. No convincing model has been proposed to explain this very curious feature. When an explanation is forthcoming, it will probably need to be applicable to earlier coinages too, for we see the same thing in the Short Cross and Long Cross periods, and indeed from later Anglo-Saxon times. In general terms the evidence seems to suggest that monetary transactions involving long-distance transfers predominated over payments within the ten- or twenty-mile orbit of ordinary farming life. Neither taxation nor the activities of travelling merchants would alone seem sufficient to account for the extreme national uniformity of the hoards, which extends even to the proportions of Scottish and continental sterlings included.

An unfortunate consequence of the thorough mingling of the currency is that there seems to be little prospect of analysing the regional or topographical patterns of monetary circulation through a study of the proportions of coins of different mints.

Secondly, the hoards reveal the rate at which older coins went out of circulation. More recent issues account for a larger proportion of the coins in the hoards than a comparison of the bullion figures would have led one to expect. Thus only a third as much pro rata of the coinage of Fox Groups I-IX as of Groups XI-XV survives in the Boyton hoard (c. 1324), implying that at least two-thirds of the original total output of Groups I-IX had somehow disappeared from use. In the rather later Aberdeen hoard (c. 1336) about half as much of the earlier Groups survives,[36] but this is because the later Groups have by then also begun to disappear, bringing the ratio up again. There were various reasons for the losses. Just as foreign silver was brought to the English mints, so merchants trading across the Channel presumably needed from time to time to hand in their English silver at foreign mints. The merry-go-round effect on bullion stocks was made all the greater in the 1280s and in the early fourteenth century, as Miskimin[37] and Prestwich[38] have pointed out, by the interplay of mints competing for bullion, with the merchant fraternity no doubt closely aware where their own advantage lay, and perhaps also by French monetary policy, when resort was made to "mutations" of the currency.[39] Royal expenditure and subsidies abroad undoubtedly depleted the national stock of coinage-metal. Thus the total currency at any given date was liable to be smaller than the aggregate of the mint-output figures. Mayhew has estimated that the total was just over £1 million during the first quarter of the fourteenth century, sinking to half a million by about 1350, a decline that was accompanied by falling prices.[40]

Secondly, archaeological site-finds and other stray finds, although they cannot be dated closely,[41] offer evidence about an aspect of the currency on which the hoards are virtually silent. Single finds are assumed to be for the most part coins accidentally lost which their owners failed to recover. It is a general rule that the chances of a coin's being lost are much greater, the smaller the value of the coin. Halfpennies and farthings therefore figure more prominently among casual finds. Conversely the fractions were as we have seen mostly excluded from hoards.[42]

One site to which it is worth drawing particular attention is that of Meols, in the Wirral peninsula. Marine erosion of the coastline during the nineteenth century gradually destroyed part of the site of the medieval port for Chester, and over the years thousands of antiquities, including hundreds of coins, were found on the foreshore. There were over a hundred Edwardian coins, which included a good proportion of cut halves and quarters. This was the official form of small change in the Long Cross period, but with the introduction of round halfpennies and farthings in 1279-80 the centuries-old practice of cutting pennies was finally ended. But not, apparently, in Cheshire. Presumably insufficient of the round fractions found their way there to meet local needs and people responded by cutting coins in the traditional way. Exact statistics of the Meols finds cannot be compiled, but it seems that cut halves, round farthings, and cut farthings were plentiful.[43]

A similar site is the vanished seaport of Dunwich, where hundreds of coins of the twelfth and thirteenth centuries have been picked up on the beach as the cliffs have crumbled. "So far as I can gather", wrote Hancox, who originally described the finds in 1908, "from those who regularly search for these pieces, the proportion of whole pennies to cut money is at the rate of one penny to four halves and five quarters, and they cover a period from William I to Henry III." But at Dunwich there were no cut coins of the Edwards. Hancox enumerates 3 pennies, 25 halves, and 53 quarters of the Long Cross coinage and 10 pennies, 6 round halfpennies, and 15 round farthings of the Edwards.[44]

Both Meols and Dunwich illustrate the very rapid expansion of the currency in the twelfth and early thirteenth century. At Dunwich there are 6 Norman coins, 3 of Stephen, 12 of Henry II, 145 Short Cross, and 130 Long Cross. The port was already in decline in the second half of the thirteenth century, so the smaller numbers of Edward pennies do not afford a true comparison. At Meols, there are roughly 6 Norman coins, 80 later coins up to Short Cross, 100 Long Cross, and 140 Edwardian coins. The last figure may reflect the considerable length of time for which some of the Edward pennies remained in circulation.[45]

If sufficient details could be compiled, site finds might also add to our information about the currency by helping to demonstrate whether the thorough mixing of coins from different mints, which the hoards reveal, was a feature confined to hoards. One could imagine a situation in which there were two more or less coextensive patterns of monetary circulation, and that a penny on leaving the mint might tend either to find its way into the coffers of the well-to-do and to be moved over considerable distances in payment for large transactions, or to spin off into some quiet backwater of village life and to stick there, passing from hand to hand to meet simple needs.[46] The detailed work remains to be done on this topic, but a preliminary impression is that there are proportionately rather fewer finds of coins of the provincial mints, for example in the Oxford region, that the hoards would have led one to expect.

A third kind of evidence comprises documentary references which show how much coinage was in the hands of an individual at a particular moment in time. Manorial records may show a reeve as holding a certain amount of cash when the accounts were scrutinized; and surprisingly large sums were found in the hands of traders at annual fairs. Mention of pollards and crockards or of foreign coins proves beyond any dispute that actual coin was in question. Much documentary material, of course, offers evidence for the history of prices, for the social distribution of wealth, and so on, without contributing anything directly to numismatic reasearch into the currency of the Edwardian period (to which this bibliographical survey is limited). In the attempt to put information and ideas derived from the coinage itself at the service of historians, the main distinction to be emphasized is between the history of the mints and the history of the currency.

The Edwardian sterling was a coin of international importance, which provided much of the currency of Scotland and Ireland as well as of England. The Scottish national coinage adhered to the same standard and was of a similar design; the Irish issues were of the sterling type; and the English penny was widely imitated on the continent. The Scottish and Irish coins have been classified with reliance on exactly the same concepts as the Fox brothers used, to the same very high standards of scholarship, and with much the same finality. Recent writings to consult are those of Stewart[47] and of Dolley and Seaby.[48]

The continental sterlings, which were struck by many rulers in northern France, the Low Countries, the Rhineland, and Westphalia, present much wider and more diffuse numismatic problems, and they have not yet all been studied in the same degree of detail as the British coinages. Those which turn up regularly in British hoards include coins in the names of Guy de Dampierre, count of Flanders, Arnold V, count of Looz, Jean d' Avesnes, count of Hainaut, John the Blind of Luxembourg, and Gaucher de Châtillon, count of Porcien, as well as deliberate imitations inscribed with Edward's name. There were few imitations of halfpence, which would have been more difficult to utter in worthwhile quantities; but a heavily die-linked hoard of them was found at Hull.[49] The only general catalogue of continental sterlings is that of Chautard, written more than a hundred years ago, which now has a very old-fashioned appearance.[50] Brief summaries listing the types are available.[51] A synthesis which sought to characterize the monetary connections between England and the continent and to distinguish successive phases of imitation was made by Berghaus in his thoroughly documented study, "Die Perioden des Sterlings in Westfalen, dem Rheinland, und in den Niederlanden", published in 1947.[52] The early imitations, which were proscribed in England in 1299/1330, included the barehead coins of Namur, coins with the shield of Brabant, and a spate of issues on which the prince wears a chaplet of roses - coins named in the documents as <u>rosarii</u>. All these were popularly known as pollards and crockards. They gave way in the early fourteenth century to a preponderance of much closer copies showing a crowned head very like that of Edward, but still with a continental legend. Thirdly there are deceptive imitations with more or less blundered legends that correspond, on a casual inspection, with those on English coins. This same theme was taken up by Rigold, in a more accessible article, "The trail of the Easterlings".[53]

There is a useful amount of documentary evidence, but surprisingly little hoard-evidence from the continent by which the imitations might be more exactly dated, and many of the older British hoards in which they occur are from the 1320's and 1330's - too late to be critical. Recent discoveries have however begun to force a revision, and to show that some categories of the imitations began earlier than had been thought. The Broughton hoard, concealed c. 1290, already contains several varieties, including one with a crowned head,[54] and Miss Archibald has pointed out that the same varieties were present in the Coventry hoard (B) of 1937, deposited at much the same date.[55] She will confirm this general conclusion in publishing the Kings Lynn hoard of 1972, again concealed c. 1292-3 and containing various continental sterlings.[56] By an ordinance made in the Exchequer, the collectors of customs were required from 1294 to confiscate counterfeit coins if they exceeded 4d in the pound, and there are wool custom accounts from Newcastle, for example,[57] which itemize the amounts of money forfeited under the ordinance by owners of goods sailing out of that port.

A fourth type of imitation comprises very close copies of the Edwardian prototype. Stylistic groups have been recognized among them, which are however anomalous in the context of the English series. One such group was good enough to deceive even the Fox brothers, who included it in their scheme under Group Xb, thus sowing the seeds of some confusion over the Durham issues of bishop Bek and the suspension of temporalities.[58] The early date (in the 1280s) of some of the imitations found in England has long been understood, but it was not clearly appreciated that many are continental in origin. One group is connected by a die-link with the mint of Alost, and another plentiful group is now known to have been struck by Gaucher de Châtillon, count of Porcien and constable of France, in his mint at Yves, alongside stylistically similar coins in his own name.[59]

The scale on which imitative sterlings were struck in the 1290s was considerable, and the attacks upon them, which figure prominently in legislation and accounts of law-enforcement of the time, were no doubt inevitable as a result of their numbers alone, apart from any political considerations. In the Mellendean hoard, concealed c. 1295, from near Berwick, 108 coins out of 532 were foreign. There are several other interesting hoards from Scotland (but not from England) consisting largely or even entirely of continental coins, which had presumably been sorted out by some merchant, and set aside to be used separately. In the Kirkcudbright hoard of 1851 there were 87 such coins, nearly all crockards, in a total of 92; the Galston hoard contained 231 coins of which 224 were foreign; all 138 coins in the Cleuchhead hoard were foreign; all 4 coins in a little find from Fyvie similarly were foreign.[60]

In the early fourteenth century, by contrast, imitations normally madé up only 2 or 3 per cent of the contents of hoards.

By the English king the imitations were seen as a threat because their intrinsic value was uncertain. They might be either light-weight or of less than pure silver, or both, and there was a real risk that Gresham's Law would operate - as adumbrated, perhaps, by the Scottish hoards just mentioned - and that bad money would tend to drive out the good, thus destroying the well-deserved reputation of the English sterlings for reliability, and damaging commercial confidence. It is in this context that research into the weight and fineness of the coins, particularly the continental coins, is of interest. Chemical analyses of the English coins have shown that sterling was indeed synonymous with quality.[61] Metrological studies, which need to be based on a statistically large enough sample from a single hoard-source, equally show that in broad terms the 22.2-grain standard was very well maintained; in detail they have raised intriguing questions about weight-control, culling, wear and tear, and selective hoarding.[62] It should be added that the hoards do not reflect the alleged clipping of the coinage, which, embroiled with prejudice against the Jews, provoked a political furore in the late thirteenth century;[63] but hoarders may well have been careful to exclude clipped coins.

Finally, what contribution have all the detailed numismatic researches of the last hundred years made? It will not, I hope, appear too unenthusiastic to say that the heart of the matter lies in the documentary records of mint-output, and that the numismatist's main function has been to erect an <u>apparatus criticus</u> around those records, and to round out the picture for mints or for periods from which output-figures have not survived, by means of estimates based for example on the proportional occurrence of the relevant coins in hoards.

Old-fashioned and misguided notions about the extent of the monetary sector of the economy die hard. Throughout the thirteenth century the use of coinage was in fact pervasive, not just in towns and ports and among the merchant class, but in villages throughout the land. Numismatic evidence, in particular stray finds of halfpence and farthings, is of value in exemplifying this and, potentially, in studying its regional aspects. In more general terms the same conclusion might be drawn from the volume of the currency, for which again one must rely on numismatic calculations deriving from hoards.

The very rapid increase in that volume of currency between 1180 and 1216, which it has been possible to date quite accurately and to quantify by numismatic arguments, seems to offer a more than sufficient explanation for inflation and for the monetization of the economy from much the same date, - <u>prima facie</u> a more convincing explanation than Postan's "pressure of population" thesis, which, considered critically, seems a rather shaky structure of demographic argument, pointing ostensibly towards a link between a modest rate of change in the population, considerable change in price levels, and sweeping change in agricultural economics.

A quantitative understanding of the currency, of how it was used, and how it changed, is a prerequisite of historical judgements about royal monetary policy: before one can say whether the decisions of governments concerning the coinage were wise, one must be informed not only about the decisions, but also about the problems with which government had to contend. Prestwich's study of Edward I's currency in the context of English economic history, and Mrs. Mate's detailed political study of the same topic are models of this kind of historical writing.[64] They are truly monetary history, as distinct from the lengthy preparations in which numismatist are employed - sometimes, one is tempted to feel, with no urgent intention on their part to come to the final purpose. The work of Prestwich and Mate is in this sense the beginning of as big a step forward as was the work of the Fox brothers.

Happily it does not exhaust the historical interest of the Edwardian coinage. The aspect where perhaps the greatest uncertainty remains is the circulation of the currency. How did coins get from place to place? Who held them? What was the balance, in quantitative terms, between commercial use on the one hand, and on the other the royal finances: income in the various forms of taxation, and expenditure on administration and warfare? Did the balance vary significantly between the north and the south of England? How far had a money economy penetrated into Wales? (One should mention here the curious topic of leather money.)[65] Had Edward's disbursements for his Welsh war made a difference?[66]

The connections between coinage and war are very much to the forefront, and one obvious reason why we have so many Edwardian hoards from Scotland and northern England lies in the sporadic warfare of the period. But one must avoid facile conclusions: if hoards were concealed in the face of a military threat or because of general insecurity and lawlessness, and - more to the point - if their owners failed to dig them up again because they were killed or prevented in some other way from recovering their property, it does not tell us anything about the ways in which they had come by their wealth. The use of coinage might still, on this evidence, be associated overwhelmingly with trade and commerce. And there is no correlation between the amount of money found in hoards from a region, and the amount of currency which circulated in that region. It might be more relevant to ask whether stray finds from Scotland include halfpennies and farthings.

There is a natural, if romantic, tendency to speculate whether very large hoards, containing perhaps ten thousand coins, might not be military treasure chests or the like; but ten thousand pence only amount, after all, to a little over £40, which would not have been an especially large amount to transact. Nevertheless, many of the largest hoards are from Scotland, which was a relatively poor country, and they may reflect military spending in the 1320s and 1330s either directly or at a remove.

Particular emergencies have been suggested as the occasion for the concealment of hoards, as for example the two finds from Neath Abbey, which have been associated with the pursuit and capture of Edward II nearby in the autumn of 1326.[67] The enormous Tutbury hoard, containing perhaps 200,000 coins, is no doubt to be connected with the downfall of Thomas of Lancaster in the spring of 1322.[68] The Yorkshire finds from Bootham, Knaresborough Scotton, and Wyke, all apparently concealed c. 1325-30, have been associated with Scottish incursions into the north of England c. 1328 following Edward II's downfall. And a group of hoards from south-west Scotland, some of which are dated by Group XVd, and others which may have been equally late, have been associated with the campaigns of Edward Balliol in the 1330s. Similarly there are numerous hoards from Perthshire and the east coast of Scotland where the terminus is the 1320s but where it is more likely that the dates of concealment are 1333-6.[69] Before the concealment of hoards can be linked with historical events, it is essential that the coins should be reliably and closely dated;[70] even then, while many of the suggestions are no doubt true few if any of them can be proved absolutely.

A final example will illustrate the difficulties. Oman was seeking to link coinage and warfare by a proposition of a different kind when he observed that under Edward II the only year when there was a really large issue of coinage was 1314, when London struck 30,000 lb and Canterbury 35,000 lb worth of pence - no doubt to pay the army which was destroyed at Bannockburn that summer.71 Students today will be inclined to judge this idea irresponsible in the absence of any sort of proof or supporting evidence, especially since almost all the bullion in question was foreign silver, and since one would not really expect a king to lay his hands on cash in the form of coin new from the mint. Leaving that aside, however, if money had been put into circulation in that way, one might have expected to see some trace in the proportional composition of hoards concealed in the years immediately following. And as a preliminary, one might be forgiven for assuming that it would be possible to comment on such a straight-forward assertion as Oman's, first, by saying which of the Fox groups was in issue in 1314. Unfortunately this is not so. Group XI had begun shortly before the death of bishop Bek of Durham in March 1311. Group XIII dies were still being made in 1317 when bishop Beaumont received the temporalities. As Group XII is very scarce, it is not certain whether dies of Group XI, XII, or XIII were in use in 1313/14. The hoard statistics suggest that it may have been the tail-end of XI. Any concentration of these in northern hoards would hardly show up. In any case, a more convincing explanation of the sudden flurry of minting activity would refer to the abrupt halting of coinage output in France at just the moment when it rises in volume in England - a shift which seems to have been due to a mutation in the French currency. The fortunes of the mints in England, Flanders, and northern France were, indeed, interlinked throughout the fourteenth century, and the basis of their monetary history is that these were the wealthy members of a north-west European economic community.

NOTES

1. Sharp 1785.

2. Fox and Fox say that he had no family arms; but cf. Senior 1964-5.

3. Bartlet 1779. On de Bury's coins, Purvey 1959.

4. Fox and Fox, 1912, 189f., quoting 4 May 1317 for the resumption of the temporalities by Beaumont. For the adminstrative background, see C. M. Fraser, A History of Antony Bek, 1283-1311, 1957, pp. 181-3 etc. See further Blunt 1961, and Dolley and Stewart 1954. The arguments have been rehearsed in Jones 1965 and Dolley 1965. See especially North 1968, p. 13 no. 11: the royal coins begin during IXb and end during Xa (1302-3), and occur again in Xc-f (2nd bust). The coins described as Xb, reading EDWARR, which North discusses, have since been reinterpreted as unofficial issues having no bearing on the question (Mayhew 1974a). For the late Edwardian period, see also Purvey 1959, Jones 1959, and Jones 1961.

5. Sainthill 1852.

6. Officially, 243 coins were to be cut from the Tower pound. This was reckoned as equivalent to 5,400 Troy grains (cf. the Troy pound of 5,760 grains). -Lyon, in BNJ XXXVIII (1969), 205 n. 4. The Tower pound is discussed further in C. S. S. Lyon, "Some problems in interpreting Anglo-Saxon coinage", Anglo-Saxon England V (1976), 173-224 at p. 186. H. A. Miskimin (EcHR 2nd ser. XX, 1967, 35-52) suggested the Tower pound was exactly three-quarters of the (pre-Elizabethan) avoirdupois pound of 15 oz. or 7200 grains.

7. Evans 1871.

8. The logic of this is not rigorous. Bek might have begun his issues with unmarked coins, like those of Robert of Holy Island.

9. Blunt 1961; B. H. I. H. Stewart, "Stefanus R", NC 1972, 169-75 at pp. 174 f. These rare halfpennies fall into Edward III's second coinage of silver, i.e. they post-date the Fox sequence of Groups I-XV.

10. Fox and Fox, 1911, pp. 116-7; Stewart 1964, at pp. 300 and 302-3; Mate 1972, at pp. 47-8.

11. The technique has been recreated by a modern student, who found it surprisingly quick and easy to do. For photographs of punches, see Sellwood 1962. For surviving medieval dies see Allen 1941.

12. G. Macdonald recognised its merits, and tried to develop it further, in his study of the Blackhills and Mellendean hoards (NC 1913), but by the time his paper was in proof, the Fox brothers' work was

already appearing. For a modern appreciation of Burns' work, see Tatler and Stewart 1962.

13. Fox and Fox 1909-13.

14. Blunt 1931. There is an up-dated summary in Stewart 1967 (Appendix I, pp. 128-31). A new variety is published in North 1975a.

15. Tatler 1957.

16. North 1966.

17. Dolley and Tatler 1963; Tatler and Stewart 1962.

18. Woodhead and Stewart 1966 distinguish IXa^1 from IXa^2. Archibald 1971 comments on the definition of IIIc, d, and e.

19. Fox and Fox 1917; North 1968.

20. Crump and Johnson 1913.

21. For useful enlarged photographs, see Harris, Purvey, and Woodhead 1964, and Harris and Woodhead 1966.

22. One can estimate the output of pennies of the provincial mints in Classes II-IV (1280- ca. 1290) by the ratios in which they occur in the hoards. Thus in the Broughton hoard, the 69 coins of Bristol, Bury, Chester, Durham, Lincoln, Newcastle, and York appear to represent some 60 million coins.

23. Fox and Fox 1910, pp. 109, 112f., 125-7 and pl. V describe about 20 specimens from 7 classes and a very limited number of dies, with reverse die-links between the classes. The two in the Dover hoard were from obverse dies 5 and 6 (Dolley 1957).

24. Stewart 1963, 1964, Mate 1969.

25. Tatler and Stewart 1962.

26. C.E. Blunt and J.D. Brand, "Mint output of Henry III", BNJ XXXIX (1970), 61-6.

27. See below pp. 67-69.

28. P.D.A. Harvey, "The English inflation of 1180-1220", Past and Present LXI (1973), 4-9; id., "The Pipe Rolls and the adoption of demesne farming in England", EcHR 2nd ser. XXVII (1974), 345-58.

29. F. Dumas and J.D. Brand, "The British coins in the Gisors (1970) hoard", BNJ XL (1971), 22-43.

30. See Rigold, below pp. 67-69.

31. Craig 1953; Reddaway 1967.

32. Thompson 1956.

33. Dolley 1968.

34. Boyton, Broughton, Dover, Newbury, Oxford, Avebury, and Grittleton.

To these can be added the important Mayfield hoard (Archibald 1971).

35. Woodhead, Stewart, and Tatler 1966. Note also the interest of the Broughton, Mellendean, and Dover hoards, as reflecting the proportions of issues before the recoinage of 1300.

36. Mayhew 1976.

37. Miskimin 1963.

38. Prestwich 1969.

39. Cazelles 1966.

40. Mayhew 1974.

41. Archibald 1974.

42. See Rigold, below pp. 59-80.

43. Metcalf 1961.

44. Hancox 1908; Seaman 1972.

45. Archibald 1974. The chances of a coin's being lost will be _inter alia_ in direct proportion to the length of time for which it remained in circulation.

46. On the theory of monetary "reservoirs", see D. M. Metcalf, "The changing relationship of coinage to money in the nineteenth and twentieth centuries", _Seaby's Coin and Medal Bulletin_ 1976, 75-8, 112-9.

47. Stewart 1967, 1971.

48. Dolley 1968, Dolley and Seaby 1968.

49. Metcalf 1964, Weiller 1967, Banks 1968.

50. Chautard 1871. It is still necessary to consult the earlier works of V. Gaillard, _Recherches sur les monnaies des comtes de Flandres_, 1852, R. Chalon, _Recherches sur les monnaies des comtes de Hainaut_, 1848-57, id., _Recherches sur les monnaies des comtes de Namur_, 1860, and P. O. van der Chijs, _De munten der voormalige graven en hertogen van Gelderland_, 1852. See also A. Dieudonné, _Monnaies féodales françaises_ (Manuel de numismatique française, IV), 1936, and Berghaus 1951.

51. Meert 1960, North 1968.

52. Berghaus 1947.

53. Rigold 1951.

54. North 1966.

55. Namely coins of Alost of Gui de Dampierre with bare head, of Valenciennes of Jean d'Avesnes with rosetted head, and of Arnhem of Renaud with crowned head. Archibald 1971 b.

56. _CH_ I (1975), 93.

57. J. Conway Davies, The wool customs accounts for Newcastle upon Tyne for the reign of Edward I. Archaeologia Aeliana 4th ser. XXXII (1954), 220-308, at pp. 224 and 275ff.

58. Mayhew 1974.

59. Mayhew 1975a, 1976.

60. Thompson 1956, Dolley 1968; Dolley 1961.

61. Harris 1961.

62. Dolley 1957a, b, Robertson 1969, Dolley and Seaby 1968, on loss of weight by wear, Archibald 1971a, M. M. Archibald, " The Attenborough Notts., 1966 hoard" , BNJ XXXVIII (1969), 50-83, Mayhew 1975d. A list of weights of the Loch Doon coins (Woodhead, Stewart, and Tatler, 1966) exists in duplicated form.

63. Mate 1972.

64. Prestwich 1969, Mate 1972. See also M. Mate, " High prices in early fourteenth century England - causes and consequences" , EcHR 2nd. ser., XXVIII (1975), 1-8.

65. The History of Allchester, written in 1622, and printed in Kennett's Parochial Antiquities, p. 696, contains the following passage: " King Edward I his leathern money, bearing his name, stamp, and picture, which he used in the building of Carnarvon, Beaumarish, and Conway Castles, to spare better bullion, were, since I can remember, preserved and kept in one of the towers of Carnarvon Castle" . See also D. M. Metcalf and C. E. Blunt, "Three early discoveries of 'leather money' ", BNJ XXIX (1958-9), 353-6.

66. See M. Prestwich, War, Politics, and Finance under Edward I, (London 1972).

67. Dolley 1957a, b.

68. Dolley and Pagan 1963. On the reliability of the figure of 200,000, see Blunt in NCirc. 1976, 227.

69. Mayhew 1975c.

70. Dolley 1968.

71. Oman 1931. His statement needs to be modified to take account of the large issues of 1307-09.

SELECT BIBLIOGRAPHY

The items have been arranged in order of publication, in order to illustrate the progress of numismatic research into the Edwardian coinage.

1779-1908

J. Sharp, " Observations on the coinage of England, with his letter to Mr. Thoresby, 1698/9" , Bibliotheca Topographica Britannica vol. VI, no. XXXV, 1785.

B. Bartlet, " The episcopal coins of Durham, and the monastic coins of Reading, minted during the reigns of Edwards I. II. and III. appropriated to their respective owners" , Archaeologia V (1779), 335-9.

E. Hawkins, " Counterfeit sterlings" , NC XIII (1850-1), 86-94.

R. Sainthill, " Coins of Edward III. and Edward V. " , NC XIV (1851-2), 20-30.

J. Chautard, Imitations des monnaies au type esterlin frappées en Europe pendant le XIIIe et le XIVe siècle, (Nancy, 1871).

A.J. Evans, " On a hoard of coins found at Oxford, with some remarks on the coinage of the first three Edwards" , NC NS XI (1871), 264-82.

E. Burns, The Coinage of Scotland, (Edinburgh, 1887).

H. Montagu, "Further notes concerning Bishop de Bury and the Durham coinage", NC 3rd ser. XV (1895), 290-300.

C.G. Crump and A. Hughes, " The English currency under Edward I" , Economic Journal V (1895), 50-67.

E.R.H. Hancox, " Finds of mediaeval cut halfpence and farthings at Dunwich" , BNJ V (1908), 123-34.

1909-55

H.B. Earle Fox and J.S. Shirley-Fox, " Numismatic history of the reigns of Edward I., II., and III" , BNJ VI (1909), 197-212; VII (1910), 91-142; VIII (1911), 137-48; IX (1912), 181-206; X (1913), 95-123. (In 1912 J. Shirley Fox changed his name to J. Shirley Shirley-Fox.)

C.G. Crump and C. Johnson, " Tables of bullion coined under Edward I, II, and III" , NC 4th ser. XIII (1913), 200-45.

H.B. Earle Fox and J.S. Shirley-Fox, The pennies of Edward I, II, and III" , NC 4th ser. XVII (1917), 279-97.

L.A. Lawrence, " On a new type of penny of Edward I" , NC 5th ser. III (1923), 56-9.

C.E. Blunt, " The mint of Berwick-on-Tweed under Edward I, II, and III" , NC 5th ser. XI (1931), 28-52.

C. Oman, The Coinage of England, (Oxford, 1931).

D. Allen, " The Boyton find of coins of Edward I and II" , NC 5th ser. XVI (1936), 115-55 (with a contribution by G.C. Dunning).

D. Allen, " Dies in the Public Record Office" , BNJ XXIII (1938-41), 31-50.

P. Berghaus, " Die Perioden des Sterlings in Westfalen, dem Rheinland und in den Niederlanden" , Hamburger Beiträge zur Numismatik I (1947-51), 34-53.

S.E. Rigold, " The trail of the Easterlings" , BNJ XXVI (1949-51), 31-55.

J. Craig, The Mint, (Cambridge, 1953).

R.H.M. Dolley, " A late nineteenth-century find of Edward pence from Falhills Wood in Scotland" , BNJ XXVII (1952-4), 215-8.

R.H.M. Dolley and B.H.I.H. Stewart, " The 1953 Bootham treasure trove" , ibid., 281-93.

1956

J. D. A. Thompson, Inventory of British Coin Hoards, A.D. 650-1500 (Royal Numismatic Society Special Publication I) (Oxford, 1956)).

1957

R.H.M. Dolley, " The Dover hoard, the first English hoard with groats of Edward I" , (with a contribution by P.E. Lasko) BNJ XXVIII (1955-7), 147-68.

R.H.M. Dolley, " A nineteenth-century Scottish hoard of Edward pence", ibid., 196-201.

G.L.V. Tatler, " A note on the transition between Types I and II of the pennies of Edward I" , ibid., 288-93.

R.H.M. Dolley, " A find of pence of Edward I and II at Neath Abbey" , ibid., 294-8.

R.H.M. Dolley, " A further find of Edward pennies at Neath Abbey" , ibid., 555-9.

R.H.M. Dolley, " An interesting new variety of the sterling of Namur" , ibid., 654-5.

1959

P.F. Purvey, " The XVd Durham pennies of Edward III" , BNJ XXIX (1958-9), 322-5.

F.E. Jones, " 'Edwardus Rex Ain' : de Bury or Hatfield? - a new approach to an old problem" , ibid., 326-33.

1960

J.J. North, English Hammered Coinage, vol. II, Edward I to Charles II, 1272-1662, (London, 1960).

G.S. Robinson, " The silver pence from the mint of the bishops palatine of Durham" , Antiquities of Sunderland XXII (1960), 63-85.

C. Meert, " European sterlings of Edwardian type" , Seaby's Coin and Medal Bulletin 1960, 134-8.

1961

D.M. Metcalf, " Some finds of medieval coins from Scotland and the north of England" , BNJ XXX (1960-61), 88-123.

F.E. Jones, " 'Edwardus Rex Ain' - further postscript" , ibid., 363-5.

R.H.M. Dolley, " A small find of continental sterlings from Aberdeenshire" , NC 7th ser. I (1961), 169-70.

C.E. Blunt, " Ecclesiastical coinage in England. Part II. After the Norman Conquest" (The President's Address), ibid., i-xviii.

E.J. Harris, " Analyses of English hammered coins" , Seaby's Coin and Medal Bulletin 1961, 390.

1962

D. Sellwood, " Medieval minting techniques" , BNJ XXXI (1962), 57-65.

G.L.V. Tatler and B.H.I.H. Stewart, " Edwardian sterlings in the Montrave hoard" , ibid., 80-7.

1963

H.A. Miskimin, Money, Prices, and Foreign Exchange in Fourteenth Century France. (New Haven, 1963).

B.H.I.H. Stewart, " Medieval die-output: two calculations for English mints in the fourteenth century" , NC 7th ser. III (1963), 97-106.

R.H.M. Dolley and G.L.V. Tatler, "The 1958 Whittonstall treasure trove", Archaeologia Aeliana 4th ser. XLI (1963), 65-84.

R.H.M. Dolley and H.E. Pagan, " An early nineteenth-century discovery of Edward pennies at Knaresborough Priory" , BNJ XXXII (1963), 117-26.

1964

B.H.I.H. Stewart, " Second thoughts on medieval die-output" , NC 7th ser. IV (1964), 293-303.

E.J. Harris, F. Purvey, and P. Woodhead, " Notes on English halfpence and farthings, 1279-1660" , Seaby's Coin and Medal Bulletin 1964, 122-7, 165-9, 202-5.

D.M. Metcalf, " A fourteenth-century hoard from Hull" , BNJ XXXIII (1964), 80-2.

B. Senior, " The episcopal marks on the coins of the prince-bishops of Durham" , NCirc. LXXII (1964), 259-61, 284-5; LXXIII (1965), 4-5, 33-4.

1965

F.E. Jones, " The episcopal marks on the coins of the prince-bishops of Durham" , NCirc. LXXIII (1965), 5-6.

R.H.M. Dolley, " Bek, Beaumont, Bury, and Hatfield - some neglected hoard-evidence" , ibid., 35-6.

1966

E.J. Harris and P. Woodhead, " Notes on English halfpence and farthings" , Seaby's Coin and Medal Bulletin 1966, 4-6.

P. Woodhead, " An unrecorded variety of Edward II" , NCirc. LXXIV (1966), 2-3.

J.J. North, " The Broughton hoard" , BNJ XXXV (1966), 120-7.

P. Woodhead and I.H. Stewart, " The Renfrew treasure trove, 1963" , ibid., 128-47.

R. Cazelles, " Quelques réflexions à propos des mutations de la monnaie royale française (1295-1360)" , Le Moyen Age LXXII (1966).

1967

I.H. Stewart, The Scottish Coinage, (London, 1967).

T.F. Reddaway, " The King's Mint and Exchange in London, 1343-1543" , EHR LXXXII (1967), 1-23.

R. Weiller, " Medieval coins of Luxembourg in the British Museum" , NC 7th ser. VII (1967), 183-8.

1968

R.H.M. Dolley, " The Irish mints of Edward I in the light of the coin-hoards from Ireland and Great Britain" , Proceedings of the Royal Irish Academy LXVI C, no. 3 (1968), 235-97.

J.J. North, The Coinages of Edward I and II, (London, 1968).

R.H.M. Dolley and W. Seaby, " A parcel of Edwardian sterlings in the Ulster Museum" , Seaby's Coin and Medal Bulletin 1968, 161-6.

F. Banks, " The 1868 hoard from the Albert Dock lock pit, Hull" (with a contribution by D.M. Metcalf and L.K. Hamblin, " Analysis of the metal contents of coins from the Hull hoard"), BNJ XXXVII (1968), 65-72.

1969

M. Prestwich, " Edward I's monetary policies and their consequences" , EcHR 2nd ser. XXII (1969), 406-16.

M. Mate, " A mint of trouble, 1279-1307" , Speculum XLIV (1969), 201-12.

M. Mate, " Coin dies under Edward I and II" , NC 7th ser. IX (1969), 207-18.

P. Woodhead, I.H. Stewart, and G.L.V. Talter, " The Loch Doon treasure trove, 1966" , BNJ XXXVIII (1969), 31-49.

I. Stewart, " Style in medieval coinage" , NC 7th ser. IX (1969), 269-89.

A.S. Robertson, " The Renfrew (1963) coin hoard" , Glasgow Archaeological Journal I (1969), 72-4.

T.J. Robertson, " An unusual Edwardian penny" , Seaby's Coin and Medal Bulletin 1969, 201.

1970

P. Woodhead, " Two finds of Edward pennies", BNJ XXXIX (1970), 78-83.

A.S. Deshazo, "A new Xb/IXb mule", NCirc LXXVIII (1970), 494.

1971

M.M. Archibald, " The Skegby, Notts., 1967 hoard" , BNJ XL (1971), 44-56.

M.M. Archibald, " The Mayfield (Sussex) 1968 hoard of English pence and French gros, c. 1307" , Mints, Dies, and Currency ed. R.A.G. Carson, (London, 1971), pp. 151-9.

I. Stewart, " Scottish mints" , ibid., 165-289.

M. Dolley, " A neglected 14th century coin-hoard from Co. Antrim" , NCirc LXXIX (1971), 278.

1972

M. Mate, " Monetary policies in England, 1272-1307", BNJ XLI (1972), 34-79.

R. Seaman, " A further find of coins from Dunwich" , ibid., 27-33.

1973

J.J. North, " Some notes on Edwardian pence. (i) A fictitious variety of the mint of Bury St Edmunds; (ii) A very rare variety of Class IXb; (iii) A trial obverse inscription in Class X" , NCirc LXXXI (1973), 428, 472.

B.H.I.H. Stewart, " Some Edwardian hoards from Scotland" , NC 7th ser. XIII (1973), 134-43.

1974

J.J. North, " Some notes on Edwardian pence. (iv) The anomolous variety of Class " Xb" ; (v) A " mysterious" mark on the pence of Edward II; (vi) A Class XII penny of the Durham mint; (vii) Punctuation marks on the pence of Edward II; (viii) A die-link and mule of the Berwick-on-Tweed mint" , NCirc LXXXII (1974), 10-11., 146-7., 193-4., 239-40.

N.J. Mayhew, " A Canterbury-Durham die-link" , ibid., 389.

N.J. Mayhew, " Numismatic evidence and falling prices in the fourteenth century" , Economic History Review 2nd. ser., XXVII (1974), 1-15.

M.M. Archibald, " English medieval coins as dating evidence" , Coins and the Archaeologist, ed. J. Casey and R. Reece (British Archaeological Reports IV, Oxford, 1974) pp. 234-71.

1975

N.J. Mayhew, " Gaucher de Châtillon and the imitation of sterlings in the name of Edward of England" , Revue Belge de Numismatique CXXI (1975), 109-16.

N.J. Mayhew, " La chronologie des esterlins de Jean d' Avesnes" , Revue Numismatique 6th ser., XVII (1975), 172-81.

N.J. Mayhew, "The Aberdeen Upperkirkgate hoard of 1886" , BNJ XLIV (1975), forthcoming.

N.J. Mayhew, " A tumbrel at the Ashmolean Museum" , Antiquaries Journal LV (1975), 394-6.

J.J. North, " An unpublished halfpenny of Berwick-on-Tweed" , NCirc LXXXIII (1975), 56-7.

J.J. North, " Contemporary forgeries of Edwardian pence" , ibid., 194-5.

J.J. North, " The Holme Cultram, Cumberland, hoard" , ibid., 332-3.

1976

N.J. Mayhew, " Imitative sterlings in the Aberdeen and Montraive hoards" , NC 7th ser. XVI (1976), 85-97.

M.M. Archibald and F.E. Jones, " The Middridge Shildon, Co. Durham, hoard" , Coin Hoards II (1976), 115-6.

APPENDIX

AN ESTIMATE OF THE TOTAL OUTPUT OF THE ENGLISH MINTS DURING THE "CROSS-AND-CROSSLETS" COINAGE, 1158-80

Method of statistical estimation: dies

In view of the variable output of individual dies (of which there is ample evidence), the most appropriate statistical method appears to be that described and used by Lyon (1970):

"A relationship which does not depend on the assumption of equal output per die, but relies instead on the assumption that every coin struck had an equal chance of surviving to be included in the corpus. When this assumption is valid, the proportion of surviving coins which are not the only representatives of the obverse (or reverse) dies from which they were struck is a good estimate of the proportion of the total output of the type which was struck from the known obverse (or reverse) dies."

This may be summarized as

$$\frac{\text{non-singletons}}{\text{known coins}} = \frac{\text{output from known dies}}{\text{total output}}$$

As the survival-rate has varied between the Classes (coins/estimated total dies, equals for Class C, 1.32; for Class F, 0.61) the estimates of total dies have been made separately for each Class within each mint (except that Carlisle and Newcastle have been treated as one mint). This procedure gives a grand total equivalent to 1,044 "dies" originally used. (This is a convenient if imprecise way of saying that the known dies represent c. x% of the original total output, which would be accounted for by 1,044 dies if the average output of the unknown dies was the same as the output of the known dies. It was undoubtedly lower, and the actual total would therefore be higher.)

Almost exactly the same number of obverse and reverse dies are known. It does not follow that the same number of each was originally made. But as the figures are mostly close to parity, except at London and Ipswich, a ratio of approximately 1:1 has been assumed. If a multiplier suitable to the expected life of reverse dies is to be applied to obverse die statistics instead, the estimate ought probably to be doubled in respect of the coins minted at London and Ipswich, i.e. increased from 1,044 to 1,344.

Method of estimation: coins per die

The choice of a multiplier is a matter of taste. It applies to a notional average derived from the known dies, as explained above. Known obverse dies account for c. 65% of the output.

In the reign of Edward I the overall average (for a reverse die) was close to 20,000 coins, and it was 14,000 under Edward II. Under Henry III at Shrewsbury, Brand has shown that it was very close to 20,000, at a mint which used roughly 20 reverse dies in a year. The mints were then far busier. Roughly 80% of the Cross-and crosslets dies were used in quite active mints (defined as mints using more than 40 dies during the reign), so under-use of dies is not likely to be a major factor in the overall estimate, and it is in any case largely allowed for already by the method of estimation used. A multiplier of 14,000 gives a total of 19 million coins, while 20,000 would give 27 millions. Some small extra allowance should probably be made for the uncertain and illegible coins, BMC 812a-79, some of which may well be from known dies. (If they were mostly from known dies, their effect on the estimate would be neutral or even negative.) A cautious statement might be that the total output of Cross-and-crosslets coins lay between 10 and 30 millions, with 20 millions as a reasonable guess. When set against the total of 400-450 millions for Long Cross, the margin of uncertainly hardly matters.

Appropriateness of the sample

The sample is large. There are more coins in it than there were obverse dies originally used. This has a bearing on most of the detailed considerations which follow.

The British Museum's collection of Cross-and-crosslets coins, catalogued with amazing patience and care by D. F. Allen, might be expected to minimize the apparent occurrence of die-duplicates, since duplicates are not normally acquired for the collection. If this were so, an estimate based on the assumption that the collection was a random sample in respect of die-duplication would point to a far larger mint-output than the true one. For various reasons, however, the coins in the catalogue approximate to a suitable sample for purposes of estimation. Thus:

1. The coins are so badly struck that two or three examples of a single die have often been retained, where they were available, to supply the complete legend or design. Many duplicates entered the collection because at the time of acceptance they could not be read in full (BMC p. xv), i.e. it was not realized that they were duplicates.

2. The size of the collections is for many mints obviously such that one has several examples from each of the dies that was ever extensively used. By the same token, the size of the sample provides an estimate with unusually narrow margins for sampling error.

3. The 922 identifiable coins in the collection are dominated by three large blocks, which helps to give a numerically balanced picture; and cross-linkage between the blocks offers some sort of check. The entire Lark Hill hoard, of 208 Cross-and-crosslets coins, was acquired, as was a large part of the Leicester hoard (158 out of 238). The third block consists of coins from the Tealby hoard. They amount to only 6 or 7 per cent of the hoard, but the 10% of the hoard that escaped the melting-pot was probably selected on the basis of legibility more than anything else. Figures calculated from the Lark Hill hoard alone indicate a much smaller total output than that proposed above -

not more than ca. 450 obverse dies - but this may be largely explained by the virtual absence of Class F and by "clustering" of dies within the hoard.

4. Another 360 identifiable coins are incorporated into Allen's die-analysis in footnotes. There are often several specimens from the same dies as the British Museum coin. The additional coins cover the richest private collections of the day (L.A. Lawrence, R.C. Lockett, F. Elmore Jones, A.H. Baldwin Ltd., etc.) as well as other museums. Where a hoard has been dispersed, therefore, it is likely that many of the legible coins from it have become accessible to Allen by various routes. Sometimes Allen records "a similar coin", and he states (BMC p. 1) that this indicates that the dies of the coin "have not been checked against those of the coin in the catalogue; such coins may or may not be from the same dies." For purposes of estimation these coins have been counted as different dies, and this may have produced a final estimate significantly on the high side. Mr Elmore Jones, whose eye and visual memory for dies is phenomenal, has discovered numerous additional die-links overlooked even by Allen (see, for example, BMC 820a and p. cxviii).

5. An independent check of the accuracy of Allen's cataloguing, and on the validity of his sample, is provided by a more recent study of the Cross-and-crosslet coins of the Lincoln mint. H.R. Mossop's The Lincoln Mint (1970) provides a corpus of 168 specimens (against Allen's 78), with sometimes more than ten coins from a die. It pushes the total of known obverse and reverse dies from 46 and 48 to 58 and 59, but yields a marginally lower original total than BMC (66 obverse dies instead of a global estimate of 69).

6. As a check on the selective survival-rate of the coins, it may be noted that the survival-rate (coins/estimated dies) is not significantly higher for minor mints. Unless dies at those mints were much underused, therefore, there is no reason to think that numerous coins of the common mints have gone into the melting-pot. London coins (where there might be more of a temptation to shirk the task of checking every possible die) do seem to have had a genuinely lower survival-rate. Carlisle and Newcastle, Chester, and Hereford have had a high survival-rate.

The overall impression from items 1-6 is that the facts on which the statistical calculations have been based diverge from a suitably random sample in such a way that they probably yield an overestimate. As the main object of the exercise is to establish the fact that the English currency was relatively small in 1180, this is an error in the right direction.

Volume of currency

After the initial recoinage in 1158, the overall output of the mints fell away, as illustrated in the diagram below (which is based on Allen's chronology, BMC p. lxxiv, and on the adjusted total of 1,344 dies). The output of London and Canterbury within the totals is shown by the shaded portions of the histogram.

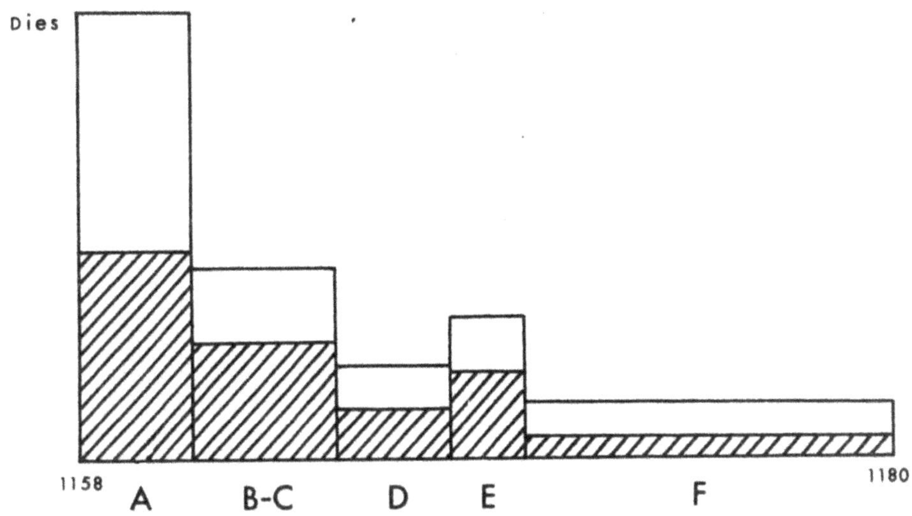

It is therefore likely that, as a result of normal losses from the stock of coinage (cf. thirteenth and fourteenth-century evidence), the currency in 1180 was appreciably smaller than the sum of mint output of the years 1158-80.

	Coins						Known obverse dies					
	A	B	C	D	E	F	A	B	C	D	E	F
Bedford	1	.	.	.	.	.	1	.	.	.	.	.
Bristol	10	3	.	4	1	4	8	1	.	1	1	2
Bury	7	11	18	4	4	17	4	1	2	2	2	10
Canterbury	49	18	67	29	23	33	28	10	40	19	16	21
Carlisle/Newc.	25	.	32	11	15	20	5	.	10	3	5	7
Chester	5	.	.	6	.	.	2	.	.	1	.	.
Colchester	8	.	8	.	5	.	6	.	3	.	2	.
Durham	18	4	7	.	.	.	2	2	1	.	.	.
Exeter	21	3	5	4	.	.	12	2	4	1	.	.
Gloucester	17	.	.	.	.	.	7	.	.	.	.	.
Hereford	9	.	4	.	.	.	3	.	1	.	.	.
Ilchester	8	3	3	4	.	1	5	2	2	1	.	1
Ipswich	.	8	21	13	7	37	.	2	9	4	4	26
Launceston	2	.	.	.	.	.	1	.	.	.	.	.
Leicester	12	.	.	.	.	.	6	.	.	.	.	.
Lewes	.	.	.	.	1	3	.	.	.	.	1	2
Lincoln	22	10	20	14	10	2	13	6	12	7	6	2
London	79	22	48	18	12	23	54	14	27	9	9	15
Newark	2	.	.	.	.	.	1	.	.	.	.	.
Northampton	30	.	11	4	.	.	18	.	5	2	.	.
Norwich	41	9	16	6	.	.	25	6	6	3	.	.
Oxford	16	.	.	2	4	.	11	.	.	2	3	.
Pembroke	2	.	.	.	.	.	2	.	.	.	.	.
Salisbury	6	.	.	.	.	.	5	.	.	.	.	.
Shrewsbury	3	.	.	.	.	.	2	.	.	.	.	.
Stafford	4	.	4	.	.	.	2	.	1	.	.	.
Thetford	38	.	15	19	.	4	19	.	3	8	.	3
Wallingford	6	.	.	.	.	.	3	.	.	.	.	.
Wilton	14	.	.	.	.	.	7	.	.	.	.	.
Winchester	24	.	13	2	1	.	17	.	5	1	1	.
York	45	.	3	8	.	.	23	.	1	4	.	.
- add												
Total	523	91	295	148	83	144	292	46	132	68	50	89
Grand Total						1285						677

	Non-singletons						Estimated total dies					
	A	B	C	D	E	F	A	B	C	D	E	F
Bedford	0	.	.	.	.	.	1	.	.	.	.	.
Bristol	4	3	.	4	0	4	20	1	.	1	1	2
Bury	4	11	18	3	3	11	5	1	2	3	3	16
Canterbury	36	12	42	15	10	19	38	15	64	37	37	37
Carlisle/Newc.	25	.	31	11	14	17	5	.	11	3	5	8
Chester	4	.	.	6	.	.	2	.	.	1	.	.
Colchester	4	.	7	.	5	.	12	.	3	.	2	.
Durham	12	4	7	.	.	.	3	2	1	.	.	.
Exeter	16	2	2	4	.	.	16	3	10	1	.	.
Gloucester	14	.	.	.	.	.	8	.	.	.	.	.
Hereford	8	.	4	.	.	.	3	.	1	.	.	.
Ilchester	5	2	2	4	.	0	8	3	3	1	.	2
Ipswich	.	8	18	13	5	17	.	2	11	4	6	56
Launceston	2	.	.	.	.	.	1	.	.	.	.	.
Leicester	9	.	.	.	.	.	8	.	.	.	.	.
Lewes	.	.	.	.	0	2	.	.	.	.	1	3
Lincoln	15	7	13	11	6	0	19	9	19	9	10	4
London	38	19	33	13	6	14	112	16	39	12	18	24
Newark	2	.	.	.	.	.	1	.	.	.	.	.
Northampton	19	.	10	4	.	.	29	.	6	2	.	.
Norwich	24	6	15	5	.	.	42	9	6	4	.	.
Oxford	9	.	.	0	2	.	20	.	.	4	6	.
Pembroke	0	.	.	.	.	.	2	.	.	.	.	.
Salisbury	2	.	.	.	.	.	15	.	.	.	.	.
Shrewsbury	2	.	.	.	.	.	3	.	.	.	.	.
Stafford	3	.	4	.	.	.	3	.	1	.	.	.
Thetford	29	.	14	15	.	2	25	.	3	10	.	6
Wallingford	5	.	.	.	.	.	3	.	.	.	.	.
Wilton	10	.	.	.	.	.	7	.	.	.	.	.
Winchester	13	.	12	2	0	.	32	.	6	1	2	.
York	32	.	3	5	.	.	33	.	1	7	.	.
- add							112	18	50	16	24	80
Total	346	74	235	115	51	86	559	85	233	114	115	238
Grand Total						907						1344

MINT OFFICIALS UNDER EDWARD I AND II

Mavis Mate

Recent events have shown how important it is for a ruler to choose his servants wisely.[1] Edward II, more than his father, has been criticized by historians for his selection of ministers. Piers Gaveston and the Despensers are not worthy companions for Robert Burnell. But what of the lesser members of his household and administration. Were they too unworthy foreigners or greedy, self-seeking natives? As yet, little is known about them. A look at the mint personnel during both reigns can help answer this question and also suggest why men were prepared to accept positions of responsibility under the crown.

The most obvious reward for service was salary. Mint employees were frequently paid more money when they did more work and these new, high salaries had a tendency to linger on after the need for them had passed. The doorkeepers at London and Canterbury, e.g., in the early years of Edward I's reign received just 13s. 4d. a year. During the recoinage of 1279-81 their salary jumped significantly to 3d a day (£4. 11s. 3d. a year), because of the extra work they had to do. When the recoinage was over, and their work-load was lightened, their new pay continued. Even during the lean years, 1291-8, when few merchants were coming to the London mint, the porter there continued to receive 3d. a day.[2] After the recoinage of pollards and crockards, however, the salary of the doorkeeper at Canterbury was reduced from £4. 11s. 3d. a year to £2. 12s. (1s. a week), because "the flood of merchants had lessened".[3] In 1301, when even fewer merchants were coming to the mint, his salary was cut still further, to £1 a year, and it stayed that way for four years. When merchants started to bring larger quantities of foreign silver to the mint once more, his salary returned to its former level and this time did not drop when the influx of silver ceased. Even during the last years of Edward II's reign, when little silver was brought to the London mint and none at all to the mint at Canterbury, both porters were paid the high salaries of £4. 11s. 3d. a year, which had been established during a time of peak minting activity.[4]

When men held more than one office, they were also paid more, but they sometimes had great difficulty in collecting their money. When Boniface Galgani was granted the joint positions of assayer and exchanger at both London and Canterbury, he was promised one hundred marks a year. He thus became the highest paid mint official, as the Warden received only 2s. a day (£36. 10s. a year). His salary, however, was slow to be paid. Despite forceful complaints in 1287, he did not receive any money from November 1285 until July 1290, when he was granted four hundred marks, the arrears of four years wages.[5] After he left England, his offices were shared among his two nephews, one working at Canterbury, and one at London. They were promised one hundred marks a year each, but there is no record of any money being paid to them. The nephew at London, Lapus Philip, failed to keep adequate records and his offices were taken from him. His brother, Lapinus Roger, was then appointed assayer at both London and Canterbury and promised £20 a year, the same salary as the new exchanger at London.[6] Shortly after he took office, however, the extra work involved in the recoinage of pollards and crockards earned him a raise and he and Roger de Frowyk, the London exchanger, were both paid £26. 13s. 4d. Once the pressure of work was over, their salaries were restored to their former level. Lapinus should then have recived £20 a year for his work as assayer and £20 a year for his work as exchanger at Canterbury. After September 1301, the Treasurer, Walter de Langton, refused to let the Warden pay Lapinus any wages as assayer, on the grounds that he was already being paid as exchanger. For the next six years Lapinus worked as assayer without pay. On the accession of Edward II and the fall of Walter de Langton, he petitioned the new king for his arrears, and agreed to accept ten marks a year for his work as assayer instead of the £20 to which he was entitled.[7] Eventually this compromise was accepted. He was given his back pay and for the rest of Edward II's reign received £26. 13s. 4d. whenever he held joint positions of assayer and exchanger at Canterbury.

Although he was born in Florence, Lapinus Roger settled down in England and devoted his whole working life to the service of the mint. He first became assayer and exchanger at Canterbury in 1292 on the departure of his uncle. Later, on the disgrace of his brother, he took over the position of assayer and exchanger at Canterbury for life. While he was in the city, he sometimes acted as attorney for the archbishop of Canterbury and the Frescobaldi, as well as serving as deputy Warden of the mint.[8] Later, he married a Kentish girl and raised his family there, becoming, in effect, a naturalized Englishman. As a result of his marriage he was admitted as a freeman of the City of Canterbury in 1311.[9]

Under Edward II, however, he was forced to spend more time in London. In 1310, when the Master of the Money, John de Pontoise, was imprisoned for making £14,680 which exceeded the standard by a quarter grain,[10] Roger took over his office and continued to hold it until 1317. During that time, the position of exchanger at Canterbury was given to John de Ramsey, the "brother" of the London exchanger, Roger de Frowyk, who supervised his work.[11] From 1317-19, Lapinus returned to Canterbury, but his successor, Giles de Hartesbury, proved incapable of minting coins in accordance with the royal specifications and was subsequently imprisoned for making money that was "less weak and of better alloy than it should have been".[12] Roger was then reappointed Master of the Money and continued to serve until the fall of Edward II. At that time he lost all his offices. Gawainus de Southorp became the Master of the Money and John de Pontoise, the former Master of the Money and later keeper of the dies, was appointed assayer and exchanger at both London and Canterbury.[13] Lapinus reminded the king that he had been appointed assayer and exchanger at Canterbury for life. Two years later these offices were restored to him and he was allocated the arrears of the fee.[14]

Roger de Frowyk, the London exchanger, also had a record of long service, keeping the position of exchanger for thirty years, from 1297 to 1327. He came from a family of London merchants and his brother, Henry, a pepperer, was alderman from 1272-86.[15] Frowyk himself was a prominent London goldsmith and was active in City affairs. He served as alderman of Langbourn Ward from 1312-24, and, in 1313, was chosen one of the assessors of the fifteenth.[16] He probably accepted the mint appointment because of the opportunities it provided to supply goods to the king and members of the court. In 1306, e.g., he received payment from the Wardrobe for gold goblets and plates and other valuables worth £664. 8s. 8d.[17] Three years later he was paid £322. 8s. 6d. for goods supplied just between July and November.[18]

Other merchants were willing to serve the mint in various capacities, in the hope, perhaps, of similarly furthering their trading ventures. William de Lisle, a merchant of Kent, became keeper of the dies at Canterbury in 1317.[19] John de Ramsey, a London goldsmith, and the brother of Roger de Frowyk, worked first as exchanger at Canterbury and later as keeper of the dies at London.[20] When Lapinus was appointed Master of the Money in 1311, he returned to Canterbury as exchanger and the Wardenship of the dies was given to John de Markenfield, who was either a London goldsmith, or an important royal clerk or both. There are several references to a John de Markenfeld, goldsmith of London, in the Memoranda Rolls,[21] and a man of the same name worked as King's Remembrancer in 1310 and later as chancellor of the exchequer.[22] So the same man was either acting in both capacities, or there were two different men with the same name.

In addition the Wardens of the Exchange often had close connections with trade and the City of London. Bartholomew de Castello had served as alderman of Cripplegate since 1260. But as he was also a household official and royal clerk, he probably served the king as mush as the City.[23] After Castello's disgrace in 1279, Edward chose one of the most important men in London, Gregory de Rokesle, to take charge of the mint.[24] Rokesle belonged to one of the leading London aldermanic families. Nominally a goldsmith, he also traded in corn, fish and cloth, as well as exporting wool and importing wine. He had become Mayor of London in 1274 and held that office until 1281. Later he was Mayor again from 1284 until July 1285 when the City was taken into the king's hands. He continued, however, to hold office of Warden until his death in 1291.

At this time the Treasurer, William de March, chose an obscure royal clerk, William de Wymondham, to succeed Rokesle. Before he joined the royal service, Wymondham had worked for the archdeacon of Chester as bailiff and receiver of his revenues,[25] but he does not seem to have had any connection with the City of London or with a trade. Why then was he chosen? It may just have been intended as a temporary appointment, for Wymondham was not formally appointed until nearly a year later, 5 May, 1292.[26] But it may also have been part of Edward's plan to subject the City to royal power and break the authority of the old-established London families. Between 1285, when the City was taken into the king's hands, and 1298, when self-government was restored, the old patriciate was destroyed as a political force. Aldermen were chosen from among the newer trades, but had not yet formed close links with the crown. With few people in the City that he knew well or trusted, the king appointed royal clerks to head the mint. When Wymondham fell into disfavor, he was replaced by Peter de Leicester, as Baron of the Exchequer, who had earlier served as clerk of the receipt of the Exchequer and one of the justices of the Jews.[27] Leicester, in turn, was replaced by another royal clerk, John de Sandale, who was continually employed on royal business in Gascony and England.[38] In 1305, however, Edward appointed Sandale chamberlain in Scotland, a position which needed all his time and attention. The king replaced him as Warden with John de Everdon, the parson of the church of Stoke Basset, who later became dean of St. Perter's Church, Wolverhampton and a Baron of the Exchequer.[29]

Edward II, at the beginning of the reign, returned to the practice of appointing merchants as Wardens, although his first appointment, that of Amerigo de Frescobaldi, was hardly calculated to conciliate the City, where anti-alien feeling was strong.[30] This appointment may have resulted from Edward's indebtedness to the Frescobaldi, or, more simply, their friendship with Piers Gaveston. At any rate, it was generally unpopular. Many Barons distrusted the Frescobaldi and their influence over the king and among the first demands of the Ordainers was one for their arrest. Later they specifically asked that an acceptable Warden be placed in the exchange.[31] When the Frescobaldi fled the country, the exchange, after the temporary wardenship of its clerk, John de de Cockermouth,[32] was granted once more to a leading London merchant, John de Lincoln.

Lincoln was a member of one of the new London families who came into prominence after Edward I's seizure of the City in 1285. His father had been elected one of the bailiffs of the cordwainers in 1300 and was sheriff of London from 1304 to 1305.[33] Lincoln junior, a cordwainer like his father, had been appointed a collector of customs at London in 1309 and the following year was elected alderman of Bassishaw Ward. He kept both offices for a while after his appointment as Warden, and so maintained his close connections with the City. In February 1315, however, Lincoln gave up the Wardenship, perhaps, because he was too busy with his mercantile pursuits, for the following year he gave up the collectorship of customs as well "as he had no leisure for it".[34]

His successor, William Trente, was a wine merchant, who had received many marks of royal favor and seemed equally at home in the City and at Court. Edward I, in November 1301, had appointed him King's Butler or Chamberlain for life and four years later, because of his loyal service, appointed him for life gauger of his wines throughout England and Ireland.[35] Royal patronage did not disappear with the death of the king, for Edward II, in January 1310, granted him the manor and town of Ware with the park there and the domain land at Kerswell in county Hereford for a £100 a year. A year later he was told that he need not pay the £100 for four years until he had recovered the money that the the king owed him.[36] During this time he was also active in City affairs. He served as Coroner to 1305. In 1309 he became alderman of Broad Street Ward and in January 1316 he was one of the representatives elected by the City to attend the parliament at Lincoln.[37]

Trente's sudden death in June 1316 ended the close relationship between the Wardenship and the City that had been maintained since the beginning of Edward II's reign. The king first gave the exchange to John de Cockermouth, a long-time mint official and royal clerk. Cockermouth started his royal service as serjeant to John de Kirkby, the King's Remembrancer, and later became King's Remembrancer himself.[38] He also worked as clerk of the exchange in 1303-5.

On the accession of Edward II he was given this office again and kept the positio until 1311 and perhaps until February 1315.[39] Although Cockermouth's wardenship was only brief, for the rest of his reign, Edward II continued to appoint royal clerks to head the mint and exchange. Augustine le Waleys of Uxbridge had served as clerk to justice William de Bereford before he became Warden in January 1317.[40] When he gave up the exchange on August 12, 1320, Edward appointed William de Hausetede, who, in the past, had worked for the bishop of London.[41] Haustede, however, died two years later and Robert de Haselshaw, provost of Wells, became Warden and remained in office until the accession of Edward III.[42]

Why did Edward II, like his father, begin appointing clerks, not merchants, as Wardens of the Exchange? It could, of course, have simply been administratively more convenient. Yet, it is possible, although by no means certain, that the switch was connected with the political problems facing the king. London citizens had strongly supported Thomas of Lancaster and his demand for the maintenance of the Ordinances. In April 1316, shortly before William Trente's death, Lancaster had retired to his estates, and real power was now resting with Aymer de Valence and other supporters of the crown.[43] Edward, therefore, no longer had the same need to conciliate the City, He was, however, still anxious to control it, and, after suspending the mayoralty for a few months in 1321, maintained restrictions on the freedom of elections until 1326. As a result of these actions, discontent was rife in the City, and the king may have found it hard, if not impossible, to find a London merchant of stature willing to accept the responsibility of the Wardenship.

Moneyers, like mint officials, were drawn from the ranks of merchants and royal clerks and many of them appear to have been equally closely connected with the cities of London and Canterbury. Unfortunately it is always difficult, if not impossible, to tell whether the same man was both moneyer and alderman, or whether these offices were held by two different men with the same name. Yet under Henry III it was clearly customary to grant the office of moneyer to London merchants and royal clerks for their maintenance,[4] so it is quite likely that Edward I continued this practice. Again, under Edward II, many of the workmen of the exchange and mint were also described as "merchants carrying on merchandise in the City".[45] The basic problem of identification, however, still remains. Was the Richard de Gloucester, who acted as temporary Warden during the absence of William de Wymondham, and was described as a leading moneyer in 1301 and again in 1310, the same man who served as the alderman from Basishaw and Cornhill Wards from 1295 to 1323?[46] Did the royal clerk, John de Kingston, who acted as constable of Edinburgh Castle, also serve as moneyer at London.[47] Did Walter de Gloucester, Baron of the Exchequer and escheator south of the Trent, also hold the position of moneyer?[48] At present these questions cannot be satisfactorily answered, but too many moneyers have the same name as royal clerks and London merchants for it to have been coincidence in every case.

In addition it is quite likely that brothers and cousins worked together in the same mint or some members of a family would work at London and others at Canterbury. Five men bearing the name Chigwelle, e.g., were moneyers at London about 1300. Two of them, Walter and William, are known to have been relatives of Homo de Chigwelle, the alderman of Queenhithe Ward from 1315-29, who was also Mayor of London several times.[49] Another, John de Chigwelle, was described as "valletus et familiaris" of the Treasurer.[50] It is possible that all five men were related, but this is by no means certain. Similarly it is known that three Chilhams worked at London and five at Canterbury, but the relationship between them is not clear.[51] The Chilhams were a long established Kentish family, whose members had served as sheriff of Kent and controlled property within the City of Canterbury as well as manors outside,[52] so it is not surprising that some of their members should hold positions in the Canterbury mint. Two of the Canterbury moneyers, however, seem to have been active in the royal service as well. A Nicholas de Chilham was one of the king's yeoman, a vallettus of the royal household, and Thomas de Chilham a clerk, went abroad with Queen Isabella in 1314.[53] The Chigwelles and the Chilhams were not the only examples of family service within the mint. Between 1280 and 1319 four Herts, four Bonseriants, three Downs, four St. Albans, three Shordichs and three Youngs worked at London.[54] Some of these men could have been brothers and cousins, and others were probably father and son, and, of course, some of them must have been unrelated.

Relatives of mint officials were also employed as moneyers. Robert Lapyn, a moneyer at Canterbury, was clearly the son of Lapinus Roger.[55] John de Waltham, a London moneyer, was the brother of the London clerk of the exchange, Richard de Waltham.[56] At Canterbury, Thomas de Tonyford worked as clerk of the exchange during the whole of Edward II's reign, and, during, that time, a John and Richard de Tonyford were employed as moneyers.[57]

All mint employees enjoyed important privileges, but they continually had to make concessions to preserve them. As early as 1219 they were free from tallage,[58] and by 1234 they had the right of being tried by the Warden.[59] In 1260, however, when Henry III tallaged the cities of London and Canterbury, he sought a "reasonable tallage" from the moneyers as well. They insisted that they had not been accustomed to contribute to tallages in the past, but eventually promised the king two hundred marks on the condition that he confirmed the liberties of the exchange.[60] Again, under Edward I, to persuade the king to maintain their privileges, they agreed to accept 1½d. less from each pound of silver that was minted.[61] In return the king gave them a new charter. On 5 December 1280, he promised them that they would be exempt from all tallages, that they would not be placed on assizes, juries or recognitions and that they could stand trial before the Warden in all cases concerning them, except those pertaining to free tenement and the royal crown.[62] A few weeks later, the first cut in the mintage rates occurred.

Despite their official exemption from tallage and subsidies, mint officials were often asked to contribute "of their own free will", or were assessed on the goods they held as a merchant. Thus the executors of Gregory de Rokesle were repeatedly asked to pay the five hundred marks that Gregory owed from an eighteenth levied on his goods within the City of London, even though he was Warden at the time.[63] In 1298 the moneyers at the London mint paid £5. 6s. 2d. towards a fifteenth being collected in London, but they did pay their contributions through the Warden and not the regular tax collector.[64] Three years later, the Sheriff seized the goods of the leading moneyers in an attempt to collect payment on an another subsidy. When the king sent a royal writ ordering the City officials to desist, the Mayor replied that the moneyers were not being taxed by reason of their office, but "as our fellow citizens, trading with us and enjoying the freedom of the City". Eventually a compromise was reached, whereby the sheriff restored the goods seized in distraint to the moneyers, who, in turn, temporarily accepted the City's point of view and promised to pay £40 towards the tax.[65]

At Canterbury local officials were equally zealous in trying to collect money from their privileged fellow citizens, and sometimes resorted to violence. In February 1301, for example, the bailiff and sub-bailiff broke the windows of the house of Thomas de Chilham, one of the Canterbury moneyers. A few months later, they came again and seized two brass jars worth 4s. and carried them away, claiming that Thomas owed them 4s. for a tallage. Even when Thomas paid them 2s., they still kept the two jars, The case eventually came before the exchequer court and the bailiffs said that Thomas "of his own free will" had conceded 4s. for his portion of the tallage and that when had paid only 2s., they seized the two jars. Thomas, however, denied this, insisting that he had not assented to any tallage, and that he had only paid the 2s. because the bailiffs seized the jars.[66] The resolution of this case is not recorded, but, in 1306, the Canterbury moneyers were told that they did not have to make any contributions to the thirtieth and twentieth and the tax collectors received an allowance for the £12. 9s. 9 3/4d. that had been assessed on the moneyers' goods.[67]

In an attempt, perhaps, to resolve this conflict, Edward II, in 1309, renewed his father's charter to the moneyers and agreed that they would not only be free from tallages, but all aids, prises and contributions of any kind. But he added that if the Warden and other ministers of the exchange granted the king a contribution of their own free will, by themselves, or with the community of the realm, then this aid was to be assessed and levied from the moneyers by the Wardens. The Wardens themselves were to be taxed by the Barons of the Exchequer.[68] Despite this grant, tax collectors continually tried to obtain contributions from moneyers and mint officials. The king, in turn, sent repeated writs to the Barons of the Exchequer, telling them not to molest mint workers or burden them with taxes, and insisting that any distraint which had been put on them was to be relaxed.[69] Even so, it often took a long time for the royal writs to have any effect. It was not until 1324 for example, that the moneyers at Canterbury were finally exonerated from a tax that had been levied on them in 1313.[70]

These disagreements between the moneyers on the one hand and exchequer and City officials on the other arose for a number of reasons. When the Mayor and Alderman of the City of London, under Edward II, tried to collect a contribution from the mint officials, they used the same argument that had been used in 1301, that the moneyers were being taxed, not as officials, but, "by reason of their mercantile pursuit".[71] This time, however, they do not seem to have succeeded in convincing the moneyers, for there is no record of any contribution being made. In addition when parliament granted a subsidy, the Barons of the Exchequer tacitly assumed that the consent of the moneyers was included with the consent of the rest of the realm and so the only privilege they were concerned with was the right of mint officials to be assessed by the Wardens, not the regular tax-collectors.[72] Mint officials, however, insisted that they should not be charged with aids or contributions "by reason of any grant that the community of the land had made in parliament, or out of parliament".[73] The king accepted the position of the moneyers, and, on receipt of their complaints, was willing to write to the Barons ordering them not to compel mint workers to make a contribution. But each time a tallage or subsidy was levied, the battle was fought anew, and occasionally moneyers, rather than put up a long fight, did pay of their own free will.[74]

These privileges, however hard they were to maintain, do help to explain why so many clerks and merchants were willing to accept positions as moneyers and mint officials. In addition a salary that was by no means negligible, and opportunities, particularly for goldsmiths, to supply the court, were added incentives. But by far the strongest reason for joining the mint seems to have been the tie of family relationship. Men frequently became moneyers, exchangers or clerks of the exchange because their father, brothers or cousins were already working there. Consequently the mint under Edward I and II was a close-knit organization, with no clear shift in personnel. Men such as Lapinus Roger and Roger de Frowyk happily served father and son. Both kings chose officials from merchants and royal clerks in accordance with the political climate of the time. Continuity, not change, was the keynote of mint administration during this time.

NOTES

1 In this article the following abbreviations have been used for records in the Public Record Office, London. E. 13 Exchequer, Plea Rolls: E. 101 Exchequer, King's Remembrancer, Accounts Various: E. 159 Exchequer, King's Remembrancer, Memoranda Rolls: E. 368 Exchequer, Lord Treasurer's Remembrancer Memoranda Rolls: E. 372 Exchequer, Lord Treasurer's Remembrancer, Pipe Rolls: E. 404 Exchequer, Warrants for Issue: SC. 1 Special Collections, Ancient Correspondence: SC. 8 Special Collections, Ancient Petitions.

2 At Canterbury there is no record of any salary being paid to the door-keeper during the Wardenship of William de Wymondham, from 1291-6, when the mint was closed.

3 The new salary came into effect on 29th September, 1300 (E. 372/150)

4 E. 372/174, m. 32d. The Warden had some difficulty in persuading the Barons of the Exchequer to allow him the money he had spent on wages. In the end it was agreed that as all the mint officials had remained in office on the king's insistence in order to make thin white money for Gascony, the Warden could use some of the £700 profit received from the Gascon coinage to pay wages at London and Canterbury (SC. 8, File 16 no. 761: Parliament Rolls, ii, 399a: CPR, 1327-1330, p. 518).

5 E. 159/61, m. 6d.; E. 372/135, m. 1.

6 He was formally appointed on 5 July, 1299 (E. 101/288/30).

7 E. 368/78, m. 24d.

8 E. 368/79, m. 131: E. 368/80, m. 107: E. 101/289/9: Registrum Roberti Winchelsey ed. Rose Graham, Canterbury and York Society, vol. LI, p. 398.

9 "The Earliest Canterbury Freemen's Rolls, 1298-1363" by Sylvia Thrupp and Harold B. Johnson, Documents Illustrative of Medieval Kentish Society ed. F.R.H. DuBoulay, Kent, Arch. Soc. XVIII, 1964 p. 197.

10 E. 368/81, m. 41d.

11 E. 368/95, m. 82. The position of assayer was given to Stephen Bek CPR, 1317-21, p. 394).

12 "minis debilis et maioris allaii" E. 368/89, m. 29.

13 Edward had written to the Treasurer and Barons of the Exchequer on 12 November, 1318 asking them to let "our dear friend", John de

Pontoise, have the wardenship of the dies (E. 368/89, m. 171), but according to the mint accounts, he did not formally take over until 5 February, 1319 (E. 372/164, m. 33d.).

14. SC. 8, File, 68, no. 3300. Later, in 1331, when Edward III decreed that no gold money should be used in the kingdom, he put Lapinus Roger in charge of the exchange table at Dover (E. 101/674).

15 For full details of the family history of the Frowyks, see Sylvia Thrupp, The Merchant Class of Medieval London (Chicago, 1948) p. 342-4.

16 Calendar of Letter Books of the City of London ed. R.R. Sharpe (London, 1889) A. p. 143: E. pp. 24, 145.

17 E. 101/369/11.

18 E. 404/481 file 14.

19 He wastthe son and heir of Walter de Lisle (E. 368/83, m. 79d.). In 1315 he was described as a valet of John de Lisle (E. 368/85, m. 184).

20 It is known that he held the position of keeper of the dies from 1307-11 (E. 101/289/9 no. 12: E. 101/289/11) and it is quite possible that he was appointed in 1301 when he gave up his office of exchanger, as the name of the keeper is not given at that time.

21 E. 368/88, m. 108: E. 368/91, m. 137d.

22 T. F. Tout, The Place of Edward II in English History (2nd ed,. Manchester, 1936)

23 He had worked as a clerk to chancellor Burnell (Gwynn Williams, Medieval London from Commune to Capital (London, 1963), p. 252).

24 During the recoinage, Orlandinus de Podio, one of the Riccardi, acted as joint Warden.

25 E. 159/65, m. 38.

26 E. 372/144, m. 26.

27 E. 159/66, m. 17: E. 159/70, m. 66d. Leicester became Warden on 2 December, 1296.

28 He became Warden in October 1298 (E. 159/73, m. 51d.). In'1297 he had gone to Gascony as controller of receipts and payments and, after his appointment as Warden, he returned there in September 1299 to audit some accounts (CPR 1292-1307, pp. 98, 140, 247, 440, 586).

29 CPR, 1292-1301, p. 272: CCR, 1302-7, pp. 131, 163, 175, 201-3: CPR, 1301-7, pp. 149, 202.

30 The appointment dated from 20 August, 1307 (CFR, 1307-19 p. 2).

31 Annales Londonienses, The Chronicles of the Reigns of Edward I and II, ed. William Stubbs (London, Rolls Series, 1857) I, p. 200.

32 He was Warden from 9-20th October 1311.

33 Cal. Letter Books, London, B, p. 159, C, p. 57. His father died in 1306, Letter Book C, p. 282.

34 He remained alderman until 1319. CCR, 1307-13, pp. 275, 321, 385: CFR, 1307-19, p. 275: Cal. Letter Books, London, C, pp. 126-141, 282.

35 E. 368/86, mm. 86, 87d.

36 E. 368/80, m.5; E.368/84, m. 58d.

37 Cal. Letter Books, London, E. p. 25.

38 E. 13/25. He was a canon of the priory of Blessed Mary, Carlisle (E. 368/85, m. 101d.) and acted, on occasion, as attorney for the Treasurer, John de Sandale and on Sandale's death was one of his executors (E. 368/85, m. 18).

39 He was named in the mint accounts from 1307-11, but from 1311 to 1315 the name of the clerk was not given, which probably indicates that it hadn't changed. In February, 1315, Richard de Waltham became clerk (E. 101/289/7: E. 101/289/11: E. 372/161, m. 44: E. 373/164, m. 33).

40 E. 368/89, m. 9d.: CFR, 1307-19, p. 351.

41 E. 368/78, m. 71d.

42 With little silver coming to the London mint and the mint at Canterbury closed, he had nothing to do and tried to give up his office. Edward II, however, insisted that he remain in office as long as money was being made at London for Gascony (SC. 8, File 16, no. 761). While he was in office, he acted as clerk of the Treasurer (E. 368/94, m. 52d.).

43 J.R. Maddicott, Thomas of Lancaster, 1307-22 (Oxford, 1970): J. R.S. Phillips, Aymer de Valence, Earl of Pembroke, 1307-24, (Oxford, 1972).

44 CPR, 1247-58, pp. 408, 468, 539, 580. In 1260 the king's surgeon was made a moneyer (CPR, 1258-66, p. 73).

45 Cal. Letter Books, London, D p. 260.

46 Munimenta Gildhallae Londoniensis, ed. H. T. Riley (Rolls Series, London, 1859), ii, 185-6: E. 101/289/9: A.E. Beaven, The Aldermen of the City of London (London, 1908).

47 A John de Kingston is mentioned as a leading moneyer in 1307 in Munimenta Gildhallae Londoniensis, ii, 185-6 and again in 1310 in E. 101/289/9. For the activities of the royal clerk see CPR, 1281-92, pp. 295, 348: CPR, 1292-1301, pp. 305, 388: CPR, 1301-7, pp. 390, 394: CPR, 1313-17, pp. 242, 383.

48 His name appears three times amongst the list of moneyers in E. 368/89, m. 40 d., which suggests that he held the appointment for some time.

49 Sylvia Thrupp, The Merchant Class of Medieval London (Chicago, 1948) p. 333.

50 E. 13/24, m. 46.

51 Hubert, John and Ralph Chilham worked at London and William, Roger, Henry, Thomas and Nicholas were moneyers at Canterbury (E. 368/89, m. 40d.).

52 For further details, see William Urry, Canterbury under the Angevin Kings (London, 1967) pp. 48-51.

53 CPR, 1292-1301, p. 505: CPR, 1301-7, pp. 160, 383: CPR, 1313-17, p. 86.

54 E. 368/89, m. 40d. Richard and Roger le Hert were clearly working together under Gregory de Rokesle (SC. 1/26 no. 10) and from the list it appears as if John, William and Richard le Hert were all employed in about 1307. John William, and Roger are also mentioned again, so that they appear to have been permanent employees.

55 In 1321 John Sauvage granted Lapinus Roger and Robert, his son, three hundred acres of marsh in county Kent (CPR, 1317-21, p. 559).

56 Calendar of Wills Proved and Enrolled in the Court of Hustings, London, 1258-1410, ed. R.R. Sharpe (London, 1889-90), i, 94. Richard de Waltham became clerk of the exchange in February, 1315 and kept his office until the accession of Edward III.

57 Richard de Tonyford was still working at the mint under Edward III "The Kent Lay Subsidy of 1334/5" Documents Illustrative of Medieval Kentish Society ed. F.R.H. DuBoulay, Kent, Arch. Soc., XVIII, 1964.

58 E. 159/3, m. 1.

59 CPR, 1232-7, p. 127: CCR, 1242-7, p. 364.

60 CPR, 1258-66, pp. 89-90.

61 SC. 8, File 120, no. 5977.

62 E. 159/77, m. 32d.

63 E. 159/66, m. 27d.

64 E. 159/71, m. 97d.

65 Cal. Letter Books, London, C, p. 103: Munimenta Gildhallae Londoniensis, ii, 183-6. The leading moneyers attending this meeting were John de Kingston, Ralph de Chilham, William and Henry de Chigwelle, John atte Down and Richard de Gloucester.

66 E. 13/24, m. 55d.

67 E. 159/79, m. 19: E. 159/80, m. 90.

68 Foedera, Conventiones Litterae et Cuiuscunque Generis Acta Publica ed. Thomas Rymer (London, 1929), ii, 67.

69 E. 368/80, m. 62d. (14 July, 1310): E. 368/82, m. 55 (29 July, 1312): E. 368/85, m. 108 (20 May, 1315): E. 368/86, m. 22 (2 November, 1315): E. 368/86, m. 63d. (24 April, 1316).

70 E. 368/94, m. 54d. The men affected were John de Bishopgate, William Gilemyn, Robert atte Bridge (braciator), Henry de Chilham, Thomas de Chilham, Robert Lapin, Lapinus Roger, John Hubert, Thomas le Taillour, Stephen de Hoo, Nicholas de Chilham (braciator), William atte Forde, Roger Elys, Thomas Doul (braciator).

71 _Cal. Letter Books_, _London_, D, p. 260.

72 _CFR_, _1319-27_, p. 254.

73 SC. 8, File 120, no. 5977.

74 Richard de Tonyford contributed to the Kent lay subsidy of 1334/5. _Documents Illustrative of Medieval Kentish Society_, ed. F.R.H. DuBoulay, Kent, Arch. Soc., XVIII, 1964.

CURRENCY AND THE ECONOMY OF EARLY FOURTEENTH CENTURY ENGLAND

Michael Prestwich

In recent years historians have come increasingly to recognise the importance of monetary factors in determining price movements, and in turn, of the whole course of economic development. Whereas A. L. Poole writing in 1951 did no more than connect the price rises of the late twelfth century to the onset of 'a period of agricultural prosperity',[1] P. D. A. Harvey has recently suggested that the explanation may lie in the sudden and striking influx of a mass of silver entering England in payment for wool exports.[2] A similar explanation has been put forward for the observable rise in prices in the first decade of the fourteenth century.[3] More important, perhaps, for the first half of the fourteenth century as a whole is the converse argument, seeing the period as one of deflation. It has been suggested that silver stocks were far from constant, and that the currency was subject to a very appreciable rate of loss, the result of wear, hoarding and export.[4] If changes in the currency did have marked effects on the economy of medieval England, then they should emerge clearly in this period. It is tempting to link the decline in the quantity of coin in circulation with the indications of economic depression in the years preceding the Black Death.

Such views are not universally accepted. While admitting the possibility that short term price changes may be affected by recoinages, a possibility graphically demonstrated by D. L. Farmer,[5] M. M. Postan has cast much doubt on the more general implications of monetary changes, stressing instead the significance of demand levels resulting in particular from demographic change.[6] Examination of admittedly scanty Genoese price evidence from the late twelfth and early thirteenth centuries suggests that the inflation of that period was not a purely English phenomenon, and that it was induced by an increased demand for goods rather than by an increase in the volume of coin in circulation.[7] A. R. Bridbury, conceding what he terms 'the subterranean existence' of the belief that the fourteenth century saw the onset of a silver famine, allowed that general price movements in this period might be monetary in origin. He did not, however, accord monetary factors much importance since 'the evidence shows unequivocally that they had no effect whatsoever on the relativity of wages and prices'.[8] The purpose of the present article is to examine some of the historical, rather than numismatic, evidence for the significance of the monetary changes of the period.

There is no need to provide more than a brief recapitulation of the evidence of the mint accounts: The fourteenth century began with the royal success in recoining the recently imported pollards and crockards into sterling, and the mints continued to work at a hectic pace until a peak was reached in 1309, their activity fuelled by large-scale purchases of foreign silver. Output then dropped, with production virtually ceasing in the 1320's. Some recovery took place in 1335, when the weight of the coinage was reduced slightly, 253 pence being taken from the pound, rather than 244, but it was not until a further change in 1344, with 270 pence being taken, that mint activity rose to levels comparable with the initial years of the century. These levels were not long maintained however, and production again began to fall in the late 1340's.[9]

The fluctuations in mint output must be seen against the evidence of currency losses through wear and export of bullion. The changes in the pattern of foreign trade are discussed elsewhere in this volume by T. H. Lloyd,[10] but another factor of significance was the export of coin as a result of war. This might occur in various ways. Considerable sums were paid to the Scots as protection money in the course of Edward II's reign: Durham paid £2,000 in 1313,[11] and Ripon promised 1,000 marks in 1318,[12] while a contemporary estimate put payments from the palatinate of Durham in this period at £20,000.[13] There is no way, unfortunately, of calculating the total received by the Scots in this way,[14] but it is tempting to suppose that some of the hoards dating from these years found in Scotland represent the fruits of such extortion. The defence of English possessions in France was probably a greater drain. There was the war of St. Sardos in 1323-5, while English expenditure abroad rose to exceptional levels in the late 1330's with the onset of the Hundred Years War.

Unlike his grandfather, who had exported large quantities of bullion in support of his war effort from 1294-97, Edward III sent surprisingly little money directly overseas to pay subsidies to his allies and to finance his armies. The keeper of the wardrobe took only about £5,865 with him in cash from England in 1338, and £4,896 in 1340. Yet between those years Edward III raised and spent about £400,000 in the Low Countries. Much of this was derived from loans made abroad by banking firms such as the Bardi and the Peruzzi, who advanced at least £106,000 in 1338-9,[15] but a substantial proportion represented the diversion of funds which would otherwise have come to England. Almost £8,000 is recorded as being paid over in customs duties in the Low Countries by English merchants, who made the payments to Edward's agents there rather than at the export ports. Substantial quantities of English wool were seized by the crown both at home and from English merchants in the Low Countries, and although the prices obtained for this wool were poor, Edward appears to have received almost £90,000 from this source.[16] In normal circumstances much of the proceeds of wool sales overseas would have been brought back to England by the merchants who had exported it; now, the proceeds were all spent on the king's extravagant military schemes, and did not augment the stock of domestic currency. Loans from Englishmen made in the Low Countries also represented a drain on bullion stocks: William de la Pole advanced over £33,000 by November 1338, and at least £37,000 between December 1338 and Midsummer 1339, for much of which he was merely acting as an intermediary for other English merchants.[17] This too was money spent abroad which would normally have come to England. So, although there is surprisingly little evidence of a direct flow of silver from England to the Low Countries in support of Edward III's war effort, there is every reason to suppose that the first phase of the Hundred Years War, that involving heavy expenditure on the purchase of alliances on the continent, witnessed in practice a very heavy drain on the English stock of currency.

It seems likely, too, that silver was being exported from England in exchange for gold at this period. Exchange rates are difficult to work out, particularly since the Italian companies were able to impose artificially high valuations on the florin. In the first decade of the fourteenth century the exchange rate for the florin varied from 2s. 6d to 2s. 8d., although the Frescobaldi were able to obtain a rate of just over 3s. in an account with the crown.[18] By 1339 an official rate of 3s. for the florin operated between the king and the Italians, but there are references to higher rates in the mid 1330s.[19] French gold coinage fluctuated considerably, the écu being valued at 3s. 9 1/4d. in 1341 on one occasion, and in 1343 at 3s. 7d and 3d. 4d.[20] The florin certainly appears to have been overvalued, and it made good sense for the Italians to import gold and export English silver, evading the bullionist regulations of the period.[21] Calculations can also be made from the account books of the company of the Peruzzi for the exchange rates of sterling against the Florentine money of account. These show that a rate of 1: 10.87 for the period 1324-31 fell to as little as 1: 9.25 on occasion by 1339. English coin appears to have been abnormally cheap in the years 1337-9, and the alteration in rates cannot be explained by changes in the metal content of the coinage. Confidence on the continent in Edward III and his military ambitions was low, and this was reflected in the value accorded to English coin. With English silver cheap, an outflow from the country was only to be expected.[22]

The evidence of military expenditure and of exchange rates suggests, therefore, that the stock of English sterling currency was being depleted from the middle of Edward II's reign, and that a massive outflow was taking place in the late 1330s. It is not possible to produce any exact calculations to compare with the estimates worked out from numismatic material by N. J. Mayhew, who has suggested that the level of currency stocks fell from over £1,000,000 to about £500,000,[23] but the general picture is clearly a similar one. It is necessary to make one qualification. Despite the rigid bullionist legislation, foreign coin did circulate in England to some extent, making good part of the deficiency. By the 1340's there is certainly evidence of the use of foreign gold coin in transactions in England, particularly the French écu. Such agreements as the recognisance of the Prior of the Hospital promising in 1347 to pay Thomas Harewold of London 1,450 écus,[24] and records of robberies of florins and écus are surely indicative of the situation.[25] Poor quality foreign black money was found in circulation in Dover in 1341,[26] and in the following year the sheriff of Middlesex was ordered to make an elaborate proclamation, forbidding the use of counterfeit money from overseas.[27] By 1348 there was a parliamentary complaint against the importation of 'lushbournes' from the Low Countries.[28]

In assessing the economic consequences of the state of the currency in the first half of the fourteenth century it is worth considering contemporary opinion. At the time monetary matters were regarded as highly significant. When the king's council met the civic authorities at York in 1301 to discuss the problem of high prices in the city, one of the reasons suggested was the recent influx of pollards and crockards,[29] and other evidence exists to show that prices were severely affected in the short term by this phenomenon at the turn of the century.[30] Suspicion and resentment of the crown's monetary policies never, of course, reached the heights they did in France, but there was certainly widespread concern and uncertainty. Edward II's denials, as in 1309, that any change in the currency was envisaged were, like so many of his statements, accorded little credit,[31] and in the Ordinances of 1311 it was laid down that the king should not change the money without the consent of the baronage in parliament. Edward III was not notably scrupulous about consulting parliament on currency questions, and in 1346 a petition protested against his policies, demanding that in future changes should only be made with parliamentary consent, a point conceded by statute in 1352.[32] That same year saw the Statute of Treason include the importation of 'lushbournes' in a very limited list of offences, where it stands rather incongruously alongside personal attacks on the king, his immediate family, and his justices.[33] Suspicion of the coinage at a local level is indicated by such incidents as the refusal of men in Devon in 1339 to use the new halfpennies and farthings.[34] The early stages of the gold coinage caused much difficulty, shown by such evidence as the commission to the bailiffs of Windsor to enquire into those refusing to accept the king's money at the ordained prices, and to imprison those found guilty.[35] An important contemporary comment dating from 1339 is that of a popular song: 'Il y a tant escarceté monete inter gentes, Qe houme puet en marché, quam parci sunt ementes', and 'gens non est leta cum sit tam parca moneta'.[36] The evidence suggests that the first half of the fourteenth century was a period of unusual uncertainty about the currency in England. An initial, erroneous conviction that the high prices of the early years of the century were the result of the lowering of the standard of the coinage was, by the 1330's, succeeded by alarm at the shortage of sterling coin and concern at the circulation of foreign coin of dubious quality. It was clearly considered that the state of the coinage had implications for price levels and indeed the general health of the economy.

How does the evidence of prices fit into this pattern? Discussion is rendered more difficult by the fact that the best compilations of prices so far produced terminate, with the exception of wool, in 1325,[37] while the disastrous grain harvests of 1315-16 severely distort the price history of the second decade of the century. Fluctuations in harvests, combined with the effects of animal diseases, dominate price changes in the short term, while over the long term changes in patterns of production and demand make it hard to single out price movements of a monetary origin.[38] It is perhaps permissible, however, to examine the figures for one staple product, and to detect some indications of monetary factors at work by comparing production levels with prices. Calculations based on wheat yields and prices have strongly suggested that the undoubted price rise of the period 1306-10 was the result of the inflation of the currency.[39] One method of doing this is to compare the ratio between yields and prices over periods of several years. In the period 1307-14, the ratio was 1:1.72, falling to 1:1.57 between 1324 and 1330. The years when the currency appears to have been at its lowest level saw the ratio fall further, to 1:1.31, and from 1342-49 there was a recovery to 1:1.55. The relationship can also be shown graphically, as in figure 1. A comparison between two years of almost identical yields, 1331 and 1342, reinforces the point. In the first case prices rose in the subsequent year to 9.17 shillings per quarter, and in the second, to only 4.83. It should be noted, however, that prices in 1331 and 1332 were unusually high in relation to yields. The most startling year was perhaps 1339, when the harvest fell to catastrophic levels reminiscent of 1315 and 1316, but prices rose to no more than an average 7.17

Figure 1. GRAIN PRICES AND YIELDS 1300–48

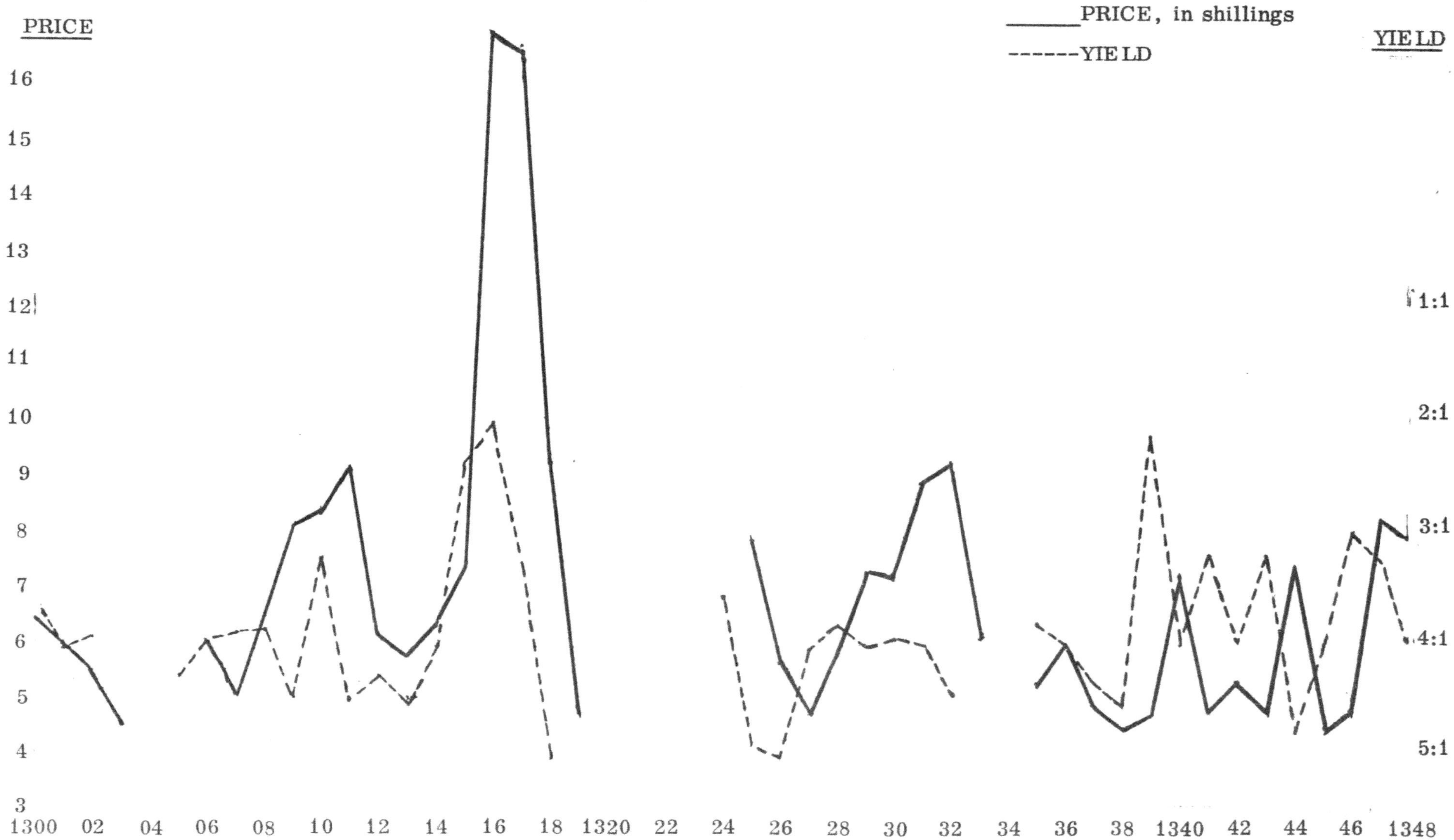

shillings. All of these calculations are from the evidence of the Winchester estates only.[40] What seems most significant is that the onset of really low prices was coincident with the outbreak of war with France, occurring long after the production of coin at the mints had slumped. A similar pattern has been observed for wool prices, but here the decline in prices began before the dislocation of the wool trade resulting from the war, with the crown's intervention in the wool trade, and a monetary explanation certainly has its part to play in any explanation of wool price fluctuations.[41]

It does not seem likely that changes in demand could account wholly for these fluctuations in price levels. The famine years of the second decade of the century undoubtedly caused a fall in population, and it is questionable whether these losses, perhaps amounting to as much as 10%, were made up in the years preceding the Black Death.[42] The probable chronology of population change, therefore, does not correlate at all closely with the changes in price levels, and it seems better to accept the views of contemporaries such as Adam Murimuth, who specifically attributed low prices in the 1330's to a lack of money. This lack was even recognised by the government and parliament in negotiating the unusual tax of a ninth taken in 1341, taken in kind rather than coin, because of the great shortage of money in the land'.[43]

What were the effects of the changes in the quantity of coin and of consequent price levels in this period? Part at least of the answer should be provided by wage statistics. If Bridbury is correct in assuming that wage rates fluctuated in remarkable unison with prices, that would have maintained real wages at a constant level,[44] and so minimized the effects of currency disturbance. However, the wage evidence is not so simple and clear cut. The statistics collected by Lord Beveridge and his researchers are far from reliable, and in general agrarian wages, for such tasks as threshing and reaping, do not appear to show a consistent trend, either rising or falling, in the first half of the fourteenth century.[45] However, it is worth noting that the years of real crisis, the late 1330's did see some wages fall alongside prices. Phelps-Brown and Hopkins noted this period as witnessing one of only three falls in the rates they calculated for the wages of building craftsmen over seven centuries,[46] and there is some evidence of a fall in craftsmen's wages on the Winchester estates in the late 1330's and early 1340's.[47] Manorial wages fell markedly on the Clare estates at the same time.[48] However, in general the first half of the fourteenth century did not see such striking movements of wage rates as to suggest that monetary changes were provoking any long term readjustments to the commonly accepted levels of pay.

It has been suggested that the high prices of the initial years of the fourteenth century provided a stimulus to the maintenance of the techniques of 'high farming',[49] and we might also expect to find the deflation of the second quarter of the century prompting landlords to abandon demesne production in favour of a leasehold system. It is, of course, extremely difficult to relate changes in managerial technique to any precise chronology, and it becomes hard to distinguish between high prices resulting from inflation and the famine prices of 1315-17. M. Mate in discussing the effects of these phenomena has rightly pointed to another problem, the often illusory character of manorial profit figures.[50] It seems probable that the earl of Lancaster had begun to lease out his demesnes on a substantial scale before the famine struck, in an attempt to cover his heavy expenditure.[51] On the other hand, the evidence from Bolton Priory shows that levels of investment, largely in building, were never higher than in the years 1303-9, the period of monetarily induced inflation, and those years witnessed an undoubted move toward the direct and centralised management of the Bolton demesnes.[52] No national pattern, however, can be clearly established.[53] In the years after the famines, when prices began to fall, an acceleration of the movement toward leasing can be observed. At Ely a marked decline in income has been noted from 1325-33, with a consequent shift from grain production for the market.[54] On the Beauchamp estates acquisition of new property proceded on a much smaller scale in the 1330's and 1340's than in previous periods.[55] Even so, exceptions can be found to the general pattern of leasing and reducing demesne acreages. The little manor of Langenhoe in Essex saw a substantial increase in demesne production in the 1340's.[56]

The years of acute monetary deflation, the late 1330's and early 1340's were also years of agricultural depression. Much the most striking evidence for this is the Nonarum Inquisitiones. This is a document that must be viewed with some caution, for it is the result of an enquiry into the poor yields of the ninth authorised in 1340. There had been great difficulty in raising cash from the sale of the produce collected, partly because the government set unrealistically high minimum prices.[57] Throughout the country jurors proferred explanations for the failure of the assessment to reach the expected levels, such as the poor bean harvest resulting from dry weather, and the fact that much land was too poor to be worth cultivating. One theme which runs through the text is particularly relevant to the present discussion: that of poverty. In many cases the tenants were said to be too poor to cultivate the land. The costs of agriculture are rarely blamed, although at Fawnesly (Northants) it was stated that the yield of grain barely paid for the seedcorn.[58] Nor are rents considered, although it seems unlikely that they would have fallen with prices: at Ely, certainly, land rents were not appreciably reduced in the second quarter of the century, and on some estates they rose.[59] The main financial burden mentioned in the returns is that of royal taxation, a burden not responsive to economic conditions to any appreciable extent. At Reading the town was said to be impoverished because of lack of trade, and the inhabitants reduced to poverty by 'various heavy aids granted to the lord king, and because of payments for the keeping of the seas'. At Sunbury in Middlesex, the parishioners had sold their animal stock 'because of too much taxation', and at Swaffham Prior in Cambridgeshire it was said that the land could not be sown as a result of the poverty of the villagers.[60] This latter plea echoes precisely the Song of the Husbandman of Edward I's time, where the complaint is that seedcorn has to be sold in order to pay taxes, so that the land is left fallow.[61]

It may seem surprising that medieval levels of taxation should have been considered so severe as to drive men into a state of destitution, and a measure of exaggeration must certainly be allowed for in interpreting the Inquisitiones Nonarum. If, however, the currency really stood at little more than £500,000, then a single fifteenth, raising some £38,000, was a substantial burden. Yet the late 1330's saw lay fifteenths and clerical tenths being levied annually, while the country had in addition to bear the weight of purveyance and wool taxation.[62] At least during the period of collection the money raised in taxes was removed from circulation, and even if it was not exported in support of the the war effort it would have taken a considerable time to filter back to the level of the local peasant ecomony from which much of it was derived. Detailed tax assessments, where they survive, suggest that the implications of taxation could be very severe in monetary terms. The assessment for Colchester in 1301 has long been in print. In that year coin was included in the list of taxable articles, but in the majority of cases none was in fact listed. William Unglefoot, however, had 18d. in coin. His total assessment came to 12s. 4d.: he had to pay 11½d. in tax. A wealthier man, John Saher, was assessed at £2 12s., of which 5s. was in coin 'for trade'. He paid 3s. 1 3/4d. in tax.[63] Obviously it was very easy to conceal coin from the tax assessors, but the indications are are that few men possessed any substantial quantity of coin as a cash reserve, and that the demands of tax collectors might well reduce that reserve very considerably.[64] J.R. Maddicott's suggestion that high mortality in 1342, as indicated by heriot payments, may be explained at least in part by high taxation, seems very plausible.[65] The evidence of widespread poverty fits very well with the arguments put forward by A.R. Bridbury in attempting to explain the way in which demographic evidence of mortality in the Black Death fails to correlate with the economic indicators, suggesting that much of the populace had reached such depths of impoverishment prior to 1348 that they were performing no effective economic function at all.[66]

What other economic effects might be attributed to the monetary problems of this period? It has been suggested in general terms that the shortage of coin in later medieval Europe provided an incentive for the development of credit techniques,[67] and it is striking that two very similar complaints about the crown's use of tallies as a means of credit date from years when coin was scarce. The Evesham chronicler complained about the unprecedented use of tallies by royal purveyors in 1297,[68] and in 1339 the Song against the King's Taxes advised Edward III to melt down his plate and coin it, abandoning the use of wooden tallies, so that he would eat off wood and pay with silver, rather than eat off silver and pay with wood.[69] The crown's use of credit, however, making use of wardrobe indentures and tallies, was not so much a direct reflection of the shortage of coin in the country as of the failure to raise sufficient funds by way of taxation to match expenditure. The fact that on occasion debentures might circulate for years before they were paid off was equally more a consequence of the crown's insolvency and of its reluctance to pay off unimportant creditors than a genuine response to difficult economic circumstances. Nor is there evidence to suggest an increase in the private use of credit in the first half of the fourteenth century. The Italian merchant companies were important in providing exchange and credit facilities in England, and it was certainly convenient for the younger Despenser to pay £300 to the earl of Norfolk in 1324 by simply ordering his bankers, the Peruzzi, to transfer the funds to Norfolk's bankers, the Bardi.[70] Such operations seem unlikely, however, to represent a response to a bullion shortage, and the first half of the fourteenth century did not see an increase in Italian activity in England, rather the reverse. A different form of credit may have been represented by the use of tokens as coinage, but despite the ample archaeological evidence for the existance of jettons, there is no documentary indication of their use as substitute coins.[71]

The natural response to the lack of coin in the country was not, in fact, to develop credit mechanisms, but to introduce policies likely to attract silver into the country, and this is what Edward III attempted to do in the 1340's, with some success. Regulations ordered all merchants to bring back two marks of silver into England for each sack of wool they exported, and a gold coinage was introduced. Initially this was intended as a rival and replacement for the florin, an international coin whose export from England was permitted, clearly in the hope that silver would be imported in exchange for gold.[72] The reduction in the weight of the silver coinage in 1344 also permitted the mint to offer a more attractive price for silver, making it more competitive with its continental rivals. There was no thought of the possibility of expanding forms of credit to compensate for the deficiency of coin in circulation.

It should be pointed out that, for all the undoubted concern and uncertainty that existed over the currency in the first half of the fourteenth century, England suffered far less than her continental neighbours from monetary problems. English records do not have the constant notes of currency changes that feature in the accounts of St. Martin de Tournai, where we find such entries as 'de die in diem erat mutatio monete, ita quod nulla certitudo esse poterat de solidis atque libris'.[73] Salamon de Ripple may have been trying to take advantage of the state of the coinage in 1335 when he reportedly weighed money paid for a fifteenth and tenth in Kent against specially selected heavy coins,[74] but there was never any need to adopt the complex systems of indexation devised in France as a protection against currency fluctuation in this period.[75]

Yet even if the situation was more serious in France and the Low Countries, there is no reason to ignore the monetary situation in analysing the English economy of the first half of the fourteenth century. It was one factor among many, and its influence is not always possible to isolate. The disasters of the famine years, the changes in the structure of England's overseas trade, the probable course of demographic development and shifts in the organisation of agriculture combined with the deflation of the coinage to make the period from the second decade of the century one of recession and poverty. The normal wastage rate of the currency was aggravated by heavy military expenditure and the fact that profits could be made by merchants exporting silver from the realm. As a result, relatively low prices reflected not good harvests, but a shortage of coin, a shortage exacerbated by the heavy rate of royal taxation in the initial stages of the Hundred Years War. The deflation was not a gradual process, but became particularly marked in the late 1330's. Contemporaries considered that land was going uncultivated as a result of poverty, and that poverty owed something at least to the acute monetary crisis of that period. The contrast with the initial years of the century, when foreign silver came to the English mints in massive quantities, causing a demonstrable monetary inflation, is a striking one, and the history of the first half of the fourteenth century shows that there can be circumstances when a degree of inflation is vastly preferable to the reverse process.

NOTES

1. A. L. Poole, *From Domesday Book to Magna Carta* (Oxford, 2nd ed. 1955), p. 54.

2. P. D. A. Harvey, "The English Inflation of 1180-1220", *Past and Present* LXI (1973), 25-9.

3. M. C. Prestwich, "Edward I's Monetary Policies and their Consequences", *EcHR* 2nd ser. XXII (1969), 415-6; M. Mate, "High Prices in Early Fourteenth Century England: Causes and Consequences", *ibid.*, 2nd ser. XXVIII (1975), 1-16.

4. N. J. Mayhew, "Numismatic Evidence and Falling Prices in the Fourteenth Century", ibid., 2nd ser. XXVII (1974), 1-15.

5. D. L. Farmer, "Some Livestock Price Movements in Thirteenth Century England", *ibid.*, 2nd ser. XXII (1969), 13.

6. M. M. Postan, *The Medieval Economy and Society* (London, 1972), pp. 235-41, 248-9.

7. W. N. Bonds, "Some Industrial Price Movements in Medieval Genoa (1155-1259)", in *Economy, Society and Government in Medieval Italy*, ed. D. Herlihy, R. S. Lopez, V. Slessarev (Kent, Ohio, 1969), pp. 124-35.

8. A. R. Bridbury, "The Black Death", *EcHR* 2nd ser. XXVI (1973), 578.

9. A convenient graph of mint activity is provided by N. J. Mayhew, *loc.cit.*, 11.

10. See Lloyd below pp. 96-124.

11. J. R. Maddicott, *Thomas of Lancaster* (Oxford, 1970), p. 149.

12. G. W. S. Barrow, *Robert Bruce* (London, 1965), pp. 341-2.

13. R. Nicholson, *Edward III and the Scots* (Oxford, 1965), p. 51, n. 1.

14. The fact that the Scots promised to pay £20,000 to the English in 1327 should not be taken as an indication that this was equivalent to English losses: see Barrow, *op.cit.*, p. 367. The payment should, however, be offset against the money taken by the Scots in their raids.

15. E. B. Fryde, "Financial Resources of Edward I in the Netherlands, 1294-98: Main Problems and Some Comparisons with Edward III in 1337-40", *Revue Belge de Philologie et d'Histoire*, XL (1962), 1186-7.

16. E. B. Fryde, "Financial Resources of Edward III in the Netherlands, 1337-40", *ibid.*, XLV (1967), 1143-4, 1149, 1161, 1169.

17 Ibid., 1153, 1160.

18 Les Livres des Comptes des Gallerani, ed. G. Bigwood and A. Grunzweig (Acad. Royale de Belgique, comm. royale d'histoire, 1961-2), I. 6-12 and passim; Public Record Office, E 101/126/21.

19 See for example CCR 1337-39, pp. 230, 571; CCR 1339-41, pp. 622, 452, 660. There are also many references to 'royal florins', presumably French royals: they were valued at 3s. 2½d. in 1333 and at 3s. 9d. in 1336: CCR 1333-37, pp. 106, 575. This coin was roughly equivalent to the Florentine florin: see E. Fournial, Histoire Monétaire de l'Occident Mediéval (Paris, 1970), p. 88.

20 CCR 1343-46, pp. 48, 121. Many further examples of exchange rates can be found in the Patent and Close rolls.

21 For an important general discussion of this question, and of the role of the Italians, see R.H. Bautier, 'L'or et l'argent en occident de la fin du xiiie siècle au début du xive siècle', Académie des Inscriptions et Belles-Lettres, Comtes-Rendus (1951), pp. 169-74.

22 I Libri di Commercio dei Peruzzi, ed. A. Sapori (Milan, 1934), pp. 285, 370; E. Ames, 'The Sterling Crisis of 1337-1339', Journ. Econ. Hist., XXV (1965), pp. 496-522.

23 Mayhew, loc. cit., 7.

24 CCR 1346-49, p. 250. For a reference to attempted import of écus from Flanders to England in 1344, see CCR 1343-46, p. 386. The coin was on this occasion seized by the French.

25 See for example CPR 1348-50, pp. 173, 586; CPR 1350-54, pp. 446, 452.

26 CCR 1341-3, p. 105.

27 Ibid., p. 685. See also the commissions of 1343, CPR 1343-45, pp. 81-2, and the proclamations of 1347, CPR 1345-48, p. 303.

28 CCR 1346-9, p. 492. A case of the importation of these coins had come up in 1346: CPR 1345-48, p. 514.

29 York Civic Ordinances, ed. M.C, Prestwich (York, 1976), p. 14. Interestingly, the royal authorities appear to have claimed that pollards and crockards were of equal standard to English sterling coins. On this question see Mayhew and Walker below pp. 125-46.

30 D.L. Farmer, 'Some Grain Price Movements in Thirteenth Century England'. EcHR 2nd ser. X (1957), 210.

31 M. Mate, loc. cit., 10.

32 P. Spufford, 'Assemblies of Estates, Taxation and Control of Coinage in Medieval Europe', XIIe Congrès International des Sciences Historiques, Studies Presented to the International Commission for the History of Representative and Parliamentary Institutions (Vienna, 1965), pp. 122-5.

33. Statutes of the Realm, I (Record Commission, 1810), 320.

34 CCR 1339-41, p. 270.

35 CCR 1343-46, p. 467.

36 Anglo-Norman Political Songs, ed. I. S. T. Aspin (Anglo Norman Text Soc., 1953), p. 111.

37 See the works by D. L. Farmer, cited supra, notes 5, 30, and T. H. Lloyd, The Movement of Wool Prices in Medieval England (EcHR supplement no. 6, 1973).

38 D. G. Watts, 'A Model for the Early Fourteenth Century', EcHR 2nd. ser., XX (1967), 545, compared prices over two lengthy periods, 1261-1310 and 1331-50, finding that in general prices of animal products, such as cloth, hides and butter, rose, while grain prices fell.

39 D. L. Farmer, 'Some Grain Price Movements in Thirteenth Century England', EcHR 2nd ser. X (1957), 217-8; M. C. Prestwich, 'Edward I's Monetary Problems and their consequences', ibid., 2nd. ser. XXII (1969), 415.

40 Figures derived from J. Z. Titow, 'Evidence of Weather in the Account Rolls of the Bishop of Winchester', EcHR 2nd ser. XII (1960), (1960), 381-402.

41 Lloyd, op. cit., p. 18, and see the tables and graphs on pp. 46, 63, 66.

42 I. Kershaw, 'The Great Famine and Agrarian Crisis in England 1315-1322', Past and Present LIX (1973), 36-50.

43 A. Murimuth, Continuatio Chronicarum, ed. E. M. Thompson (Rolls Ser., 1889), p. 89; N. M. Fryde, "Edward III's Removal of his Minister and Judges", Bull. Inst. Hist. Res., XLVIII (1975), 152.

44 Bridbury, loc. cit., 582-3.

45 The best evidence available is of course that of the Winchester estates, but discussion based on this material should be postponed until the publication of Dr. Titow's work on Winchester wages, and Dr. Farmer's study of wages in the forthcoming Agrarian History of England and Wales, ii.

46 E. H. Phelps Brown and S. V. Hopkins, "Seven Centuries of Building Wages", in Essays in Economic History II, ed. E M. Carus-Wilson (London, 1962), 174.

47 I owe this information to the kindness of Dr. J. Z. Titow.

48 G. A. Holmes, The Estates of the Higher Nobility in XIV Century England (Cambridge, 1957), p. 91.

49 M. Mate, loc. cit., 15-16.

50 Ibid. For a good summary of the problems of manorial profit figures, see I. Kershaw, Bolton Priory (Oxford, 1973), pp. 43-7.

51 Maddicott, Thomas of Lancaster, pp. 31-2.

52 Kershaw, Bolton Priory, pp. 36-7, 120-22.

53 See the cautionary remarks of J.Z. Titow, English Rural Society, 1200-1350 (London, 1969), p. 52, where 'an explanation in terms of a sudden change in the general economic situation' is ruled out.

54 E. Miller, The Abbey and Bishopric of Ely (Cambridge, 1951), pp. 105-6.

55 Holmes, Estates of the Higher Nobility, pp. 113-4.

56 R.H. Britnell, 'Production for the Market on a Small Fourteenth Century Estate', Ec.H.R. 2nd. ser. XIX (1966), pp. 384-5.

57 N.M. Fryde, loc. cit., 152.

58 Inquisitiones Nonarum (Record Commission, 1807), p. 26.

59 Miller, Abbey and Bishopric of Ely, pp. 110-11; Holmes, Estates of the Higher Nobility, pp. 103, 114.

60 Inquisitiones Nonarum, pp. 10, 198, 211.

61 The Political Songs of England, ed. T. Wright (Camden Soc., 1839), pp. 149-52.

62 The financial burdens of this period are well summarized by J. R. Maddicott, The English Peasantry and the Demands of the Crown (Past and Present supplement no. 1, 1975), pp. 46-7. See also W. Stubbs, Constitutional History of England II (4th ed., 1906), 397 n. 1.

63 Rotuli Parliamentorum, i (London, 1783), 243-65.

64 For an important discussion of the question of the impact of taxation in this period, see E. Miller, 'War, taxation and the English economy in the late thirteenth and early fourteenth centuries', in War and Economic Development, ed. J.M. Winter (Cambridge, 1975), pp. 11-31. See also J. R. Hadwin, below.

65 Maddicott, The English Peasantry and the Demands of the Crown, p. 72.

66 Bridbury, loc. cit., 590-1.

67 C. Cipolla, 'Currency Depreciation in Medieval Europe', EcHR 2nd. ser. XV (1963), 418.

68 Bodleian Library MS. Laud Misc. 529, f. 87v. I owe this reference to the kindness of Dr. J.H. Denton, who lent me his transcript of part of this chronicle.

69 Anglo-Norman Political Songs, p. 111.

70 A. Steel, "The Negotiation of Wardrobe Debentures in the Fourteenth Century", EHR XLIV (1929), 439-43; G. O. Sayles, "A Dealer in Wardrobe Bills", EcHR III (1931-2), 268-73; E. B. Fryde, "The Deposits of Hugh Despenser the Younger with Italian Bankers", EcHR 2nd ser. III (1950-1), 348.

71 But see Palmer and Mayhew, below, pp.88-9.

72 Statutues of the Realm I (Record Commission, 1810), 289, 291; Rotuli Parliamentorum, II, 137.

73 Comptes et documents de l'abbaye de St. Martin de Tournai sous l'administration des gardiens royaux (1312-1355), ed. A d'Haenens (Brussels, 1962), p. 574.

74 Historiae Anglicanae Scriptores Decem, ed. R. Twysden (London, 1652), p. 2068. This incident raises the question of how common it was to weigh coinage, since Ripple's offence appears to have lain in his selection of especially heavy coins, not in the act of weighing. It is perhaps relevant to note that in 1297 specific instructions were given to tax collectors that they were not to weigh coin, but were to accept it by count: 'E qe les chiefs taxeurs preignent la moneye le roi par counte saunz peiser tiele come court en roiaume', Parliamentary Writs, ed. F. Palgrave (Record Commission, 1827), I, 55, 63. The correct reading 'peiser' rather than 'priser' is established by E 159/70, m. 123. This instruction was not repeated later, and it suggests that it may have been commoner to make payment by weight than is often thought, though Willard certainly assumed that payment by tax collectors in to the exchequer was by weight: J.F. Willard, Parliamentary Taxes on Personal Property, 1290 to 1334 (Cambridge, Mass., 1934), p. 258. See also Mayhew and Walker below.

75 E. Fournial, 'L'indexation des créances et des rentes au xive siècle', Le Moyen Age, 4th ser., XVIII (1963), 583-96.

SMALL CHANGE IN THE LIGHT OF MEDIEVAL SITE-FINDS

S.E. Rigold

It is necessary, first of all, to define, 'small change', for at no time in medieval England were there denominations so small that their loss might be ignored and not worth the trouble of searching, as may well have been the case of minims and barbarous radiates. This study covers the three or four smallest denominations available at any time, which, as long as nothing more than a silver penny was normally struck, include also the highest. It ignores those which, after the middle of the fourteenth century, were preferred for hoarding and less exposed to the wear of circulation, i.e. gold coins and groats (but not half-groats), though these too occur as isolated site-finds. It also ignores jettons, which themselves were only available from the end of the thirteenth century, and thereby does not re-open the vexed question whether these, by custom, though certainly not by statute, might have been accepted as a kind of token coinage. In view of the relatively high value, in terms of labour, of coins from half-a-groat to a farthing, it seems at first remarkable how many, rather than how few, single finds have been recorded on medieval sites: the contrast with Roman sites is strong if *Aes* or silvered *Aes* is reckoned, but not if only denarii and siliquae are told. It is only when the total of medieval casual coin finds recorded over half a century is set against the probable total production that the small proportion of coins that have survived in this way becomes apparent. By the inherent likelihood of loss this study is progressively biassed towards the smaller denominations, including cut fractions, circulating at any given time. Against the hypothesis of the circulation of jettons it may be be noted that on many, but not all, sites the total of jettons found is of the same order as that of coins, which would hardly be so it they represented minor fractional denominations.

Over nearly 30 years in the Ministry of Works and its successors I have had a view of numismatic finds from medieval excavations over most of England and Wales, though my descriptive work has been mainly confined to jettons. At the same time I have made extensive use of the record-cards of finds over a much longer period from monuments in the care of the Ministry, whether from supervised excavations or otherwise. I was left with a number of cumulative impressions, which, like most such impressions, have proved to be fundamentally right but distorted in proportion. Among these I noted:

1. that Short-cross coins were conspicuously commoner than anything earlier, though the rise, noticeable in Class 1, was accelerated under John;
2. that 'Tealby' coins were, if anything, rarer than those of Stephen;

3. that all these early finds, but perhaps less so Long-cross, had a high proportion of cut fractions;

4. that the 'Edwardian' coinage showed an increase over its predecessors at least comparable with that of Short-cross;

5. that 'Edwardian' fractions were rare, until those of the 1330's and '40's, which were quite common;

6. that most 'Edwardian' coins were in fair condition, those of the later 14th century conspicuously less so, York pence of Richard II, for instance, occurring quite often, but always very worn;

7. that 15th century pence were progressively rarer than earlier ones, and almost always ill-preserved, but that on a few sites they were relatively numerous;

8. that these 'tailings-off' at either end from a 13th-14th century climax were much greater than could be explained by the known occupation or desertion of the sites - most of the castles and religious houses dated from the early 12th century, if not before, and continued to the Tudor age.

It was this Symposium that finally induced me to verify my impressions (having long sought for somebody else to do it), by collecting and analysing all single site-finds of less than a groat and with no suspicion of coming from a hoard, whether they were well stratified of not, until they reached what seemed to be a statistically significant sample. This I set at 100 sites, collected at random from whatever source came to hand, whether the excavation was exhaustive, partial or casual, and whether the descriptions could be verified or not, provided they were adequate for the purpose. The only self-imposed limitations were (a) a deliberate culling of sources widely distributed over England and Wales and (b) a proportionate representation of classes of site that suited the available evidence very well and might be expected, as in fact it appears to do, to show significant differences between the classes. The classes and their proportions are:-

I. 33% Religious Sites, of all kinds from major monasteries to isolated parish churches, including pilgrimage-chapels (for which reason Richborough is, from the medieval point of view, a religious site), urban religious houses, but not urban parish churches (cf., however, IV).

II. 33% Fortified and Wealthier Secular Sites - Castles, including minor forts; palaces, including episcopal; major moated sites.

III. 22% Poorer Secular Sites - deserted medieval villages and farmsteads, several of them found superimposed on Roman sites, minor moated sites, including some just of manorial status, but all indicative of an essentially peasant economy.

IV. 12% Urban Sites, counting a whole city, apart from its religious houses, as a single 'site', and with particular interest in those having a resident archaeological 'unit', such as Lincoln Oxford, and York, but including also the tale from those where excavation has been more casual. I am most grateful for the kindness of those who have made unit records available to me,[1] but, to avoid an imbalance, have not asked this favour of all such units. In the case of York the information was given to me under 'secular' and 'church' sites, including Clementhorpe Priory, but these have been counted together in the 'urban' totals and then considered separately in the light of class I.

Certain kinds of site-assemblage are omitted as likely to distort the total, though useful for comparison, viz: the results of field-walking (lacking in depth), as at Tackley, Oxon.,[2] 'treasure-hunting' and beach-combing, as in the astonishing collections from Dunwich, Suffolk,[3] Meols in the Wirral,[4] both rich in cut fractions, and South Shields.[5]

The examination proceeds on the assumption that a round hundred sites yield a sample that is significant both cumulatively and within each class, an assumption supported by the pattern of distribution on either count. It is not claimed that the sample shows how much coinage existed in one phase relatively to another, or even how much was circulating and not hoarded. The use of purses and (free-hanging) pockets[6] is an imponderable factor and the sample is merely representative of how much was lost - or rejected. The latter is important: forgeries have been noticed from some sites,[7] in the Edwardian phase there seems to be an over-representation of unwanted 'marginal' coins - continental sterlings and even Scottish and Irish,[8] and in the late phases perhaps too many genuine but worn and clipped ones. The proportion of fractions, cut or round, may well be enhanced because they were easily lost - unless compensated by the fact that they are not easily found.

The period covered extends from Eadgar's reform to the renewal of fine silver in 1551, which is also that from Dunstan and Aethelwold to the dissolution of the last religious houses under Edward VI, and could be taken as one definition of the 'Middle Ages'. The central and climacteric position of the Edwardian phase in this context makes it appropriate to this symposium. This span has been divided into 10 'circulation-phases':

- I. Eadgar to the 'expanding cross' of Edward the Confessor (c. 973-1053).
- II. The Confessor's 'pointed helmet' to type XIII of Henry I (c. 1053-1125?).
- III. Late Henry I, Stephen, 'Tealby' (1125?-1180).
- IV. Short-cross (1180-1247).
- V. Long-cross (1247-1279).
- VI. 'Edwardian', including 'Florin' issues (1279-1351).
- VII. Edward III's reform to Henry IV's reduction (1351-1412).
- VIII. Thence to Edward IV's reduction (1412-1464).
- IX. Thence, including Wolsey's coinage, to the debasement (1464-1544).
- X. The base coinage (1544-1551, or to the demonetization in 1561).

The finds from each site are divided among the ten columns for each of these phases and, in addition, there are two outer columns, A and B: A for non-English coins, Scottish, Irish and continental sterlings, that are included in the total for their phase, so that this column does not affect the site-total, and B for foreign coins, including 'galley-halfpence' (soldini) that do not match the English currency, and are excluded from the phase-totals, but not from the site-totals. The 'circulation-phases' are, of course, not strictly comparable: the ideal examples are phases IV, V, and from a retrospective viewpoint, VI, where the recoinage was complete and the currency uniform; in the earlier phases the initial recoinage was perhaps not exhaustive and there were several recoinages, some certainly not exhaustive, within them, but the effect on loss was mathematically the same as if the coinage were uniform throughout; in the later phases the recoinage was notionally complete, but in practice certainly not so, as far as the lower denominations, pence and under, were concerned. We can estimate the proportion of phase VI coins surviving in the early part of phase VII from the Beulah Hill hoard,[9] and of phase VI and VII coins at the beginning of phase VIII from the Attenborough hoard,[10] and contrast these with the almost complete disappearance of any-before phase IX, by the end of that phase, from the Maidstone hoard.[11]

The totals in each phase, both for each of the four classes of site and for the whole range of sites, are added up and then adjusted to the duration of each phase. This is done by reckoning the durations in decades or half-decades. More precise divisors might be used, but in view of the uncertain length of the periods of transition and, in the earlier phases, the disputable date of commencement, a possible error of two or three years is not thought worth the extra calculation involved. The adjusted figures show the mean loss per decade over the whole phase. They do not show, for instance, any rise in circulation between the beginning of Short-cross and the heavy issues of king John, and it is doubtful whether useful figures for this could be produced without a detailed re-examination of all the material, some of it now scattered.

The graphs plot these average losses on a natural, not logarithmic, scale against the middle-points of each phase on an absolute time-scale. They are not shown as histograms but as continuous curves joining the middle-points of each phase. The reason for this is twofold: a) because, though mintage is a matter of 'stop-and-go', it is unlikely that the amount of coin in circulation ever changed so catastrophically, and (b) because, while down to phase VI the initial recoinage is taken as near-exhaustive and the amount of residual coin consequently ignored, it was certainly not so with pence and fractions in the later phases, and experiment with the harmony of the curve may give some indication of the proportion of residual coin actually circulating sc. at the middle-point of the phase. This does not altogether agree with the evidence of the hoards, where the residual coin, being heavier, might seem ipso facto more likely to be hoarded. Thus, while of the seven pence in the Beulah Hill hoard, buried c. 1364,[9] well before the middle-point of phase VII, only two are of phase VI, the Attenborough hoard, buried soon after the opening of phase VIII,[10] shows some 320 pence and below of phase VI against some 640 of phase VII and as yet only 57 of phase VIII. This might suggest a survival of some 50% from one phase to the next, but a graph making this sort of allowance looks very distorted. A graph made on the hypothesis that about a third

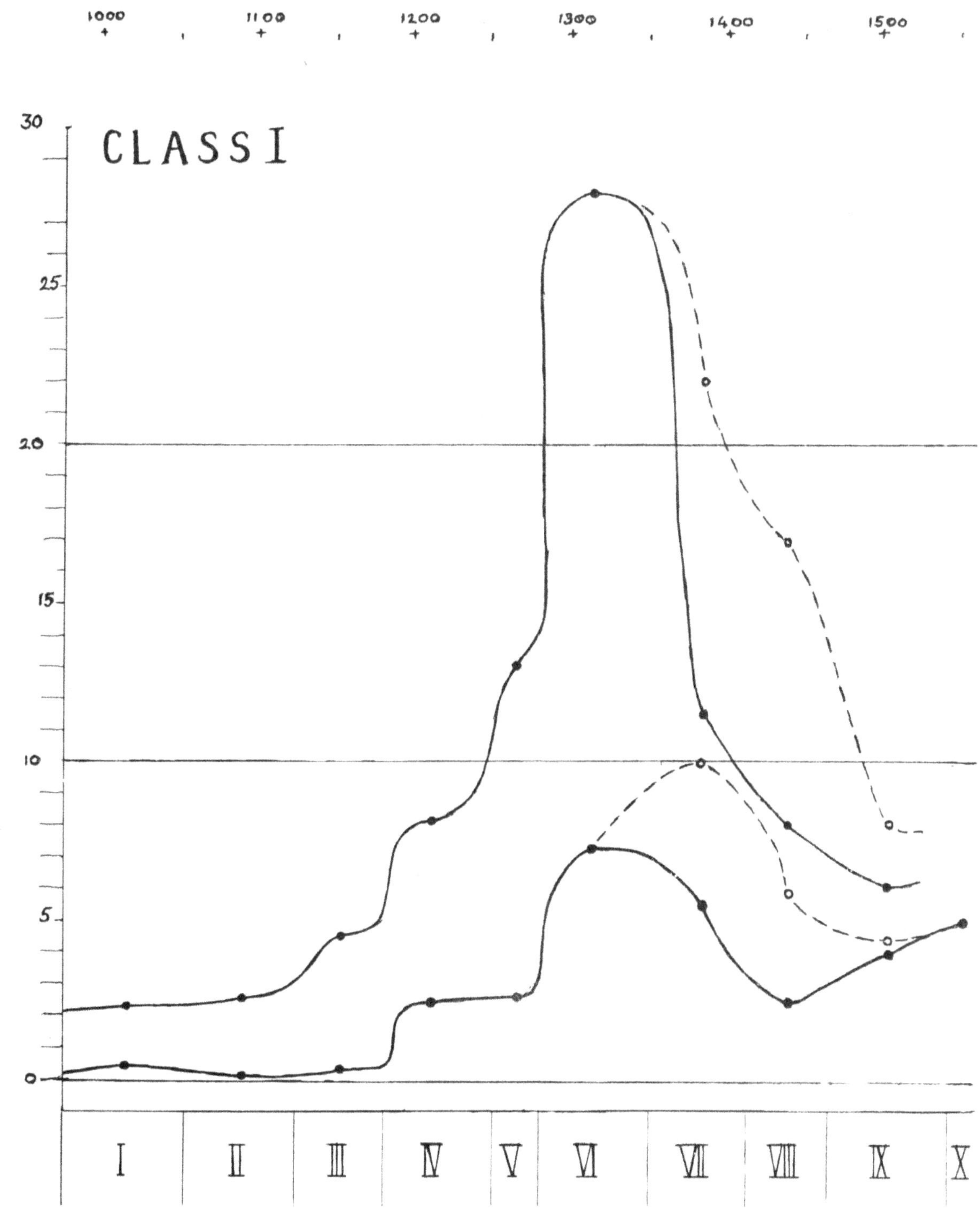

1000
1100
1200
1300
1400
1500
30
25
20
15
10
5
0
CLASS I
I
II
III
IV
V
VI
VII
VIII
IX
X

Fig. 1

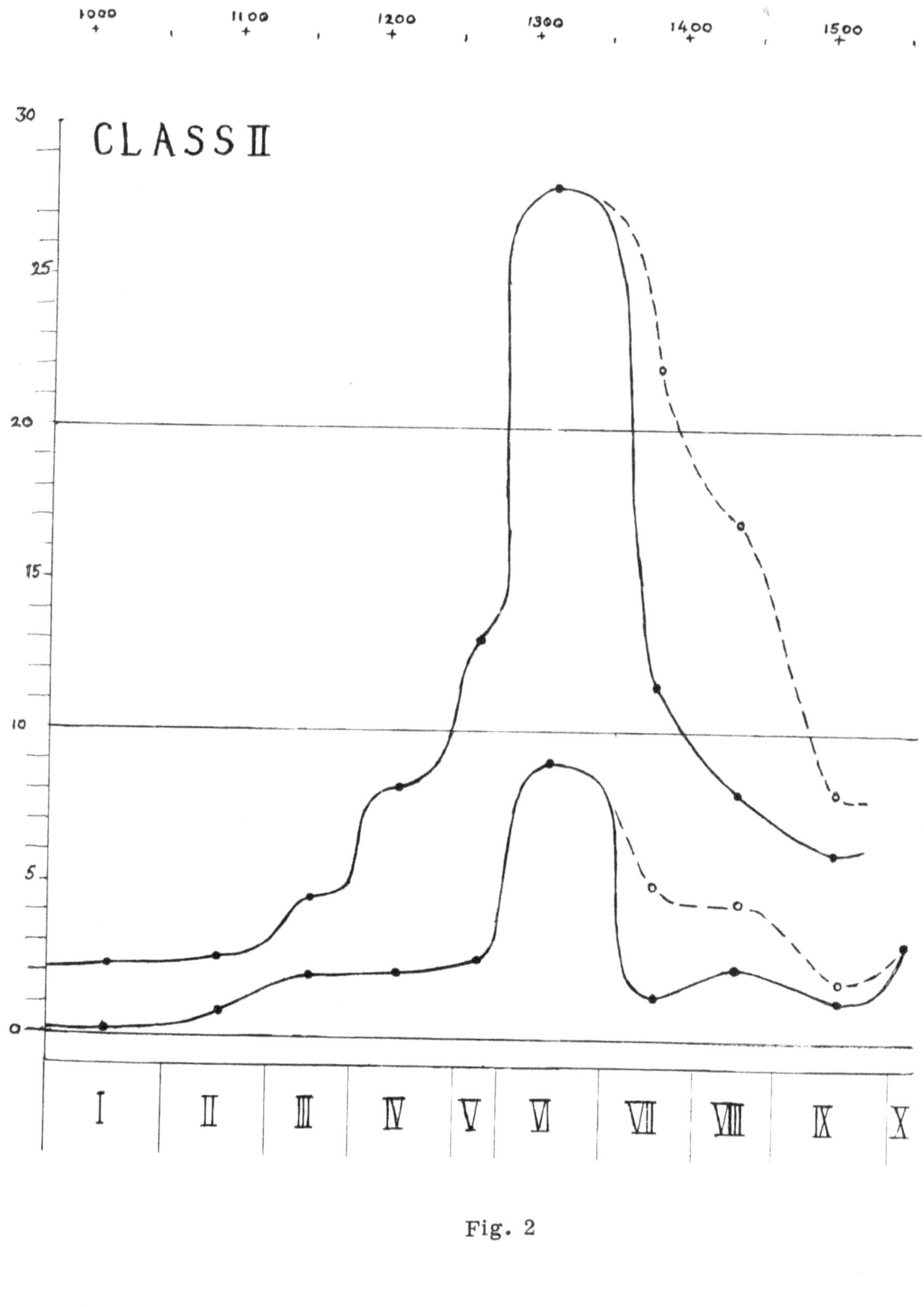

1000
1100
1200
1300
1400
1500
30
25
20
15
10
5
0
CLASS II
I
II
III
IV
V
VI
VII
VIII
IX
X

Fig. 2

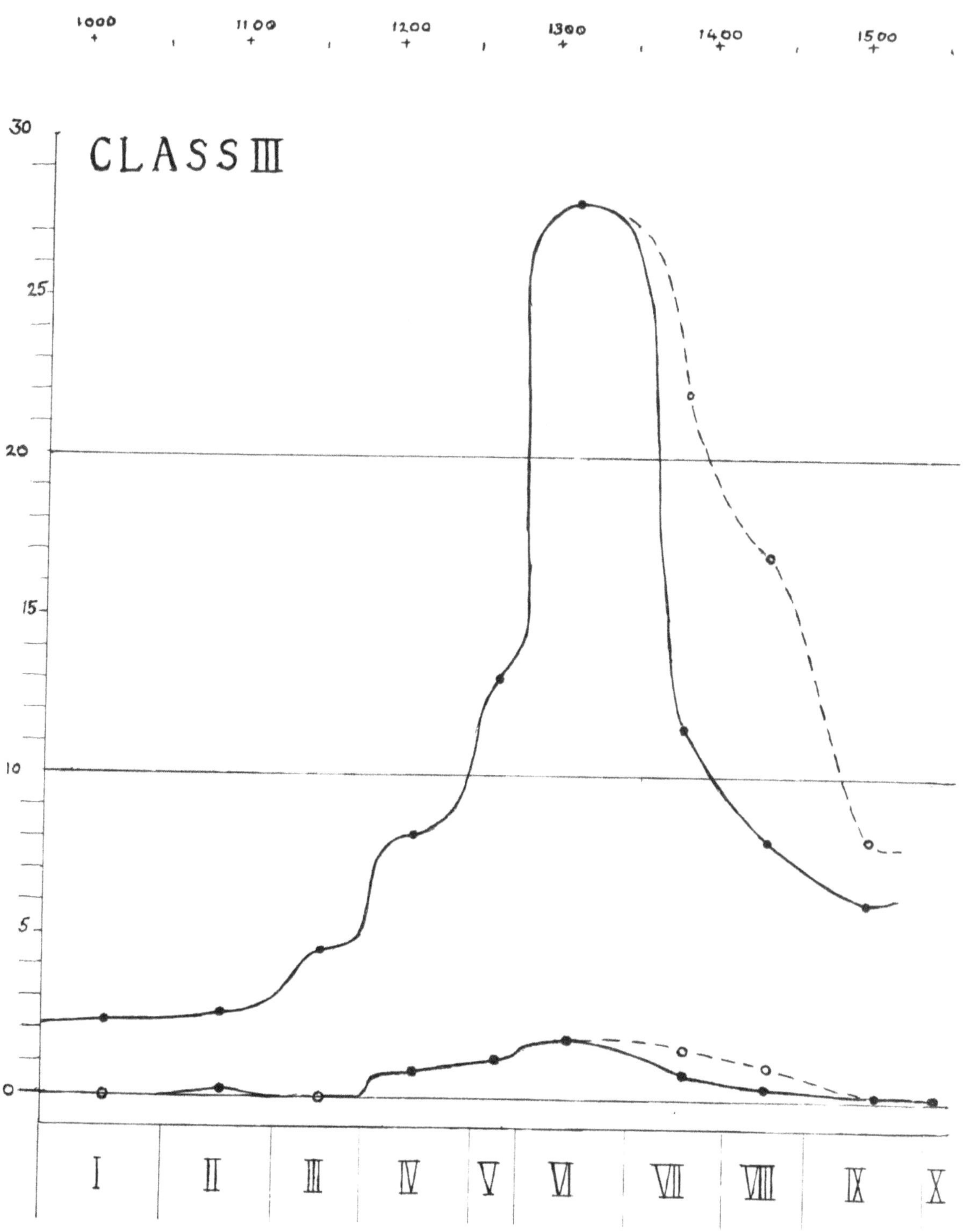
1000
1100
1200
1300
1400
1500
CLASS III
30
25
20
15
10
5
0
I
II
III
IV
V
VI
VII
VIII
IX
X

Fig. 3

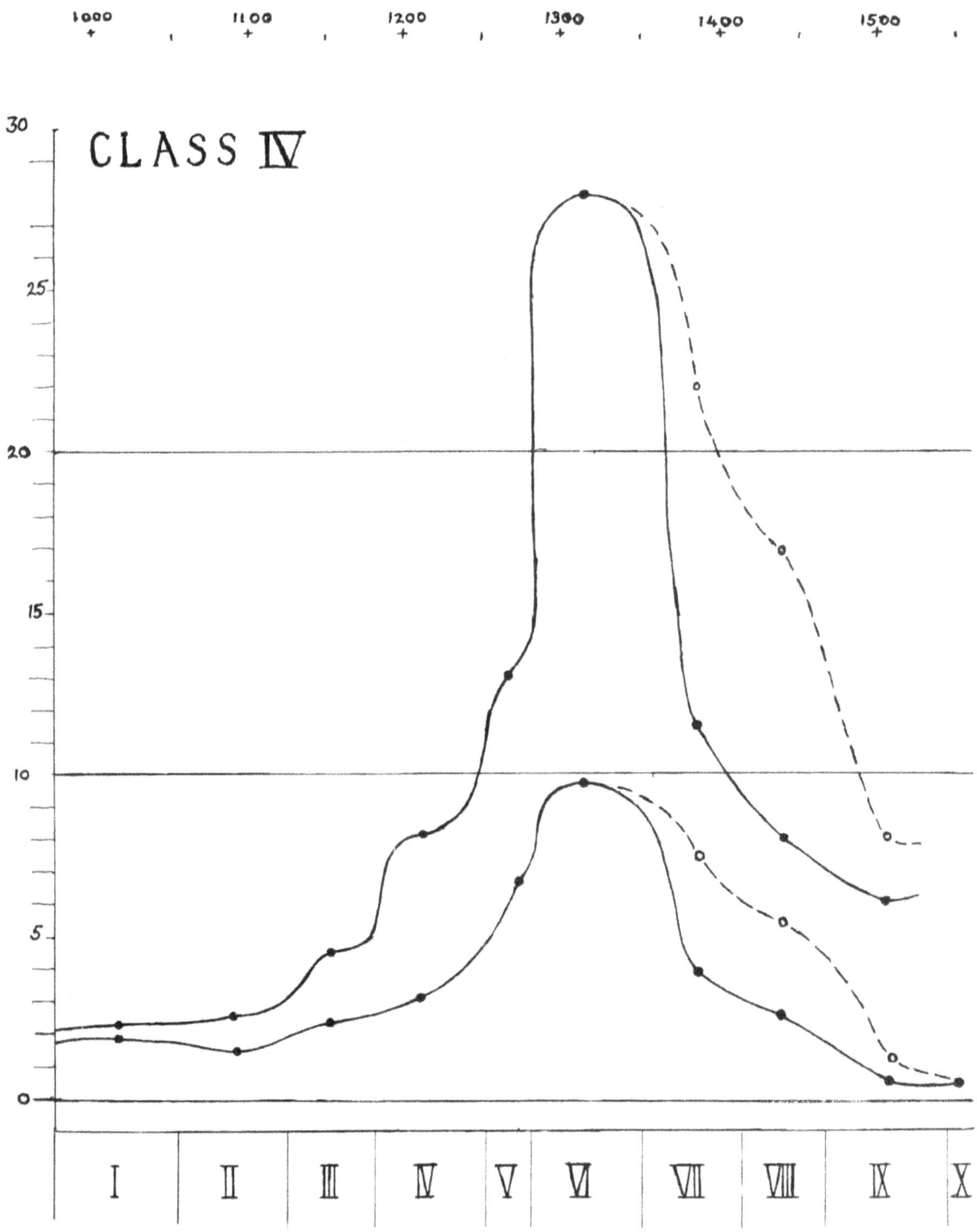

1000
1100
1200
1300
1400
1500
CLASS IV
30
25
20
15
10
5
0
I
II
III
IV
V
VI
VII
VIII
IX
X

Fig. 4

carried over from middle to middle of two successive phases and about a ninth survived over three phases produces a smooth curve and is marked in broken lines over phases VII and VIII. The consequent effect on losses in phase VI might suggest a reduction of the total by a third, but the condition of most of the coins examined suggests that this is too high and that not more than 10% or 15% are later losses. In phase IX the material is so scanty, even including a residuum, that the curve seems hardly worth extending to any meaningful end, and phase X, even if extended for the full 17 years to the demonetization, is too exceptional to respond to adjustment. Of the foreign totals those in column B are largely gathered from unrepresentative royal and coastal sites.

The adjusted mean losses per decade for each class, together with the hypothetical figures to allow for loss of residual coins in phases VII and VIII, are plotted (Figs. 1-4) against the total mean losses, with the additional, hypothetical, figures extended to class IX. The 'total' curves, with and without the hypothetical addition, are examined first, as derived from the largest and most significant sample, and the curves for the classes, where they differ materially from these, are considered in relation to this norm. Finally, the total of fractions in each phase is considered in relation to the general total for each phase, and the exercise repeated for each class, to bring out any significant differences in proportion. The resultant observations are as follows:

1. The first three phases show a steady increase. At first it appeared that phase III would rise at about the same rate as in I and II, but the final figures show an increase of about 80% from the mid twelfth century. Lest it seem that this figure is distorted by excavation at Castle Acre and other works of Stephen's time, the urban totals (class IV) point the same way.

2. The noticeable increase in Short-cross (phase IV) is somewhat muted by the higher figure for phase III. The first indications were that the increase would be between 100% and 150% (not more), but final results give less than 100%. mostly no doubt in the early thirteenth century but apparent from 1180. This is still enough to constitute an economic revolution, and surpassed only by the increase in phase VI.

3. The rise continues through phase V (Long-cross), at some 21%.

4. The increase in the Edwardian phase is apparent from the beginning of phase VI (c. 1280) and runs at over 115%, or perhaps nearer 100% if we allow for some residue in the next phase. Though not quite in accordance with the mint output figures adduced by Mr. Brand, it is obvious from a superficial glance at the material. On the economic scale it is comparable to that in Short-cross, but the historical necessity seems less clear.

5. The adjusted figures in phase VII shows falling-off to little more than a third of the Edwardian phase, though the allowance for residual coins would bring it up to about two thirds. However, the comparison is no longer perfect, since much of the silver was tied up in groats. It is perhaps better to view it in the light of the undoubted decline in popula-

tion, since loss is a function of coin-users rather than of coins, and to consider that the circulation of small change per individual may actually have increased.

6. The same considerations affect phase VIII, where the hypothetical coin-residue would point to a decline, but not as catastrophic as the absolute figures might suggest.

7. In phase IX there is actually an increase in the mean loss of small coin of recent mintage, but if the hypothetical residues are included at the same rate, there is a decline as against the augmented figure for phase VIII, and this is to be set against a documented recovery in population. Many of the sites, of course, have been excavated simply because they had now become deserted or neglected, but the urban figures show a comparable decline.

8. Phase X is too short and atypical for any adjusted figures to be useful for comparison, and many of the coins may have been thrown away after 'crying-down' rather than lost.

9. In classes I ('religious' sites) and III ('peasant' sites) the three earliest phases make a poor showing and the increase in the Short-cross phase is correspondingly sharp. Since both (the Cistercians are well represented) may be considered as largely rural and, at this period, near a subsistence economy, the sudden access of some coin in peasant hands may well be truly reflected. In class III, mostly deserted sites, the rapid decline after the Edwardian phase (VI) is only to be expected. Class I, however, behaves differently: it shows very little increase in Long-cross (phase V) and a sharp rise in phase VI, which is yet less than average in relation to that of Short-cross, as though the access of coinage around 1180 or 1200 were not followed up for a century and somewhat retarded for a century and a half. Then, once started, the rise continues, so that, with the hypothetical allowance for residual coins, phase VII would show a higher mean loss than phase VI and a much slower, in fact an arrested, decline in the subsequent phases, unlike in any other class.[12] This is not money thrown around at the Dissolution: it affects the late fourteenth and fifteenth centuries, and Benedictine as well as Cistercian houses. It may reflect some relaxation of the rule or just carelessness, but it is easier to connect it with the change to farm-rents, hired servants and the money-managed monasticism that has been observed from this period onwards.

10. In class II phases I and II are typically scanty, but not III. The mean accession of coin rises steadily from the mid twelfth century and the relative increase in the Edwardian phase is the highest of all (over 200%), then there is a sharp drop of about 50% to a level that seems to be maintained until the mid fifteenth century, followed by another decline, even on sites known to have been intensively occupied. What all this reflects of the habits of lordly households cannot be discussed here.

11. On the urban sites (class IV) all the earliest phases are relatively well represented, as befits the old-English coinage, with its many burghal mints; phase IV is curiously weak but Long-cross (phase V) shows

a strong foretaste of the Edwardian climax. Whatever the significance of this rise from the mid thirteenth century, it is not so surprising as the rapid decline in the fifteenth, even at places, such as York, that are known to have continued in prosperity. Is it perhaps at this time, rather than earlier, that we might best look for the use of jettons or lead pieces as some form of restricted token coinage?

12. The fractions, both cut and round, are presented in the form of totals for each phase in relation to the absolute totals of all coins for the phase, neither adjusted, nor with the hypothetical addition for residual coins, among which it is assumed there would have been few fractions. As before, there are corresponding totals for each class which should be compared with the totals for all the classes. It is only in phases III to VII that the samples seem large enough to be significant, but from the mid twelfth century the proportion of fractions to whole coins drops from one in less than three to one in almost five in the Edwardian phase (most of which, in fact, are the common halfpence of the 1330s and 1340s, when coinage of pence had temporarily ceased, so that the proportion for most of the phase was considerably lower). In phase VII it falls to one in eleven. Among the classes there is no strong variation from the average in classes I, II and IV, the urban sites being the most typical, but the peasant sites of class III are quite distinctive in that, in phases III to VI, fractions actually form a large majority of the small sample. Thus parsimoniously did the hind of the thirteenth century approach the novelty of coin.

CLASS I (RELIGIOUS)

	Phases	SITE TOTALS A	I	II	III	IV	V	VI	VII	VIII	IX	X	FRACTIONS B	I	II	III	IV	V	VI	VII	VIII	IX	X
1	Angmering Ch., Sx.	–	–	–	–	1	–	–	–	–	–	–	–	–	–	–	–	–	–	–	–	–	–
2	Bargham Ch., Sx.	–	–	–	–	–	–	1	–	–	–	–	–	–	–	–	–	–	–	–	–	–	–
3	Basingwerk Abb.	–	–	–	–	2	2	2	–	–	2	–	–	–	–	–	–	–	–	–	–	–	–
4	Binham Py., Nf.	–	–	–	–	–	–	–	–	1	1	–	–	–	–	–	–	–	–	–	–	–	–
5	Canterbury S. Augustine	1	1	1	–	1	–	7	2	1	4	–	1	–	–	–	1	–	5	–	–	–	–
6	Colchester S. Botolph	–	–	–	–	–	–	1	–	–	–	–	–	–	–	–	–	–	–	–	–	–	–
7	Coventry, S. Mary, Py.	–	–	–	–	–	–	1	1	–	–	–	–	–	–	–	–	–	1	1	–	–	–
8	Coventry, Whitefrs.	–	–	–	–	–	–	–	1	1	4	4	–	–	–	–	–	–	–	–	–	–	–
9	Cowton Grange, Y.	–	–	–	1	1	1	–	–	–	–	–	–	–	–	1	1	–	–	–	–	–	–
10	Easby Abb., Y.	–	–	–	–	–	1	–	–	–	–	–	–	–	–	–	–	–	–	–	–	–	–
11	Finchale, Py., Du.	–	–	–	–	–	–	3	4	–	–	–	–	–	–	–	–	–	–	–	–	–	–
12	Frocester Ch., Gl	–	–	–	–	–	–	–	–	–	1	–	–	–	–	–	–	–	–	–	–	–	–

CLASS I (RELIGIOUS) continued.

	Phases	SITE TOTALS											FRACTIONS										
		A	I	II	III	IV	V	VI	VII	VIII	IX	X	B	I	II	III	IV	V	VI	VII	VIII	IX	X
13	Furness Abb.	-	-	-	-	2	-	3	2	-	-	-	-	-	-	-	-	-	-	-	-	-	-
14	Glastonbury Tor	-	-	-	1	-	1	3	1	-	-	-	-	-	-	-	-	-	1	-	-	-	-
15	Hanslope Ch., Bk.	-	-	-	-	-	-	-	1	-	-	-	-	-	-	-	-	-	-	-	-	-	-
16	Haughmond Abb., Sa.	-	-	-	-	1	-	-	1	-	-	-	-	-	-	-	-	-	-	-	-	-	-
17	Higham Py., K.	-	-	-	-	1	-	-	-	-	-	-	-	-	-	-	-	-	1	-	-	-	-
18	Kirkham Py., Y.	-	-	-	-	-	1	2	1	-	-	-	-	-	-	-	-	-	-	-	-	-	-
19	Kirkstall Abb., Y.	-	-	-	-	3	-	1	1	-	-	-	-	-	-	-	2	-	-	-	-	-	-
20	Lindisfarne Py. Nb.	-	-	-	-	1	-	2	-	1	2	1	-	-	-	-	-	-	-	-	-	-	-
21	Michelham Py., Sx.	-	-	-	-	-	-	-	1	-	-	-	-	-	-	-	-	-	-	-	-	-	-
22	Oxford Blackfr.	-	-	-	-	-	1	-	-	-	-	-	1	-	-	-	-	1	-	-	-	-	-
23	Pontefract Py., Y.	-	-	-	-	1	-	3	3	1	3	-	-	-	-	-	1	-	1	-	-	1	-
24	Richborough K.	-	2	-	-	1	-	1	1	1	3	1	4	-	-	-	1	-	1	-	-	1	-
25	Rievaulx Abb., Y.	1	-	-	-	1	-	11	8	2	11	1	-	-	-	-	-	-	5	1	-	-	-

CLASS I (RELIGIOUS) continued.

		SITE TOTALS												FRACTIONS									
	Phases	A	I	II	III	IV	V	VI	VII	VIII	IX	X	B	I	II	III	IV	V	VI	VII	VIII	IX	X
26	Roche Abb. Y.	1	-	-	-	-	-	2	3	1	2	-	-	-	-	-	-	-	-	-	1	-	-
27	Thetford Py.	1	-	-	1	-	-	-	1	1	-	-	-	-	-	-	-	-	-	1	1	-	-
28	Thornholme Py. Li.	-	-	-	-	-	-	2	-	1	-	-	-	-	-	-	-	-	-	-	-	-	-
29	Titchfield Abb., Ha.	-	-	-	-	-	-	1	-	-	-	-	-	-	-	-	-	-	1	-	-	-	-
30	Vale Royal Abb.	-	-	-	-	-	-	-	-	1	-	-	-	-	-	-	-	-	-	-	-	-	-
31	Walsingham Py.	-	-	-	-	-	-	-	1	-	-	-	-	-	-	-	-	-	-	-	-	-	-
32	Waltham Abb., Ess.	1	-	-	-	1	-	5	-	-	-	1	-	-	-	-	-	-	-	-	-	-	1
33	Waverley Abb.	-	-	-	-	-	1	-	-	-	-	-	-	-	-	-	-	-	-	-	-	-	-
	Totals	(5)	3	1	3	17	8	51	33	12	33	8	6	-	-	1	7	1	15	3	2	3	1

Sources (abbreviated): 1, 2, 21, Sussex Arch. Coll., cxiii, lxvi, cv; 3, 4, 5, 6, 7, 10, 12, 13, 16, 18, 20, 24, 25, 26, 27, 28, 29, 30, 33, DoE (ex-Min. of Works) records (16 and 28 ex current excavations by G. Coppack and G. West); 8, Mrs. C. Woodfield; 11, Trans. Bristol & Glos. Arch. Soc., lxxxii; 14, 31, Arch. Jnl., ccxxvii, and cxxv; 15, Records of Bucks., ix; 17, Arch. Cantiana, lxxxii; 19, 23, Thoroton Society, annual excavation reports; 22, Oxford Arch. Excav. Cttee.; 32, Mr. and Mrs. P.J. Huggins and Colchester and Ess. Museum Annual Reports; 9, C. Platt, The Monastic Grange in Medieval England. (1969).

CLASS II (CASTLES, ETC.)

	Phases	A	I	II	III	IV	V	VI	VII	VIII	IX	X	B	I	II	III	IV	V	VI	VII	VIII	IX	X
		SITE TOTALS												FRACTIONS									
1	Bishop's Waltham Pal.	-	-	1	-	-	1	-	-	1	1	-	-	-	-	-	-	-	-	-	-	-	-
2	Bolingbroke Cas.	-	-	-	-	1	-	-	-	-	-	1	-	-	-	-	1	-	-	-	-	-	-
3	Castell-y-Bere.	-	-	-	-	-	-	2	-	-	-	-	-	-	-	-	-	-	-	-	-	-	-
4	Castle Acre.	-	-	3	4	-	-	3	-	1	-	-	-	-	-	-	-	-	-	-	-	-	-
5	Castle Rising	-	-	-	1	-	-	1	-	-	-	-	-	-	-	1	-	-	-	-	-	-	-
6	Conisbrough Cas.	-	-	-	-	-	-	-	-	1	-	-	-	-	-	-	-	-	-	-	-	-	-
7	Conway Cas.	-	-	-	-	-	-	-	-	1	-	-	1	-	-	-	-	-	-	-	-	-	-
8	Denbigh Cas.	1	-	-	-	-	-	3	1	1	-	1	1	-	-	-	-	-	-	-	-	-	-
9	Dover Cas.	-	1	-	-	-	1	3	-	-	-	3	-	-	-	-	-	-	-	-	-	-	-
10	Dunstanburgh Cas.	-	-	-	-	-	-	3	-	-	-	-	-	-	-	-	-	-	-	-	-	-	-
11	Eltham Pal.	1	-	-	-	-	-	2	-	-	-	-	-	-	-	-	-	-	-	-	-	-	-
12	Farleigh Hungerford C.	-	-	-	-	-	1	1	-	1	1	-	-	-	-	-	-	1	1	-	-	-	-

CLASS II (CASTLES, ETC.) continued.

	Phases	SITE TOTALS A	I	II	III	IV	V	VI	VII	VIII	IX	X	FRACTIONS B	I	II	III	IV	V	VI	VII	VIII	IX	X
13	Goodrich Cas.	-	-	-	-	-	-	-	-	1	-	-	-	-	-	-	-	-	-	-	-	-	-
14	E. Haddlesey Moat, Y.	-	-	-	-	-	-	1	-	1	-	-	-	-	-	-	-	-	1	-	-	-	-
15	Hadleigh Cas. Ess.	1	-	-	-	-	-	2	-	-	-	-	-	-	-	-	-	-	1	-	-	-	-
16	Helmsley Cas. Y	1	-	-	-	-	-	5	1	-	-	-	1	-	-	-	-	-	2	-	-	-	-
17	King's Langley Pal	-	-	-	-	-	-	7	1	-	-	-	1	-	-	-	-	-	1	-	-	-	-
18	Launceston Cas.	1	-	-	-	-	1	5	1	1	1	-	-	-	-	-	-	-	-	-	-	-	-
19	Llanstephan Cas.	-	-	-	-	-	-	1	-	-	-	-	-	-	-	-	-	-	-	-	-	-	-
20	Ludgershall Cas. Wi.	2	-	-	1	4	-	6	-	-	1	-	5	-	-	-	1	-	2	-	-	-	-
21	Lydford Fortlet	-	-	-	1	-	-	-	-	-	-	-	-	-	-	1	-	-	-	-	-	-	-
22	Old Sarum	-	-	1	1	4	-	2	1	-	1	-	1	-	-	-	-	-	-	-	-	-	-
23	Otley Pal. Y	1	-	-	-	1	1	-	1	-	-	-	-	-	-	-	-	-	-	-	-	-	-
24	Pickering Cas. Y	-	-	-	-	-	-	-	-	-	1	-	-	-	-	-	-	-	-	-	-	-	-
25	Pleshey Cas. Ess	-	-	-	-	-	-	2	-	-	-	-	1	-	-	-	-	-	-	-	-	-	-

CLASS II (CASTLES, ETC.) continued.

	Phases	SITE TOTALS												FRACTIONS									
		A	I	II	III	IV	V	VI	VII	VIII	IX	X	B	I	II	III	IV	V	VI	VII	VIII	IX	X
26	Rest Park, Y	-	-	-	-	-	-	1	-	-	3	-	-	-	-	-	-	-	-	-	-	1	-
27	Richmond Cas. Y	2	-	-	1	1	-	3	1	-	-	2	-	-	-	-	-	-	-	-	-	1	-
28	Scarborough Cas.	-	-	-	-	2	1	5	-	-	1	-	-	-	-	-	-	-	-	-	-	1	-
29	Shaftesbury Fortlet	-	-	-	1	-	-	-	-	-	-	-	-	-	-	1	-	-	-	-	-	-	-
30	Tower of London	-	-	-	-	-	-	3	-	-	-	-	-	-	-	-	-	-	-	1	-	-	-
31	Weoley Cas. Wo	-	-	-	-	1	1	-	-	-	-	-	-	-	-	-	-	1	-	-	-	-	-
32	Whichford Cas. Wa.	-	-	-	1	1	-	-	-	-	-	-	-	-	-	-	1	-	-	-	-	-	-
33	Writtle Ess, (Moat)	1	-	-	-	1	1	4	1	4	-	-	-	-	-	-	-	-	-	-	-	-	-
	Totals	(10)	1	5	11	16	8	65	8	13	10	5	12	-	-	3	3	2	8	-	-	3	-

Sources (abbreviated): 1-13 and 15-21, inclusive, 24, 25, 27, 28, 30, 32, DoE records (of which 4, 5, 6, 11, 15, 17, 18, 20 concern current or recent excavations by J. G. Coad, B. M. Morley, J. S. Johnson, H. M. Woods, P. Drewitt, D. S. Neal, A. D. Sanders and P. V. Addyman, respectively); 14, 26, H. E. J. le Patourel, Moated Sites of Yorkshire (1974); 22, material in Salisbury Museum; 23, Yorks. Arch. Jnl., xlv; 29, Proc. Dorset N. H. and Arch. Soc., lxxi; 31, Medieval Archaeol., vi-vii; 33, P. A. Rahtz, Excavations at K. John's Hunting Lodge, Writtle (1969).

CLASS III (' D. M. V.'s, ETC.,)

		SITE TOTALS											FRACTIONS										
	Phases	A	I	II	III	IV	V	VI	VII	VIII	IX	X	B	I	II	III	IV	V	VI	VII	VIII	IX	X
1	Barrow Mead, Bath	-	-	-	-	-	1	-	-	-	-	-	-	-	-	-	-	-	-	-	-	-	-
2	Bossal Vicarage, Y	-	-	-	-	-	-	1	-	-	-	-	-	-	-	-	-	-	1	-	-	-	-
3	Farningham K	-	-	-	-	-	-	-	-	-	-	-	1	-	-	-	-	-	-	-	-	-	-
4	Goltho, Li.	-	-	-	-	-	-	-	-	1	-	-	-	-	-	-	-	-	-	-	-	-	-
5	Grenstein Nf.	-	-	-	-	-	-	1	-	-	-	-	-	-	-	-	-	-	-	-	-	-	-
6	Hampton Wafer, He.	-	-	1	-	-	-	-	-	-	-	-	-	-	-	-	-	-	-	-	-	-	-
7	Hartburn Du	-	-	-	-	-	-	-	-	-	1	-	-	-	-	-	-	-	-	-	-	-	-
8	Hangleton, Sx.	-	-	-	-	-	-	-	3	-	-	-	-	-	-	-	-	-	-	-	-	-	-
9	Gt. Horkesley Es.	-	-	-	-	-	-	-	-	1	-	-	-	-	-	-	-	-	-	-	-	-	-
10	Holyoak, Le.	-	-	-	-	-	-	-	-	-	-	2	-	-	-	-	-	-	-	-	-	-	-
11	Leigh, Moat, K.	-	-	-	-	-	-	1	-	-	-	-	-	-	-	-	-	-	-	-	-	-	-
12	Keighton Nt.	-	-	-	-	1	-	-	-	-	-	-	-	-	-	-	1	-	-	-	-	-	-

CLASS III ('D. M. V.'s, ETC.,) continued.

	Phases	SITE TOTALS											FRACTIONS										
		A	I	II	III	IV	V	VI	VII	VIII	IX	X	B	I	II	III	IV	V	VI	VII	VIII	IX	X
13	Lullingstone, K	-	-	-	-	-	-	2	-	-	-	-	-	-	-	-	-	-	1	-	-	-	-
14	Lyveden, Np.	-	-	-	-	-	-	-	1	-	-	-	-	-	-	-	-	-	-	-	-	-	-
15	Newstead, Moat, Y	-	-	-	-	-	-	1	-	-	-	-	-	-	-	-	-	-	-	-	-	-	-
16	Riseholme Li	-	-	-	-	-	-	1	-	-	-	-	-	-	-	-	-	-	-	-	-	-	-
17	Stixton Mill Bd	-	-	-	-	-	-	1	-	-	-	-	-	-	-	-	-	-	1	-	-	-	-
18	Swineshead, Li.	-	-	-	-	1	-	2	-	-	-	-	-	-	-	-	-	-	-	-	-	-	-
19	Tarring, Sx.	-	-	-	-	-	-	-	-	-	-	-	1	-	-	-	-	-	-	-	-	-	-
20	Upton, Gl.	-	-	-	-	2	-	-	-	-	-	-	-	-	-	-	2	-	-	-	-	-	-
21	Wharram Percy, Y	-	-	-	-	-	-	1	1	-	-	-	-	-	-	-	-	-	-	-	-	-	-
22	Whittington, Gl.	1	-	-	-	1	2	1	-	-	-	-	-	-	-	-	1	2	1	-	-	-	-
	Totals	(1)	-	1	-	5	3	12	5	2	1	2	2	-	-	-	4	2	4	-	-	-	-

Sources (abbreviated): 1, 5, 9, 10, 21, 22, DoE records; 2, Yorks Philosoph. Soc. Annual Report, 1935; 3, 13, Arch. Cantiana, lxxxviii, lxiii, lxv; 4, G. T. M. Beresford, Medieval Clay-Land Villages (1975); 6, Trans. Woolhope N. F. Club, xxxix; 7, Arch. Aeliana, 4th ser., xlii; 8, 19, Sussex Arch. Coll. ci, cii; 11, personal inspection, forthcoming in Arch. Cantiana; 12, Trans. Thoroton Soc., lxxv; 14, Northampton Museum Journal, ii; 15, H.E.J. le Patourel, Moated Sites of Yorks, (1974); 16, Med. Archaeol., iv; 17, Bedfordshire Arch. Jnl., vii; 18, Lincoln Hist. and Arch. Notes, 1966; 20, Trans. Bristol and Glos. Arch. Soc., lxxxv, lxxxviii.

CLASS IV (URBAN)

		SITE TOTALS											FRACTIONS										
	Phases	A	I	II	III	IV	V	VI	VII	VIII	IX	X	B	I	II	III	IV	V	VI	VII	VIII	IX	X
1	Abingdon	-	1	-	-	-	-	-	-	-	-	-	-	-	-	-	-	-	-	-	-	-	-
2	Bedford	-	-	-	-	1	-	-	-	-	-	-	-	-	-	-	1	-	-	-	-	-	-
3	Canterbury	-	-	-	-	1	-	1	-	-	1	-	-	-	-	-	1	-	-	-	-	-	-
4	Chichester	-	1	-	1	2	-	-	1	-	-	-	1	-	-	-	-	-	-	-	-	-	-
5	Colchester	1	-	-	2	3	4	6	5	-	-	-	-	-	-	-	-	-	-	1	-	-	-
6	Hull	-	-	-	-	-	-	4	-	-	-	-	-	-	-	-	-	-	-	-	-	-	-
7	Lincoln	1	5	5	-	6	4	8	2	1	-	1	1	-	1	-	2	-	2	-	1	-	-
8	Oxford	5	1	-	1	2	6	16	4	2	-	-	2	-	-	-	1	3	9	-	-	-	-
9	Rochester	1	-	-	-	2	-	1	-	-	-	-	-	-	-	-	-	-	-	-	-	-	-
10	Southampton	3	-	-	4	1	-	8	1	3	2	-	3	-	-	2	-	-	1	-	1	-	-
11	Thetford	-	2	2	-	1	-	1	-	1	-	-	-	1	-	-	-	-	1	-	-	-	-
12	York	2	4	3	4	3	6	23	10	6	1	-	-	-	-	3	-	2	3	2	1	-	-
	Totals	(13)	14	10	12	22	20	68	23	13	4	1	7	1	1	5	5	5	16	3	3	-	-

Sources (abbreviated): 1, Oxoniensia, xl; 2, Bedfordshire Arch. J., ix; 3, Arch. Cantiana., lxii; 4, A. Down, Chichester Excavations, ii (1974); 5, Colchester and Ess. Museum Annual Reports, 1910 ff.; 6, Kingston-on-Hull Museum Bulletin, vii, x; 7, Lincoln Arch. Trust. records; 8, Oxford Arch. Excav. Cttee. records and Oxoniensia, iv, xv; 9, Arch. Cantiana, lxxvii, lxxiii; 10, Excavations in Medieval Southampton, ii (1975); 11, DoE records; 12, York Arch. Trust records and B.N.J., xxx.

FUNCTIONS OF THE SITE-TOTALS

The totals for each class and the sum of all the classes are expressed hereunder:

A, in their natural form;
B, adjusted to give the mean loss per decade;
C, augmented by the hypothetical residuum of one third from the previous phase, added to B, beginning with that of VI in VII.

In addition, the natural totals for all classes together are expressed as multiples of the totals of fractions, as are the overall totals, but not the phase-totals, for each class.

Class	I	II	III	IV	V	VI	VII	VIII	IX	X	Foreign B
I, natural	3	1	3	17	8	51	33	12	33	8	6
I, adjusted	0.37	0.15	0.5	2.25	2.7	7.3	5.5	2.4	4.0	(5.0)	-
I, augmented	-	-	-	-	-	-	10.0	5.8	5.25	-	-
II, natural	1	5	11	16	8	65	8	13	10	5	12
II, adjusted	0.12	0.7	2.0	2.1	2.7	9.3	1.3	2.5	1.2	(3.3)	-
II, augmented	-	-	-	-	-	-	5.0	4.6	2.25	-	-
III, natural	-	1	-	5	3	12	5	2	1	2	-
III, adjusted	-	0.15	-	0.7	1.0	1.7	0.83	0.4	0.12	(1.3)	-
III, augmented	-	-	-	-	-	-	1.5	1.0	0.25	-	-
IV, natural	14	10	12	22	20	68	23	13	4	1	7
IV, adjusted	1.7	1.4	2.2	3.0	6.7	9.7	3.8	2.6	0.5	(0.7)	-
IV, augmented	-	-	-	-	-	-	7.5	5.6	1.0	-	-
Sum, natural	18	17	26	60	39	196	69	40	48	16	27
Sum, adjusted	2.25	2.43	4.5	8.0	13.0	28.0	11.5	8.0	6.0	(10.0)	-
Sum, augmented	-	-	-	-	-	-	22.0	17.0	8.0	-	-
Ratio of fractions	18	17	2.8	3.0	3.9	4.7	11	9	10	8	-

Fraction-ratio of classes: I - 5; II - 7.7; III - 3; IV - 5.

NOTES

1. To Miss C. Colyer and the Lincoln Archaeological Trust; to Messrs. T. G. Hassall and B. G. Durham and the Oxford Archaeological Excavation Committee; to Messrs. P. V. Addyman and C. H. M. Clarke and the York Archaeological Trust.

2. Oxoniensia, II (1932), 95-6.

3. BNJ, XLI (1973), 27-33.

4. cf. BNJ XXX (1961), 111-4 for full references.

5. BNJ, ut supra, 116-7.

6. 12th century evidence is limited but large draw-cord purses are conspicuously on mid-13th century funeral effigies of both sexes (e.g. at Darlington); mid-late 14th century effigies show slits on the hips, presumably giving access to hanging pockets; heavy, usually lidded, purses are common on effigies from the mid-15th century.

7. e.g. in the sample from York.

8. Together they amount to about 15% of the Edwardian or 12% of the Edwardian plus Long-cross totals.

9. NC, 6th ser., XIII (1953), 115-122.

10. BNJ, XXXVIII (1969), 50-83.

11. BNJ, XXVII (1943), 58, 65.

12. This is also the pattern of the finds from the (generally minor) church sites in the York sample.

MEDIEVAL COINS AND JETTONS FROM OXFORD EXCAVATIONS

N.J. Palmer and N.J. Mayhew[1]

For the medieval archaeologist coin site-finds, since they can generally be more closely dated than other archaeological material, represent a useful opportunity for assigning dates to features and for cross-checking the dating evidence provided by pottery. For the numismatist, however, they can also be useful in giving some indication of the 'small change' current in medieval England. Hoard evidence is unsatisfactory in this respect, showing a disproportionate number of coins of the higher denomination, and lacking those which could be considered 'small change'. There are, however, problems to be overcome before this aim can be fulfilled. The paucity of coins on medieval sites is a byword among archaeologists: an excavation in the medieval village of Tetsworth,[2] for example, produced no medieval coins at all. Urban sites are richer, but it is certainly rare for coins to be recovered in large numbers.[3] Whether coins are found also depends on further factors such as the size of the excavated area and the methods of excavation used. Another limitation is that whereas a hoard will be closely datable, often allowing the conclusion that its constituent coins were in circulation at that date, it is very rare to find an archaeological deposit that both contains a number of coins and can be dated within a limited time. Thus one can only gain a general indication of what was in circulation, without being able to say exactly when.

To obtain, therefore, a reasonable and representative sample of medieval 'small change', it will be necessary to examine a number of sites, at the same time endeavouring to consider the archaeological and other limiting factors operating in each case. It is hoped that such a sample may be obtained by examining the coins from some Oxford excavations. Since 1967, when the Oxford Archaeological Excavation Committee was founded in order to carry out a programme of excavation in advance of the modern redevelopment of the city, a number of sites have been examined, both inside and outside the medieval city walls. The presence of the University has meant that this redevelopment has been confined to the south west corner of the city, and so the excavations, apart from that in All Saints Church, have also been concentrated in this area. It should also be remembered that this same university presence would ensure in the middle ages a cosmopolitan and mobile population, making Oxford possibly atypical among English medieval provincial towns. However, it is impossible to say whether either of these factors will distort the picture given by the coin finds from the city.

There have been seven major medieval excavations in Oxford since 1967 (Fig. 1): three on tenement sites, in Church Street, St. Aldates, and The Hamel; two on monastic sites, Blackfriars and Greyfriars; one in All Saints

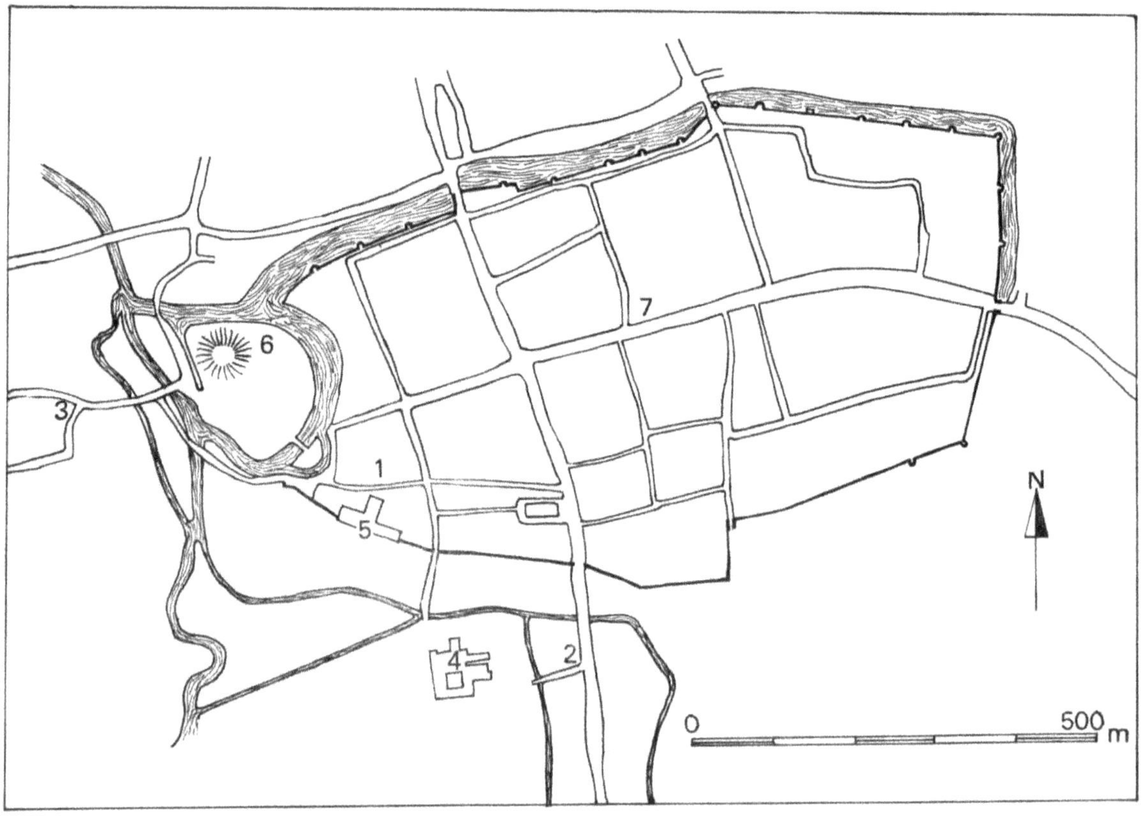

Fig 1. Excavations in Medieval Oxford

	COINS				JETTONS						
	Farthings	Halfpence	Pence	Others	English	French	Nuremburg	Others	Lead tokens	Uncertain	Post 1500 and others
1. CHURCH STREET	2	2	3		6	7	4	1		3	31
2. ST ALDATES	2	1	1	1	1	1			1?	1	25
3. THE HAMEL	4	6	6	1	3	6			1?	3	18
Total	8	9	10	2	10	14	4	1	2	7	74
4. BLACKFRIARS	1			1		4			1		6
5. GREYFRIARS											10
6. OXFORD CASTLE											4
7. ALL SAINTS							1			1	16
TOTAL	9	9	10	3	10	18	5	1	3	8	110

Fig 2. Coins and Jettons from Oxford Excavations

Church and one in Oxford Castle. Of these, the first four produced useful quantities of coins. There have also been a number of smaller excavations not producing any quantity of coins, which will not be discussed in detail.

1. CHURCH STREET[4]

The first large scale excavations of medieval tenements carried out in Oxford were those from 1968-70 on the site of 31-34 Church Street in St. Ebbes, within the medieval city, and now under the Westgate Shopping Centre. Documentary research by Dr. Hilary Turner[5] has found little to suggest that this area was either richer or poorer than other parts of Oxford. In the medieval period it was continually occupied. There was the occasional vacant site, but few remained completely so, although there was a lot of empty ground, used for the deposition of rubbish, behind the street frontages. The houses emerge from the documents as being mostly constructed of timber. Some are described as having a solar and cellar, so some, perhaps most, would have been of two storeys. The excavation covered part of two medieval tenements: about one quarter of the trench covered that known as Whitehall (31 Church Street) and the remaining three quarters, that known as Domus Mirifeld (32-34 Church Street). The documents[6] for these properties begin in 1340 and 1266 respectively, but give no indication that either was used as anything other than a dwelling house in the Middle Ages. The excavators offer the presence of a number of small hearths in Domus Mirifeld as evidence that the property may have been used for trade purposes during the late medieval period.

The excavated area was extensive (about 525 square metres) and most of the excavation was carried out by hand, only the initial clearing of the site being done mechanically, so the chances of recovering coins were reasonably high. Archaeologically the results of the excavation were disappointing: few traces of medieval structure were discovered and most of the site was taken up with a honeycomb of rubbish pits. These latter were difficult to excavate and their nature meant that the pottery found in them did not form closed groups. However, the site produced a total of fifty-nine coins and tokens.[7] Of these, thirty-one were post-1500 and three uncertain. Of the remaining twenty-five, seven were coins, including two farthings, two half-pennies and three pennies, and eighteen were jettons, including six English types, seven French types, four early Nuremburg types and one other. All the coins came from Domus Mirifeld, although similar numbers of jettons came from each tenement. The total shows more finds from Domus Mirifeld, reasonably so, since more of this tenement was excavated.

	Coins			Jettons				
	Farthings	Halfpence	Pence	English	French	Nuremburg	Others	Total
Domus Mirifeld	2	2	3	1	3	4	1	16
Whitehall	-	-	-	5	4	-	-	9
	2	2	3	6	7	4	1	

2. ST. ALDATES[8]

During 1970 and 1971 a second tenement site was excavated on the corner of St. Aldates with Speedwell Street, outside the city walls in the south suburbs, which the excavation showed to date back into the Saxon period. The documents[9] for the property begin in 1279, when the Hundred Rolls describe the corner tenement as held by Will. Rowe and worth 5s 4d. From 1339, the property was used as a shop; a deed of 1439 describes a shop beneath a solar, giving its dimensions as 10 feet along the High road and 16 feet along the lane. These measurements were confirmed by the excavation. Given the size and situation of the premises it seems likely that it was a retail shop rather than a workshop that was meant.

Although the site was much smaller than Church Street, initially covering an area of about 90 square metres as against about 525 square metres, meticulous excavation produced a stratified sequence of occupation with associated structures dating back to the Middle Saxon Period quite unlike anything recovered from Church Street. The site also produced thirty-four coins and jettons, twenty-five of them post-1500. Before 1500 there were five coins, one farthing, one cut farthing, one cut (?) halfpenny, a penny and a south German pfennig, two jettons, one uncertain, and a possible medieval lead token.[10]

3. THE HAMEL[11]

The third and most recent tenement excavation took place in 1975 and 1976 on the corner of The Hamel with St. Thomas' High Street in the western suburb of St. Thomas's, which seems to have been laid out during the twelfth century. Again the excavated area lay across two medieval tenements: the south quarter of the trench covered that known as <u>the Hall of St. Helen</u>, the northern three-quarters that known as <u>Bretels</u>. Another small trench was dug across the road in another tenement called <u>St. Frideswide's Tenement</u>. The <u>Hall of St. Helen</u> emerges from the documents[12] as a substantial property, belonging at different times to the Hospital of St. John and to Oseney Abbey and for some time in use as an academic hall. Its excavated remains were also substantial. According to the antiquary Anthony Wood the Hamel contained houses for the "mechanicall professions" of Oseney Abbey, but an excavated sequence of bread ovens from <u>Bretels</u> may be evidence that part of that tenement was for some time a bakeshop.

The site produced forty-eight coins and tokens,[13] of which eighteen were post-1500 and four were uncertain, including one possible medieval lead token. For the medieval period there were seventeen coins, including four farthings three halfpennies, three cut halfpennies, six pennies and a halfgroat, and nine jettons, three of English types, six of French. Jetton no. 88, (Pl. I, 17) Edward I, has a bust similar to that on the regal coinage (cf. Fox type VII rev: arms of John Langton, Lord Chancellor 1292 or, less likely, Walter Langton, Treasurer 1295) and the same punches may have been used to produce the obverse die as were in use for the coinage of the time. Another government official whose arms appear on jettons is John Offord, Chancellor 1345.[14] If one could assign the Hamel jetton to John Langton as Chancellor Fox Class VII might be more firmly dated to around 1292.

The most noticeable feature of the Hamel group is its sheer size. A total of twenty-six items as against twenty-four from Church Street, although the excavated area was only 249 square metres as opposed to 525 square metres. The distribution of the finds among the tenements is as follows:

	Coins				Jettons		
	Farthings	Halfpence	Pence	Half groat	English	French	Total
St. Helens Hall	2	3	3	-	-	3	11
Bretels	1	2	3	1	3	3	13
St. Frideswides	1	1	-	-	-	-	2
Total	4	6	6	1	3	6	26

Since the excavated portion of Bretels is three times the size of that of the Hall of St. Helen, the latter emerges as the more affluent tenement, although the former produced half the items found. If, however, one considers that St. Aldates produced eight finds from an area of 90 square metres perhaps the Hamel group does not seem so large. Both excavations, unlike Church Street, were concentrated on occupation layers, rather than rubbish pits.

4. BLACKFRIARS[15]

Excavations on the second site of the Oxford Dominican Priory were carried out intermittently from 1961-1975. The Blackfriars came to Oxford in 1221 and initially established themselves on St. Aldates.[16] Building on the second site seems to have begun about 1236, the Friars taking possession of their new home in 1245 and first using the church for services in the following year. By 1251, when there was a royal grant for the building of cloisters, the main part of the work must have been finished. The Oxford Blackfriars was unparalleled in size and prestige among Dominican Priories. From the outset, it was the studium of the English Province and after the general chapter of 1261 was raised to the rank of studium generale. The house was dissolved in 1538, demolition began almost immediately and today nothing remains above ground except a fragment of the gatehouse incorporated into a later cottage.

The methods of excavation were different from those used on the tenement sites discussed above. The Priory covered a large area and a number of small trenches were excavated, with mechanical assistance, for the purpose of discovering the plan of the priory buildings. Such methods serve this limited purpose but are not conducive to the recovery of coins. Nevertheless, the site did produce two coins,[17] a cut farthing and half a coin of Charles V of France, the only numismatic evidence of the establishment's international connections. There were also four French type jettons and a lead token, as well as six post-1500 jettons.

5. GREYFRIARS[18]

The site of the Oxford Greyfriars, on which excavations were carried out between 1968 and 1974, lay south of the Church Street site, in St. Ebbes, and astride the city walls. The original church lay presumably within the city wall, but in 1244 the Greyfriars received Royal permission to throw down part of the city wall and insert their church in the gap. The earlier excavations uncovered the plan of this second church, the later involved a number of trenches designed to recover that of the domestic buildings. The methods used were similar to those employed at the Blackfriars and since the buildings anyway were in a poor state of preservation, it is not surprising that no medieval coins or jettons were discovered.[19]

6. OXFORD CASTLE[20]

The two trenches dug in 1972 on parts of Oxford Castle produced much interesting information about the early history of the Castle and city in the form of Saxon pit groups and a sunken hut, but little medieval material. The only coin dating before 1500 was an exceptionally rare silver halfpenny of Eadred.[21]

7. ALL SAINTS[22]

The excavations in All Saints Church prior to its conversion to a library for Lincoln College were similarly unproductive of coins.[23] Again the site revealed Saxon occupation, this time in the form of yard surfaces and a cellar, from the top of which came a fragment of a coin of Edward the Confessor.[24] Enough medieval structure was discovered to allow the reconstruction of the development of the medieval church but the surviving features were not of a coin-producing type. One early Nuremburg jetton came from a post medieval pit. The smallness of the number of coins from the last four sites is striking. This is less the result of the methods of excavation, although this may have played a part in some cases, than simply the lack of occupation layers which judging by the number of coins coming from the tenement sites, are the layers which produce most of the coins.

Thus from Oxford Excavations between 1967 and 1976, a total of thirty-one medieval coins, thirty-five medieval jettons and three possible or probable medieval lead tokens were recovered (Fig. 2). For the purposes of examining the content of medieval small change, however, perhaps it would be as well to omit the two monastic sites, since their methods of excavation mean that the coins found are probably not a fair sample. One can also ignore the All Saints and Castle excavations since they produced no coins to speak of. We are left, therefore, with the three tenement excavations, Church Street, St. Aldates and The Hamel, which produced a total of twenty-nine coins, thirty jettons and two possible lead tokens.

A number of conclusions can perhaps be drawn from these figures. The first point to note is the meagre numbers of coins involved. Medieval small change seems to have been a scarce commodity; a comparable series of Roman excavations would have produced many times the number of coins. Secondly one may note the relatively large numbers of farthings and halfpennies. They occur in approximately the same numbers as pennies (eight farthings, nine halfpennies and ten pennies), and present a quite different picture from the hoards. In fact, there would probably be even higher numbers of the smaller denominations in circulation, since farthings, especially cut farthings, are easily missed by excavators.

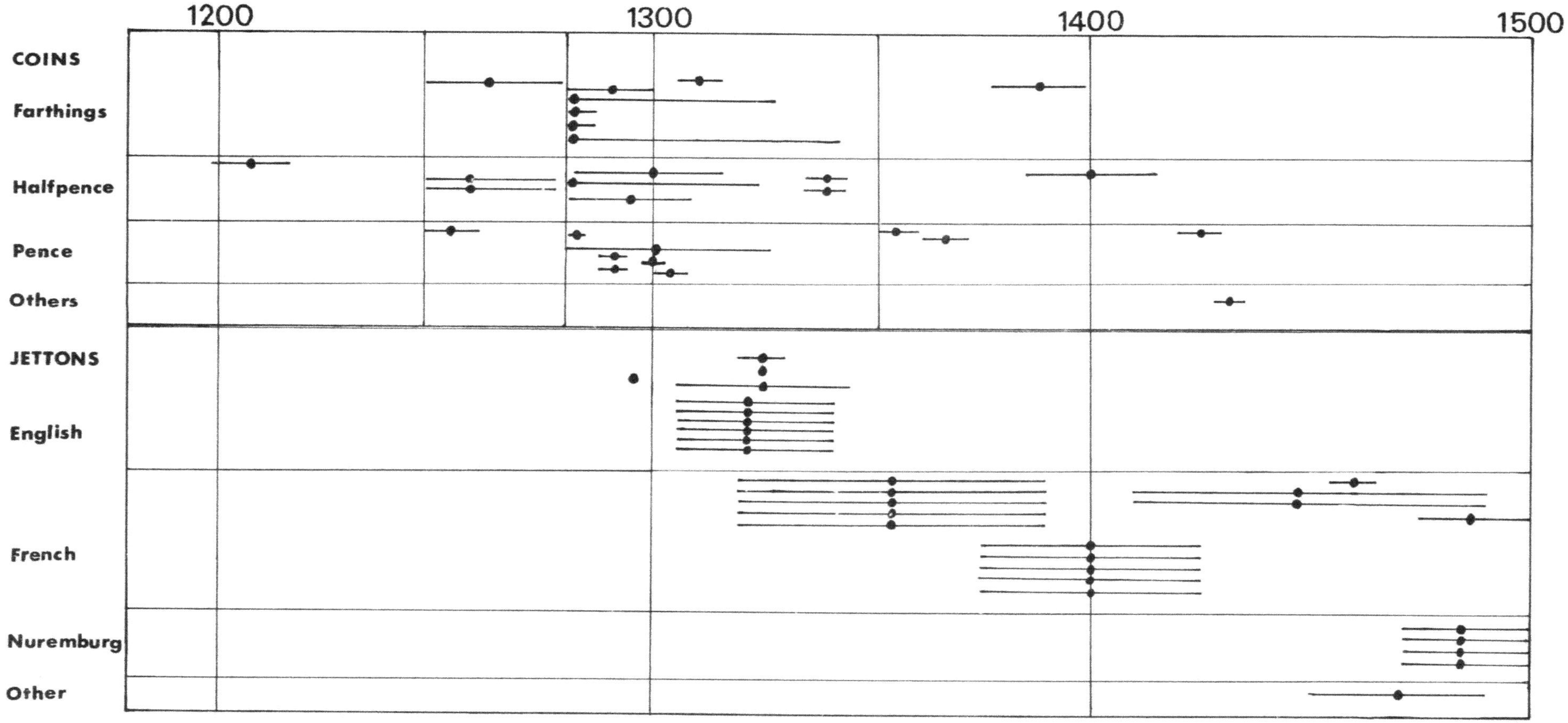

Fig 3. Date Ranges of Coins and Jettons from Tenement Sites

The picture given by the date ranges of the coins (Fig. 3) is as follows:

	1200-47	1247-79	1279-1351	1351-1500
Farthings	-	1	6	1
Halfpence	1	2	5	1
Pence	-	1	6	3
Others	-	-	-	2
	1	4	17	7

The majority of the finds come from the late thirteenth and early fourteenth centuries. If small change was scarce throughout the middle ages, it becomes especially so in the late fourteenth and fifteenth centuries. Although the city of Oxford is believed to decline in this period, the lack of small change appears to be general,[25] and the most likely explanation for this is the known decline in mint output during this period.

The final question is that of the place of jettons in the scheme of medieval 'small change'. The traditional view is that they were used exclusively as casting counters for reckoning purposes. A perhaps more attractive view is that they were used as 'small change' to supplement the meagre quantities of coins in circulation.[26] There are a number of arguments in favour of this. The first point is their ubiquity, for as many jettons were found in Oxford as coins (twenty-nine coins, in our sample, thirty jettons) and they come even from the poorest tenements. The reply to this is that large numbers of reckoning boards existed - as evidenced by the numbers mentioned in inventories. However, there were jettons in Layer 18/1 in the Blackfriars[27] which is interpreted as the dust under the choir stalls, so these jettons at least are unlikely to be from reckoning boards unless the Blackfriars church was full of money changers. A second point of interest is the fact that the same punches were used for coins and jettons. Thirdly, the fact that jettons were mutilated to prevent their circulation as coins admits the possibility that jettons were so used. Finally, the date range of the jettons (Fig. 3), compared with the coins found, is at least consistent with the theory that jettons filled the gap created by the dearth of small change in the late fourteenth and fifteenth centuries.

A further question is the basis on which they may have passed as small change. Was it the result of individual initiative or official policy? A useful analogy perhaps is the circulation of telephone gettone in Italy today. Although produced for another purpose, due to a shortage of coined small change, these tokens have come into circulation instead. Perhaps it was the same with medieval jettons.

The excavations also produced a few examples of lead tokens. For the use of these to supplement the supply of small change the archaeological and documentary evidence both in Britain and abroad is rich. Perhaps the most thorough collection of evidence yet made was that published in the Revue Belge de Numismatique by L. Dancoisne for the lead tokens of Arras in particular and Artois in general.[28] He confidently asserts that the tokens which he illustrates were used, in the thirteenth and fourteenth centuries, as small change, circulating voluntarily by convention rather than by law. While they served such a vital function they were tolerated by the authorites, but in the fourteenth and fifteenth centuries the introduction of black money put an end to official tolerance of lead tokens. Dancoisne cites three fifteenth century edicts banning the use of lead tokens and complaining that earlier bans were being ignored.

Nor was their use confined to Europe. In the early sixteenth century England was regarded as the home of lead tokens.[29] A great deal of evidence for their use was collected by Akerman[30] who records, among other things, the famous London find of 1846, to which Dolley and Seaby refer in their paper on a similar Dublin find.[31] Moulds for tokens of exactly similar type are preserved in the Department of Antiquities of the Ashmolean Museum. They were found in the Thames and are believed to have come from Osney Abbey.[32] Documentary evidence indicates that lead tokens were not always cast, but sometimes struck with dies.[33] Lead tokens of rather cruder type have also been found near Oxford. Some were found in excavations at Banbury and others, of identical type, at Abingdon, indicating a rather wider circulation for crude types than might otherwise have been assumed. Further work on tokens retrieved from the Thames, near Windsor, is in progress.[34]

In conclusion, the Oxford material provides, therefore, some indication, both of the results that can be gained by numismatic study of archaeological site-finds and of their limitations as a source of information. Apart from the size of the group the Oxford coins are not untypical,[35] but obviously many more site groups need to be studied in detail to gain a real indication of the nature of medieval small change.

APPENDIX

Note: Individual coins are identified by the numbers assigned to them in the site records (Small Find numbers). In the case of the three tenement sites, abbreviations indicate the tenement from which they come. DM is Domus Mirifeld, W Whitehall, H Hall of St. Helen, B Bretels and SF St. Frideswide's Tenement.

1. 31-34 Church Street

Coins

Farthings:	1014	Edward I-II	c 1310	London	DM
	1018	Richard II	1377-99		DM
Half pence:	1035		Late 13th-14th century		DM
	1101		Late 14th-15th century		DM
Pence:	108	Edward I	1280-2	Bristol	DM
	1134	Edward I-II			DM
	90		15th century (1420-30)		DM

Jettons

English Types:	2	Edward II	1325		W
	1060		1300-50		W
	2101		Early 14th century		W
	1107		Early 14th century		DM
	2139	(unofficial?)	Early 14th century		W
	2143		Early 14th century		W
French Types:	1012		1350-1400	Moor's Head	W
	1108		1350-1400	Moor's Head	DM
	2065		1350-1400	Moor's Head	W
	2100		1350-1400	Moor's Head	W
	28		15th century		DM
	2056		15th century		W
	1058		Later 15th century		DM

Nuremburg:	45		Late 15th century		DM
	46/2		Late 15th century		DM
	46/3		Late 15th Century		DM
	29		Late 15th century		DM
Others:	15		Mid-Late 15th century		DM

+ 3 Uncertain Jettons/Tokens
+ 31 Post Medieval

2. 79-80 St. Aldates

Coins

Farthings:	263	Henry III Cut-Long cross	1247-79 Moneyer-William	London ?
	476	Edward I	1280-1300	
Half Pence:	350	Edward I-II Cut ?	1279-1324 (probably 1280)	
Pence:	110	Edward I Class IXb	c 1300	
Other:	102	S. German or Austrian pfennig (?)	Late 14th century	

Jettons

English Types:	295	Edward II	c 1325	Berry, Pl. 4, 9
French Types:	113		c 1460	

340 Uncertain fragment (possibly - Cut Farthing of Stephen)

+ 25 Post-medieval, and 1 possible medieval lead token.

3. The Hamel

Coins

Farthings:	214	Edward I-III	1280-1343	Fox X ?	H
	159	Edward I orII	probably 1281	Fox I-III	B
	211	Edward I	c 1281	Fox III	H
	9	Edward I	c 1280	Fox III	SF
Half Pence:	36	John Cut Short cross	Moneyer-Hugh	Canterbury	H
	21	Henry III Cut Long cross		London ?	B

	67	Henry III Cut Long cross		Brockage	H
	113	Edward I	1280-3	Dublin	B
	210	Edward III	1335-43		H
	7	Edward III	1335-43		SF
Pence:	114	Henry III Long cross	Moneyer-Hugh c 1247-60	London	H
	103	Edward I	post 1300	Newcastle IXb	H
	95	Jean I Brabant-Limburg	1288-94	Chautard 97	B
	43	Jean I Brabant-Limburg	1288-94	Chautard 95-7?	B
	37	Edward III	1351-61 Pre Treaty	York	H
	14	Black Prince Anglo-Gallic	1362-72		
Halfgroat:	56	Henry VI	1430-4 pinecone mascle	London	B

<u>Jettons</u>

English Types:	167		Early 14th century	obv. Berry, Pl. 5,1	B
	161		Early 14th century	Short cross moline	B
	88	Edward I Bust of Fox type VIIb, rev. arms of John Langton, Chancellor 1292 or Walter Langton Treasurer 1295 (Pl. I, 17)			
French Types:	86	1350-1400	Moor's Head Barnard p. 113, no. 12		H
	70	14th-15th century	cf. Barnard Pl. VI, 43 but cruder		B
	16	14th-15th century	cf. Barnard Pl. VI, 47 obv. lis in field		
	5	14th-15th century			
	73	14th-15th century	cf. Barnard Pl. VI, 43 but different legends		H
	131	14th-15th century	rev. cf. Barnard Pl. VI, 47 obv. illegible		B
Other:	63	possible medieval lead token			H

+ 3 uncertain

+ 18 Post-medieval coins, tokens and jettons.

4. Blackfriars

Coins

Farthings:	1002	Henry III Cut Long cross penny Class 3c	1248-50
Other:	23	Charles V Broken half of base AR blanc	1365-c 1384

Jettons

French Types:	52	Official-Moor's Head	1360-1380
	101	Official-Moor's Head	1360-1380
	103	Official	Last quarter 14th century
	146	" French derivative"	Late 15th century or c 1500
Other:	106	Mereau in lead-alloy	Late 13th-14th century

+ 6 Post-medieval tokens/jettons.

5. Greyfriars

10 Post-medieval

6. Oxford Castle

3 Post-medieval + 1 coin of Eadred.

7. All Saints

Jettons

92 Early Nuremburg c 1490

59 Uncertain

+ 15 Post-medieval + 1 coin of Edward the Confessor.

NOTES

1. The authors would like to acknowledge help and advice from Dr. Michael Metcalf, Martin Welch, Mark Blackburn, Brain Durham, Tom Hassall, George Lambrick and the Museum of Oxford. The bulk of the paper is the work of Nicholas Palmer, while the identifications and the section on lead tokens are by Nicholas Mayhew. Despite this division of labour the authors are in agreement over their findings.

2. M.A. Robinson, "Excavation at Copt Hay, Tetsworth," Oxoniensia XXXVIII (1973), 41-115.

3. See Rigold, above pp. 59-80.

4. Interim Reports: Oxoniensia XXIV (1969), 5-11; XXV (1970), 7-10.

5. Unpublished report for O.A.E.C.

6. H.E. Salter, Survey of Oxford II, OHS NS XX (1969), 72-3.

7. Appendix 1.

8. Interim Reports: Oxoniensia XXXVI (1971), 10-14; XXXVII (1972), 143-8. Final Report: B.G. Durham, "Archaeological Excavations in St. Aldates, Oxford, 1970-2," Oxoniensia (1977) forthcoming.

9. Salter, op.cit. no. 6, 22.

10. Appendix 2.

11. N.J. Palmer, CBA 9 Newsletter 1976, 69-72.

12. H.E. Salter, Oseney Cartulary II, OHS XC (1929), 405-10, 416-28; A. Clark (ed) Wood's City of Oxford I, OHS 1889, 317-8.

13. Appendix 3.

14. G. Berry, Medieval English Jettons, (London 1974) p 39, 1c.

15. Interim Report: Oxoniensia XXXVIII (1973), 286-94. Final Report: G. Lambrick and H. Woods, "Excavations on the Second Site of the Dominican Priory, Oxford," Oxoniensia (1976) forthcoming.

16. W.A. Hinnebusch, "The Pre-Reformation Sites of the Oxford Blackfriars," Oxoniensia III (1938), 57-82.

17. Appendix 4.

18. Interim Reports: Oxoniensia XXV (1970), 10-15; XXXVI (1971) 6-8; XXXIX (1974), 59-61.

19. Appendix 5.

20. Interim Report: Oxoniensia XXXVIII (1973), 280-5; Final Report: T. G. Hassall, "Excavations of Oxford Castle, 1965-73," Oxoniensia (1976) forthcoming.

21. For further discussion on this coin, and the possibility that it is a farthing rather than a halfpenny see D. M. Metcalf, in T. G. Hassall "Excavations of Oxford Castle, 1965-73" Oxoniensia (1976).

22. Interim Report: Oxoniensia XXXIX (1974), 54-7.

23. Appendix 7.

24. PACX; BMC type iv.

25. See Rigold, above.

26. J.Y. Akerman, Tradesmen's Tokens Current in London and its Vicinity between the Years 1648 and 1672, (London 1849), 3.

27. Appendix 6, 103, 106 and two of the post-medieval jettons.

28. L. Dancoisne, " Les Petits Mereaux de Plomb d'Arras aux types de Mailles," RBN 1884, 55-65.

29. P. Grierson, "Notes on Early Tudor Coinage: 2, Erasmus's Lead Tokens," BNJ XLI (1972), 85-7.

30. Akerman, op. cit. no. 26.

31. M. Dolley and W. A. Seaby in N. Circ. Dec. 1971, 446.

32. The authors are grateful to Michael Metcalf and Martin Welch for this information.

33. G.C. Boon, Welsh Tokens of the Seventeenth Century, (Cardiff 1973), 16.

34. M. Dean, forthcoming in NC.

35. See Rigold, above.

OVERSEAS TRADE AND THE ENGLISH MONEY SUPPLY IN THE FOURTEENTH CENTURY

T. H. Lloyd

One of the most important debates which has engaged the attention of economic historians is that about the factors which contributed to European economic expansion in the early middle ages and to apparent contraction in the later middle ages. Although a number of theories have emerged the most actively discussed have been those propounded by what one may term the monetarist school on the one hand and by the demographic school on the other.[1] A common interest of these schools is the study of prices. Unfortunately, while price material is relatively abundant and changes in price levels are easily detected it is less easy to decide why those changes occurred. Supporters of a demographic model urge that the most important influence on prices was that exerted by the pressure of population upon resources, while monetarists counter with the claim that the amount of bullion, and hence of money, was a more important factor. Although the ideas of each of these schools are sometimes set out in terms which seem to imply that they are mutually exclusive this is not necessarily the case. Much depends upon the time scale of one's perspective. The present paper contains little or nothing that will weigh the balance in favour of either one school or the other as far as the whole of Europe and the whole of the middle ages is concerned, since it deals only with the experience of England during the fourteenth century. Moreover, it is not primarily concerned with price changes. Its purpose is to demonstrate possible changes in the amount of money in circulation during various periods and to link these with changes in the balance of overseas trade.

It is difficult to doubt that overseas trade was the most important factor influencing the amount of money in circulation in England during most of the middle ages. This nation produced no gold and a negligible amount of silver; consequently the money supply could be maintained only by importing bullion. A positive balance in commodity trade encouraged an inflow of bullion, while a negative balance involved an outflow of existing stocks. Even to maintain the money supply at a given level and quality it was necessary that the balance of trade should be favourable enough not merely to compensate for wear and tear on the coinage but also to provide funds for overseas expenditure by the English crown, church and private citizens. At all times such expenditure was significant and during periods of active warfare military adventures might be responsible for an actual diminution of the national bullion stock. In contrast non-mercantile activities seldom gave rise to an accretion of bullion. In general terms the stability of the English medieval coinage in comparison with that of other European countries has often been hailed as evidence that the English merchant community rose successfully to the challenge of maintaining a favourable balance of trade. However, the lack of detailed studies has enabled conflicting views to be advanced. Thus Professor M. M. Postan has written that 'the balance of payments was probably more favourable to England in the fourteenth and fifteenth centuries than in the thirteenth', while Professor H. A. Miskimin sees 'decreasing foreign earnings and increasing expenditures, with a resultant outflow of bullion' from the middle of the fourteenth century.[2] That the former statement cannot be demonstrated to be true, while the latter can be shown to be untrue is a reflection of the existing state of knowledge about medieval trade balances. The present paper seeks to remedy the deficiency for the fourteenth century, using all the unpublished customs material as well as the published figures for wool and cloth. Inevitably some speculation is involved in this exercise and the author does not wish his claims to be exaggerated. It is sufficient to show when the balance of trade was favourable, when it was unfavourable and what the rough order of magnitude of the balance may have been. Some of the statistics are presented in such a way to allow the reader to insert alternative values, but it is unlikely that the broad conclusions need to be altered.

Mint activity during the first three and a half decades of the fourteenth century may be divided into a number of clearly defined phases, in each of which volume of production is the key factor, although origin of silver and denomination of coins are also significant. (See Table 1.) The lull in activity which followed the general recoinage of 1299-1300 was short-lived, for after Michaelmas 1303 silver began to flood into the mints and by 1309 over 634,000 pounds of coin had been produced at London and Canterbury. A gap of two years in the enrolled accounts separates this somewhat exceptional period from the next, covering 10 years (1311-21), in which output ran at a much reduced level, indeed at one which may be regarded as low compared with years of normal activity in the thirteenth century. However, with an average output of almost 26,000 pounds of coin a year the picture was still cheerful compared with what was to come. Another gap of 12 months in the enrolled accounts is followed by two years in which total production was less than 2,000 pounds. In so far as the new money was produced almost entirely from foreign silver these years belong with the preceding period, but the tempo of production heralded a silver famine which lasted for a decade. In this next period (1324-35) production of coin averaged less than 500 pounds a year, although half of it was now made from old English coins or other native silver and three-quarters of the output consisted of farthings, the making of which had been eschewed during the good years, since they gave a smaller profit to the mint.

During the years 1303 to 1309 99% of new money was made from recently imported foreign silver and inevitably historians have associated mint activity with the contemporaneous boom in wool exports. Exports averaged about 28,000 sacks a year from 1297 to 1304 but 39,854 sacks a year from 1304 to 1311.[3] In fact the export boom seems to have started about 1300, was retarded, but not reversed by hostilities between Flanders and France from 1302 to 1305, and received a new impetus during the clip of 1305, which coincided with the Franco-Flemish Peace of Athis-sur-Orge. The boom began slowly to fade about the time that Edward II came to the English throne,

TABLE 1

FOURTEENTH CENTURY COIN OUTPUT (ALL RECORDED MINTS) *

	Silver				Gold					
					London		Calais		Aggregate Values in Money of Account (£ Sterling)	
	Weight of Coin (Pounds)				Weight of Coin (Pounds)		Weight of Coin (Pounds)			
Period of Account[1]	Total	Annual Average	Origin of Bullion[2]	Composition of Coin[3]	Total	Annual Average	Total	Annual Average	Total	Annual Average
1303–9	634 381	105 730	99%F	P99% F1%H negligible					642 362	107 060
9 Oct. 1311–21	259 705	25 971	99%F	P 98% F2%H negligible					263 009	26 300
7 Oct. 1322–24	3 826	1 913	E negligible	P91% F9%H negligible					3 878	1 939
1324–7 May 35	4 882	461	51%E	P26% H1% F73%					4 937	466
7 May 1335–41	10 865	2 006	83%E	H54% F46% PNil					11 449	2 114
1341–15 Dec. 43	22 496	10 187	94%F	H97% F3% PNil					23 620	10 696
20 Jan. 1344–45	57 231	34 339		All P	3 448	2 069			111 185	66 711
1345–24 June 51	37 521	6 525		P20% H77% F3%	9 810	1 706			180 387	31 372
24 June 1351–8 Apr. 57	299 445	52 077			29 444	5 121			815 966	141 907
8 Apr. 1357–11 Feb. 63	48 476	8 310			46 451	7 963			757 360	129 833
11 Feb. 1363–68	10 045	1 786			7 712	1 371	18 803[4]	3 406	410 281	72 939
1368–73	3 926	785			9 786	1 957	9 165[5]	1 767	289 172	57 834
1373–84	13 298	1 209			4 264	388	2 927[6]	266	124 487	11 317
1384–89	2 901	580			4 115	823	2 170[7]	635	97 888	19 578
1389–10 Oct. 99	7 274	727			11 469	1 147	3 960[8]	410	240 536	24 053

1. All periods of account start and end at Michaelmas (29 Sept.) except where stated otherwise

2. F = Foreign Coin
   E = English

3. P = Pence
   H = Halfpence
   F = Farthings

4. To 27 Aug. 1368
5. 27 Aug. 68–4 Nov. 73
6. From 4 Nov. 73
7. To 22 Feb. 88. Account missing 28 Feb. 88–17 Jan. 90
8. 17 Jan. 90–25 Aug. 99

* Sources C. G. Crump and C. Johnson, 'Tables of Bullion Coined under Edward I, II & III', Num. Chronicle, ser. 4, 13 (1913), with some corrections from M. Mate, 'Monetary Policies in England, 1272-1307', Brit. Num. Journal, 41 (1972) and from Miss. E. Stokes, 'Tables of Bullion Coined, 1377-1550', Num. Chronicle, ser. 5, 9 (1929), with Mss. additions for Calais.

although it cannot really be said to be at an end until 1313. There are at least two possible explanations for the recession. Either the Flemish cloth industry had momentarily reached a level of production which could not be sustained and from which the demand for wool could only fall or, alternatively, trade declined because of the growing friction between England and Flanders. This friction has been ascribed to the aid given by the latter to the Scots rebels. However, it is clear that such aid was not the cause but the consequence of the Anglo-Flemish estrangement, which was rooted in the refusal of Edward I to succour the Flemings in their struggle with France. A point of no return was reached in December 1310 when English sailors perpetrated a major act of piracy against a Flemish fleet and this led inexorably to the compulsory wool staple which was established in 1313 at Saint Omer outside the frontiers of Flanders.[4]

The mint activity of the first decade of the fourteenth century seems to have been what modern economists might describe as an export-led boom. In this period England had a highly-favourable balance of trade, based upon wool exports, and inevitably she accumulated a large amount of silver. The situation was not fundamentally new, for in all probability the wool trade had been responsible for the import of silver throughout the thirteenth century. However, in the light of Miss Archibald's figures relating to silver 'losses' it is clear that imports of silver to pay for wool may not too readily be regarded as net additions to the national bullion stock in the thirteenth century.[5] An analysis which ascribes the high level of early fourteenth century mint activity exclusively to the boom in wool exports is not acceptable to all historians. Dr. M. Mate, while conceding a connection, believes that the wool trade does not provide a sufficient explanation for this activity and she prefers a monetary explanation, which relies upon mint prices.[6] She holds that merchants who, earlier and later, had silver coined on the continent, during the years 1305 to 1310 deliberately favoured the English mint. Although there is as yet no satisfactory explanation for this behaviour the implication is that merchants were not motivated simply by the need to have large amounts of English currency in hand, but rather that they positively preferred the island mint to its continental rivals because it paid a better price for silver. If one accepts that major changes in silver flows were caused by mint policies then one has to accept the possibility of a third explanation of the boom and subsequent recession in the wool trade. By this reasoning exports may have been influenced not only by industrial demand or by military/diplomatic factors, or both, but also by national monetary policies. The boom may have been encouraged by the fact that temporarily it was more profitable to sell silver to the English mints than to those on the continent. While conceding this point it must be urged that the depth of the subsequent recession cannot be accounted for solely by a change in mint policies. Military and diplomatic factors, which have already been hinted at, and which will later be discussed more fully, must be given greater prominence.

As far as alien merchants were concerned the inadvisability of importing more silver than they needed for their immediate trade needs is established by the fact that Edward I maintained a rigid ban on the export of silver in any form. Dr. Mate has suggested that the principal reason for this was the king's determination that silver should not get to those mints which had been counterfeiting his coins. To this one may add that his resolve may have been strengthened by the refusal of merchants to pay a customs duty on money and plate either imported or exported. The Carta Mercatoria of 1303, as well as increasing the rate of duty on alien exports of wool and placing specific duties on cloth and wax had imposed an ad valorem duty of 3d in the £ on all other merchandise imported and exported. Although the charter made no mention of plate or money it is clear that at first customs officials tried to levy duty on these. An alien merchant exporting £30 sterling from Bristol in April 1303 was required to pay duty as were two others who took £24 from Boston in the following August. More important, although more puzzling, are the customs accounts for Lynn.[7] From February 1303 to Michaelmas 1305 numerous aliens paid duty on imported gold florins valued at more than £159 and on over 580 pounds of silver coin; the actual totals were considerably larger, but many coins were valued in gross with commodities. In this period there was one export of 12 pounds of silver. In the following two years notices of coin at Lynn were considerably fewer, although imports of silver totalled at least 134 pounds, while gold imports were worth £12 and gold and silver £23; there was again a single export of silver. In the earlier period the Lynn silver was described as sterlings and, on one occasion, as monete anglie, while later it was simply argentum. Although it is conceivable that all this silver consisted of genuine English coins being brought back from overseas it seems strange that no parcels of foreign silver should be taxed. Surviving customs accounts of other ports during these years contain no evidence at all of the levy of duty upon imported silver and very little upon gold.

Study of the customs particulars indicates that while some alien merchants were both importers and exporters many engaged in only one branch of trade. The question inevitably arises as to how the importers managed to repatriate their profits. Some undoubtedly entered into various types of partnership with export merchants, both alien and denizen, while the remainder presumably made use of letters of exchange. Such arrangements minimised the need for physically moving silver either into or out of the country. On balance the amount of silver introduced into England by the alien community was very small, since a small export surplus on visible trade was further reduced by what may be termed invisible imports. The latter consisted of letters of exchange made available to individuals and institutions from outside the merchant community who wished to export money from England.

Table 2 gives an estimate of the values of various branches of alien trade between the introduction of the Carta Mercatoria and its abolition by the Ordainers in 1311.[8] The figures must be regarded as little more than orders of magnitude, since there can be no question of precision. The main difficulty lies in ascribing average values to wool, cloth, wax and wine, the commodities which were not valued by the customs officials, since they paid a specific rate of duty. Most critical of all is the value which should be given to wool, exports of which by aliens averaged about 17,000 sacks a year (1304-11); this has been tentatively valued at £8 per sack f.o.b. In addition aliens exported some 400 woollen cloths a year, most of them probably re-exports, and general merchandise, including worsteds, valued at £14,360 a year. To finance these

TABLE 2

Balance of Trade, 1303-11

ALIENS

	£		£
Exports			
Wool (1304-11) 16 832 sacks at ? £8 f.o.b.	134 656		
General Merchandise	14 362		
Woollen Cloth 394 pieces	1 200		
		c	150 000
Imports			
General Merchandise	52 260		
Woollen Cloth 11 977 pieces at ? £3	36 000		
Wax 1735 cwt at ? £2	3 500		
Wine ? 15 000 tuns at £2 10s	37 500		
			129 260 + profits
Invisible Imports			
Letters of Exchange		?	10 000
Export Surplus - silver imports		c	10 000

DENIZENS

Exports			
Wool (1304-11) 22 757 sacks at ? £8 f.o.b.	182 056 + profits		
General Merchandise	?		
			200 000 +
Imports and Overseas Spending			100 000 +
Nett Export Surplus - silver imports		c	97 000

exports, totalling some £150,000 a year, aliens imported firstly general merchandise to the value of £52,260.[9] Next they imported some 12,000 woollen cloths of assise, which have been assigned an average value of £3 each. This figure is near the bottom end of the price range of imported cloth, which covered a very wide spectrum. At the upper end the finest varieties sold for £12 and more, but such cloths, dyed in grain or part grain, made up less than 5% of total imports. Some indication of an average value is provided by the terms of a loan which the king proposed to exact from all merchants in 1317. In the event only wool was taxed, but a writ proves an intention to impose a levy on all trade at a rate of about 10%, general merchandise paying 2s in the £.[10] Scarlet cloths were intended to pay one mark, cloths de colore, worth £3 and more, were to pay half a mark, while cloths worth £2, apparently the minimum price, were to pay 4s. Wax imports by aliens averaged 1,735 cwt a year and have been valued at £2, although this is possibly a little low. At the end of Edward I's reign William Servat undertook to supply 300 cwt a year for 5 years to the royal wardrobe at 65s per cwt or a lesser sum should the London price fall.[11] However, the contract was made at a time of scarcity and Thorold Rogers' figures indicate a retail price of 6d to 8d per pound. Finally we have wine imports, for which there are no volume figures during this period. Dr. M. K. James, however, estimated that in a normal year imports exceeded 20,000 tuns, with aliens handling three quarters of the trade.[12] I have therefore credited them with an average of 15,000 tuns a year at a value of 50s, the latter figure being based on the proposed levy of 5s per tun in 1317. These figures suggest that overall alien merchants imported commodities with a wholesale value of around £129,000 a year, to which a certain amount of profit must be added. This means that they needed to find less than £20,000 to finance their export trade.

It has already been mentioned that part of the alien visible trade deficit was covered by selling letters of exchange to fellow aliens who wished to export silver from England. First and foremost among the ranks of the latter was the Roman pontiff who, despite opposition, managed to extract over £40,000 from the English church during the period under consideration.[13] A series of tenths levied on the whole of the Church netted £10,451 by 1312, annates collected from certain classes of clergy grossed £18,838, common services paid by bishops and abbots appointed or confirmed by the pope approached £10,000, while other papal revenues yielded an average which can be little short of £1,000 a year. Next we have other consequences of an international church. After the conclusion of peace with France French monasteries recovered possession of the extensive lands which they owned in England and these properties must be taken into consideration. While some monasteries maintained cells in England, which had first call upon revenues, considerable sums were available for delivery abroad. In the case of the abbey of Bec the bailiwick of Ogbourne, with a regular income of over £500 a year, was reserved to the mother house.[14] There were also windfalls, such as the timber sold for £450 about 1310 to assist in the rebuilding of the church at Bec. The total value of alien priories in the early fourteenth century has not yet been ascertained, but in 1343 the Exchequer received £5,304 from sequestrated estates.[15] Nor was this their total value, since allowances had to be made for the support of brethren in conventual establishments. One must, therefore, reckon with the possibility of exports of £2-3,000 or more from the lands of the alien priories. Finally alien nobility received revenues from estates in England and gifts from the crown which they sometimes wished to export. All such sums had to be transferred by means of letters of exchange, which was not without its own risk. In 1304 Amaneus de la Bret, Lord of Albret, paid £500 in London to the Florentine company of Mozzi for letters repayable abroad, but the firm became bankrupt and the letters were dishonoured. In 1316 another Florentine company, Cornekyns, dishonoured letters for 200 marks repayable to two Luchese spicers in Champagne.[16]

If the funds transferred by alien nobles and ecclesiastics approached an average figure of £10,000 a year, which seems by no means improbable, then the net contribution of all aliens to mint acquisition of silver is reduced to £10,000 or less out of an average of £107,000 a year in money of account. The balance was supplied by the English merchant community out of the proceeds of the wool trade. From 1304 to 1311 denizen exports of wool averaged 22,757 sacks a year, which at £8 f.o.b. amounts to £182,000. To this one must add profit from the sale of wool overseas and the value of any denizen exports other than wool. This must produce a figure in excess of £200,000 a year. Since the denizen contribution to mint silver has been calculated to be around £97,000, one is left with something over £100,000 to cover denizen imports, including wine, and exports of money by all denizens, including overseas expenditure by the crown. The last item was probably smaller at this time than at any other period in the fourteenth century. While denizen exports of wool were considerably larger than alien exports natives had probably not yet displaced aliens from their leading position in the import trade. This is quite understandable, for the domination of English overseas trade by Englishmen was only just beginning and it must have been achieved more easily with commodities which originated at home than with those which were obtained abroad. While alien domination of the import trade continued denizens had of necessity to bring their cash balances home with them, some in letters of exchange, but much in hard currency which had then to be taken to the mint. Had it been possible to increase the demand for imported goods the influx of silver might not have occurred, but this was probably ruled out by the unequal distribution of wealth and established patterns of consumption. Ironically the influx of silver resulted in price inflation which may have meant that even the wealthy were not permanently better off in real terms.

The above figures, crude though they may be, provide an essential foundation for attempting to understand changes in the pattern of overseas trade and alterations in the money supply in subsequent periods. Clearly the first task is to establish a link between overseas trade and the reduction in mint output to an average of £25,000 a year from 1311 to 1321. Unfortunately, between the abolition of the Carta Mercatoria in 1311 and its restoration in 1322 the only trade figures available are those for the combined denizen and alien exports of wool. Although one is immediately struck by the coincidence of a fall in wool exports and the fall in mint output in order to propose cause and effect it is necessary to vindicate the customs record against its detractors. R. L. Baker has claimed that the falling customs figures of the second and third decades of the fourteenth century portray not a real slump in trade but a breakdown in customs' administration and an increase in smuggling.[17] In

TABLE 3

Balance of Trade, 1322-36

ALIENS

	£	£
Exports		
Wool (1323-36) 8357 sacks at ? £7 f.o.b.	58 500	
General Merchandise	c 7 000	
		65 500
Imports		
General Merchandise	27 600	
Woollen Cloth 9800 pieces at ? £3	29 400	
Wax 875 cwt at ? £2	1 750	
Wine (1322-35) 5000 tuns at ? £2 10s	12 500	
		71 250
Invisible Imports		
Letters of Exchange		? 10 000
Import Surplus - Silver exports		c 15 750

DENIZENS

Exports		
Wool (1323-9) 14 914 sacks at ? £7	104 000	
Wool (1329-36) 22 998 sacks at ? £7	161 000	
General Merchandise	?	
		(1323-9) c 125 000
		(1329-36) c 190 000
Imports and Overseas Spending		? In excess of earnings
Import Surplus - silver exports		?

his analysis the improved figures of the 1330s reflect the reform of the customs in 1331. This view is not accepted by the present writer. The improvement in customs' receipts took place long before the ordinance of 1331 and the fluctuations in exports are explicable at first against the course of Anglo-Flemish relations and later against the internal politics of Flanders. In 1311-13 wool exports still averaged 37,754 sacks a year, but then came a complete break between the two countries and a state of war existed until the death of Count Robert III in September 1322. Although friendly relations were then reestablished Flanders was almost immediately caught up in a bitter civil war, which had serious consequences for the wool trade. Exports, which had averaged only 27,027 sacks from 1313 to 1323, slumped to an average of 23,749 between 1323 and 1329. After the ending of the civil war wool exports recovered to an average of 30,945 sacks between 1329 and 1336.[18]

The recovery of wool exports during the 1330s apparently failed to bring an extra pound of silver to the English mint, which remained virtually inoperative. Although exports were still below the boom years of the early fourteenth century they were above the level of the 1280s when a great deal of foreign silver had been brought to the mint. To explain this deficiency we must again address ourselves to the pattern of trade and also consider the possibility of a lack of confidence in English currency at this time. Table 3 presents a picture of alien trade between 1322 and 1336. Since, for the sake of clarity, an overall average has been given for each commodity a brief description of trends during the course of this period is necessary. The rate at which aliens were disengaging themselves from English trade was undoubtedly slower after 1322 than between 1311 and 1322 but some disinvestment did continue. Alien wool exports averaged 8,835 sacks from 1323 to 1329 but 7,947 sacks from 1329 to 1336. General imports and exports averaged £36,311 from 1322-7, £33,951 from 1327-33 and £31,811 from 1333-6. Wax averages in the same periods were 1,437 cwt, 668 cwt, and 352 cwt, while cloth averages were 10,000, 10,621 and 7,806. Alien wine imports were adversely affected by warfare in the mid 1320s but then recovered until the 1330s, when there may have been a continuation of the decline.

In Table 3 the value of wool has been reduced to a figure of £7 per sack f.o.b. in order to take account of lower prices paid to producers, and alien investment in the average of 8,357 sacks amounts to £58,500. To this must be added an estimate of £7,000 for general exports. During this period some ports tend not to distinguish between import and export revenue, but there is sufficient evidence to establish that the actual division was much as before. To finance exports aliens imported merchandise, cloth, wax and wine to a total value of about £71,250. This means that aliens had an import surplus of about £5,750, which had to be repatriated.

As far as alien ecclesiastics and nobles are concerned there is no evidence that the earlier estimate of money exports of anything up to £10,000 a year should be revised downwards. The flow to Rome certainly continued unabated. From 1311 to 1322 about £14,000 was paid in annates and £13,400 in common services, while Edward II gave coronation gifts to Pope John XXII reputedly worth 30,000 florins or about £5,000. The king also paid 4,000 marks of the annual tribute, which had been in arrears since 1289. In addition the pope received some hundreds of pounds each year from more regular revenues, while procurations collected on behalf of papal envoys increased, the largest amount being some £5,000 levied for the nuncios who were sent to negotiate peace between England and Scotland in 1317. From 1322 to 1336 common services totalled at least £14,700 and possibly more, while the pope received anything between £28,000 and £36,000 as his share of a series of tenths levied on the church in the early 1330s. He also received 1,500 marks from the annual tribute and several substantial gifts from individual bishops.

Grouping alien merchants, ecclesiastics and nobles together we are faced with exports of money averaging £15,750 a year. Some of this was undoubtedly taken in English coin, for, despite repeated proclamations against the export of sterlings, the ban was less rigidly enforced than before, while an edict of 1324 actually authorised the export of reasonable expenses.[19] Between August 1322 and May 1323 nine alien merchants and skippers legally exported a total of £146 sterling from Lynn, while 82 pounds of silver were taken from Chichester in 1326, all paying duty of 3d in the pound.[20] In 1331 the government revived the provision of the Statute of Stepney (1299), which established exchange tables at Dover and other ports. This was probably intended to discourage the illegal export of sterlings, these being exchanged for foreign coins which could now be legally exported in certain circumstances.

Turning to denizen trade we find that an average of 19,267 sacks of wool were exported each year between 1323 and 1336, which at £7 f.o.b. gives a figure of £134,868. The addition of profits from sales, together with any other denizen exports, suggests that over £150,000 was available for repatriation or expenditure abroad. This overall average disguises the marked disparity between the 1320s and the 1330s and it is advisable, therefore, to consider separately the periods 1323-29, with its average of 14,914 sacks worth some £104,000, and 1329-36, with 22,998 sacks worth around £161,000. In the earlier period it is possible that total overseas earnings were around £125,000 a year compared with £190,000 in the later years. Were it not for the lower valuation which has been given to wool denizen earnings in 1329-36 would actually exceed those of the period 1303-11.

In considering what happened to denizen earnings the first charge must be the satisfaction of alien money exports of £15,750 a year overall. This reduces earnings in the years 1323-9 to around £110,000, which may be compared with the earlier estimate of £97,000 supplied to the mint and over £100,000 going to provide denizen imports and to satisfy other overseas expenditure, including crown spending. Even allowing for the fact that virtually nothing now came to the mint it is abundantly clear that denizen earnings were totally insufficient to finance imports necessary to compensate for the decline in alien imports, which on the basis of figures already given amounted to about £58,000 a year. The certainty of increased overseas crown expenditure compared with the base period must also be taken into consideration, since this reduces the sum available for the purchase of imports.

While there can be little or no doubt that combined denizen and alien imports in the 1320s were less than those of the first decade of the century it is an open question whether they fell sufficiently to be paid for out of current denizen earnings. It is quite possible that imports did not fall by the necessary degree and that some of the large silver balances accumulated in earlier years were now exported to cover a trade gap. It is, in any case, improbable that any fall in imports was proportionate across the whole range of desirable commodities. In the case of wine, for which there was no home-produced substitute, it is likely that except, for the war years, denizen imports increased to cover most of the reduction in alien trade. Some historians will undoubtedly speculate that savings may have been made on imported cloth and that this provided the first stimulus in the revival of the native cloth industry. It is useful to repeat that a significant fall in alien cloth imports came only after 1333 and it is an intriguing question as to whether this was due to the first success of home industry or merely to an increase in denizen imports.

The growth of denizen wool exports at the end of the 1320s increased national earnings by something like £65,000 a year, and the question arises as to what use this money was put. The most likely answer is that it led to a reduction in an outward flow of silver or an increase in imports, or a combination of both. However, a third possibility cannot entirely be ignored, which is that there was actually some inward flow of silver or gold, or both. Under certain circumstances one might logically expect to find such a flow. If, for instance, the authorities had been reasonably successful in preventing the export of silver and if home industry and consumer demand had adapted to a lower level and a new pattern of imports then scope for the re-expansion of imports might be somewhat limited. Given the slow pace of medieval economic and social change, one clearly must not press this case too hard, but the possibility remains that the demand for imported goods may not have revived as quickly as the increase in total overseas earnings. In this event merchants would once more have been obliged to bring their balances home in hard cash. But if they did, what happened to it, since it did not arrive at the mint?

This question obliges us to consider the import and circulation of counterfeit sterlings in the later years of Edward II and the early years of Edward III. The first proclamation against the use of foreign money was made in 1310, but from 1315 proclamations were made more frequently and their tone becomes more urgent. If we accept for the moment that the threat of counterfeit coins was a real one, what was the cause of it? Did it result from the latent dishonesty of merchants, or was it based on a genuine economic difficulty? The English mint, on the basis of fineness declared in the particular accounts, seems to have been reluctant to buy silver of less than sterling fineness, the reason probably being the danger of loss to the master, along the lines described in the tractatus nove monete of 1280.[21] While this prejudice could be sustained when strong silver was plentiful one might expect it to be abandoned if the only alternative to accepting weak silver was the run down of the mint. However, the acceptance of weak silver posed its own problems. In the absence of strong silver with which to mingle it weak bullion could be brought up to sterling standard only by removing some of the alloy. This was undoubtedly more troublesome and more costly than reducing strong silver by the addition of weak silver or a base metal. The mint would be obliged to pass on the extra cost to the supplier and the offering price might fall below a level acceptable to the latter. In this event merchants importing silver would dispose of it for a use other than money or, if it consisted of coins resembling official issues, might be tempted to pass it into general circulation. It is possible, therefore, that while the difficulties which overtook the wool trade were primarily responsible for the reduction in English mint activity the situation was exacerbated by a decline in the standard of such silver as was still available for import.

Dr. Mate's investigation of the accounts of the official searchers, and other evidence, has led her to conclude that during the last 10 years of Edward II's reign counterfeit sterlings made up an insignificant part of the total English money supply and this impression is confirmed by the hoards of the period.[22] It is clear that given an adverse trade balance there could be little importation of any sort of silver, unless one invokes Gresham's Law and makes good sterling and gold illegally exported commodities. The revival of the wool trade at the end of the 1320s may have provided the means for accelerating the inflow of counterfeit sterlings, although it did not in itself ensure that this would happen. There might just as easily have been a greater import of foreign gold coins.

In May 1335 parliament, after condemning the import of counterfeit money, agreed that the mint should abandon the sterling standard in favour of an alloy 10 ounces fine, although only halfpence and farthings were to be made from this metal. The latter precaution was presumably intended to protect the old penny coinage. It may seem as if this ordinance should have encouraged the mint to buy silver of less than sterling standard, even if it was not actually designed to that end. However, while it did initially stimulate the flow of foreign silver all the acquisitions were of sterling standard or finer, suggesting that a prejudice against weaker bullion was not given up. Unfortunately, the outbreak of the Hundred Years War and the complete dislocation of overseas trade soon reduced the flow of foreign silver to its former trickle. While the mint bought 1223 pounds from August 1335 to Michaelmas 1336, total acquisitions during the next 5 years were only 465 pounds. English silver, on the other hand, totalled 1986 pounds and 6600 pounds in those two periods. Some of this was newly-mined metal, but the greater part consisted of old sterlings brought for recoinage. The operation left the supplier with a profit of 10d on every pound of full weight pennies provided. What actually happened was that he brought sterlings and received back precisely the same weight in debased halfpence and farthings, with no deductions for mintage and seignorage. This can be demonstrated with the example of the vicar of St. Laurence, who on 10 August 1335 supplied the first parcel of silver for the new coinage.[23] If the £5 6s 2d which he provided consisted of full weight pennies their face value would be £5 7s 5d, while the £5 6s 2d which he received in return, if half in halfpence and half in farthings, would have a face value of £5 11s 11d, giving him a profit of 4s 6d. Rectors and vicars figure prominently among those who supplied silver to the London mint during the next few years, suggesting that they were a class of men who had the time and opportunity to cull the heavy coins which alone could provide any profit. It is currently reckoned that pennies subject to normal wear lost 2-2.75% of their weight each decade, or some 6d in the £ by value, and very few pennies were less than ten years old in 1335. A larger number of farthings had been produced since 1324, but such coins were probably subject to greater wear.

Coming to the opening stages of the Hundred Years War we find that while some money was sent out of England to support the king's military adventures the amount pales into insignificance in comparison with the diversion of the earnings of the wool trade. The greater part of all wool leaving England between August 1336 and the summer of 1343 was dispatched in the name of the king and most of the income from its sale was expended abroad unproductively. Furthermore much of the wool exported privately by alien and denizen merchants was bought with taxes assigned to them in settlement of loans made abroad to the crown and this also counts as an unproductive export. This means that throughout these years the wool trade made a very limited contribution to settling the nation's import bill. Inevitably imports declined. Between 1336 and 1343 alien trade averaged between two thirds and a half of the level of the previous period and it is conceivable that denizen imports suffered proportionately. Yet it is unlikely that imports were allowed to fall to the level where they could be paid for out of the overseas earnings which were left in the hands of the merchants. It seems far more likely that in order to sustain imports specie was exported in greater amounts than ever before. This might be reserves of foreign gold coin, or, when these were exhausted, silver. Although the situation eased after 1343 it is highly improbable that the outflow of silver was completely stopped. The Calais campaign, for instance, gave rise to a considerable loss, including a renewal of unproductive wool exports.

By 1339 parliament was fearful that a shortage of silver money might bring internal trade to a halt and requested legislation that all who exported wool be required to import silver to the value of at least 40s per sack. In 1340 it was enacted that within three months of export all Englishmen and 'other residents' should deliver to the exchanges plate to the value of two marks per sack. It is not clear what significance, if any, should be attached to the fact that plate, rather than any other form of bullion, was stipulated. To ensure compliance with the regulation merchants were required to deposit plate of equal value with the customs collectors prior to export, which would be restored to them on production of a certificate that silver had been taken to the exchanges. Initially the bullion law could not be very effective, since the wool trade remained in the grip of a crown semi-monopoly and the king was more concerned with obtaining money overseas than with ensuring the import of silver. The government certainly instructed the customs officials to collect the deposit of plate, but it seems to have valued this more as security that all exporters, including its own agents, would take their wool to the compulsory staple at Bruges than for its true purpose. Only from the autumn of 1341 when the ban on the private export of wool was periodically lifted was there a real prospect of an inflow of silver. Even now, however, there remained a serious problem, since many merchants did not enjoy sufficient liquidity to engage in trade. The obligation to pay 46s 8d for custom and subsidy and a further 26s 8d as deposit, in advance of export was a formidable obstacle. Private export was only possible at such times as the government removed this obstacle, not, however, by relaxing the deposit requirements, but by deferring payment of the subsidy of 40s until the merchants had sold their wool overseas and brought the money home.[24] Given this the new regulation apparently began to have its desired effect, for between Michaelmas 1341 and December 1343 the mint acquired 18,842 pounds of foreign silver.

The increase in mint activity provided scant relief for the country's internal economy, for in the winter of 1342-3 coin was desperately short and it was alleged that counterfeit sterlings were being imported. It was because of this that the parliament of 1343 renewed the bullion law enacted three years previously. The renewal threatened to perpetuate the difficulties experienced by wool merchants, for if the king continued to exact his subsidy in advance of export trade would remain beyond the means of most of them. It is suggested that this is the real reason why the community of English merchants now took the administration of the customs entirely into its own hands. Although they were required to pay 10,000 marks a year above the receipts for this privilege they stood to gain two very substantial advantages. Between themselves the merchants might not only devise a form of bullion security which was less onerous than hard cash or plate but they might also be able to defer payment of the customs duties. They were required to pay the king 1,000 marks a month, the balance being accounted for every quarter. This would allow individuals ample time to export wool and to repatriate the proceeds. Some time after the merchants took the customs into their own hands the bullion law seems to have fallen into abeyance, for it was reintroduced in the parliament of January, 1348, at the instigation of the king's council. A few weeks later, in the Lent parliament, the commons requested its repeal on the grounds that the Flemings would not allow bullion to be exported and that the regulation was adversely affecting the price of wool.[25]

During the middle and late 1340s the English currency was in a state of flux and in dealing with this period the historian is confronted by a number of awkward questions. In 1343 a general debasement seems to have been considered, but this was opposed by parliament on the basis of recent experience, the commons complaining that the king's ministers had refused to receive taxes proffered in the debased halfpence and farthings made since 1335. Given this opposition the only way in which the production of pennies could be resumed was by lowering the official weight. Early in 1344, therefore, orders were given for the coining of pennies of sterling fineness, but of the weight of those in general circulation. This was at first reckoned to be 270 pence to the pound weight, but subsequent indentures called for 266 and 268 before stabilising at 270 in 1346. During this period full weight old sterlings could have been recoined with a profit to the supplier of 9d to 11d in the pound. However the greater part of the existing currency was at least 20 years old and, suffering a loss through wear of some 5%, could not have been recoined. This leads one to conclude that despite the apparent relaxing of the bullion law most of the silver which came to the mint between 1344 and 1351 was newly imported. The only alternative seems to be a major dishoarding of plate or little-used sterlings. Mint acquisitions of imported silver must somehow be reconciled with repeated allegations about the illegal import and circulation of Lushebournes, a counterfeit of sterling coming from continental mints. A Hanseatic merchant was charged with importing £200, £20 and £20 on three separate occasions and it may be significant that a search order of November 1345 enjoins the arrest only of those importing more than £5 of false money.

In 1351 the weight of new sterling coins was lowered to 300 pence to the pound. This meant that virtually all the money made since the last general recoinage of Edward I could profitably be sold to the mint. Coins which had been in circulation for fifty years would have lost, on average about 13% of their original weight, while all profit did not disappear until a coin had lost 18% of its weight. Pennies made since 1344 gave a very good profit, but the debased halfpence and farthings afforded little or no margin, since average wear must have eliminated the profit of 6d in the pound which might have been obtained from full weight coins. The motivation of the 1351 currency change must remain a matter of speculation. It is not impossible that this was one of the rare occasions on which an English king manipulated the coinage for fiscal reasons. On the other hand it is possible that the government was sincere in its claim that the reduction in weight was intended to prevent a wholesale illegal export of sterlings. The Black Death, by reducing the population, had eased the pressure on the money supply and concentrated existing stocks in fewer hands. This may have made it easier for merchants to accumulate hoards, which may then have been smuggled to continental mints which were continually debasing their currency during this period.

Although earlier issues were not demonetised in 1351 the fact that almost all existing money could be recoined at a profit means that most of the currency should have passed through a mint within a comparatively short period of the weight reduction. Nevertheless, the total output of recorded mints during the six years which followed was a mere 300,000 pounds, about £375,000 in money of account. This figure, which may include dishoarded plate and some newly imported silver, must be about the upper limit of the total silver currency in 1351 and succeeding years. In relation to population the silver coinage may now have been considerably smaller than that of the early years of the fourteenth century despite the effects of the Black Death. Far from being alarmed at this fact Edward III proceeded to allow the completely free export of his new coins, although the ban on the export of old sterlings was maintained so that the king should not be deprived of his seignorage. It is quite clear that there was no shortage of money in the 1350s and it is likely that the price rises of this decade were due in some measure to monetary factors. The key to the situation lies in the recently introduced gold coinage of Edward III. Historians have tended to regard medieval gold currency as being primarily of importance in the settlement of international trade balances and have minimised its role in a country's internal economy. English experience in the second half of the fourteenth century suggests that this view is erroneous. Before 1344 England did not have its own gold currency, although the crown, the nobility and the mercantile class made use of Italian and French gold coins. In 1311 Edward II attempted unsuccessfully to ban the circulation of foreign gold, while a similar prohibition in 1331 probably had no more effect. Although this foreign gold must be regarded as part of the money supply there is unfortunately no means of estimating even its approximate amount. The immediate spur for the coining of gold in England in 1344 was a complaint by the merchants that they were compelled to sell wool in the Low Countries for florins, which were valued at a rate which caused them to lose one third of their profit. Edward III, who had been recognised by the Flemings as King of France, proposed to make a gold coin which should have common currency in England and Flanders and which, hopefully, would displace Italian and French florins. A longer term, but more important, reason for the introduction of the gold currency was the cheapening of this metal in terms of silver.[26] Prior to 1344 changes in the sterling value of gold can be demonstrated only by means of the exchange rates given to foreign coins, of which the most stable was the little florin of Florence, weighing 54 grains of nominally pure gold. The most authoritative statement of the market value of this florin in England in the early fourteenth century is found in the arbitration of a dispute between the Exchequer and the Genoese banker, Anthony Pessaigne, in December 1314. A jury of English and alien merchants found that since the previous Easter the value of the florin in London had not fallen below 3s 1d. This gives a weight ratio of 15.25:1 or, allowing for a gold purity of 191/192, a ratio of 14.18:1 for pure gold to pure silver. In the opening stages of the Hundred Years War the official rate of the florin in dealings between Edward III and his Italian bankers was 3s. Although at least one transaction appears to indicate that this was in line with the current market rate of the coin in the Low Countries contemporary sterling exchange rates of French gold coins cast some doubt on whether this was really the case. The French royal, although only very slightly heavier than the Florentine florin, was valued at more than 3s in English accounts and in May 1336 Paul de Monte Florum was allowed 3s 9d for it at the English Exchequer.[28] The ecu, or florin with the shield, weighing 70 grains of nominally pure gold, was usually valued at 4s 6d sterling in the late 1330s, although exchanges at rates up to 5s are known.[29] These official valuations of French gold at higher rates than the Florentine florin are difficult to explain and the mystery is increased by an account which shows that in 1338 Northwell, keeper of the king's wardrobe, bought ecus on the Continent for 4s sterling and passed them to his creditors at 4s 6d. The first price has the greater claim to be regarded as a genuine market rate and in fact values the ecu at about the same rate as a 3s florin. After 1340 the usual exchange rate of the ecu in royal accounts was 3s 4d-3s 5d, and the latter figure was said to be the current value in London in November 1341. At this price level we are probably dealing with the later, debased ecus of Philip VI, which were only 20 carats $2\frac{1}{2}$ grains fine, and the valuation corresponds to a 3s Florentine florin of pure gold.

When Edward III began to mint gold in 1344 he based his coins on the Florentine florin, his leopard weighing 54 grains of nominally pure gold and officially declared to be worth 3s sterling. At 266 pennies to the pound this gives a weight ratio of 13.53:1 or 12.58:1 in terms of pure metal.[30] However the official valuation of the new coins was too high, vendors refused to accept them at this rate and they were quickly withdrawn from circulation. This overvaluation of gold, a gamble which failed, had been designed to allow the king to take a large profit at the mint. With the next gold issue the rate of seignorage was slashed from 20s to 5s in the pound. The new coin, the noble, weighed 136.7 grains and was officially valued at 6s 8d, which gave gold and silver coins ratios of 11.88:1 and 11.04:1. In 1346 the weight of the noble was reduced to 128.6 grains and the ratios became 12.44:1 and 11.57:1. From the recoinage of 1351 the weight of the noble was 120 grains and the ratios with the new silver currency became 12:1 and 11.16:1.

The introduction of a gold currency kept the London mint busy throughout the 1350s and early 1360s. At times the gold issues actually exceeded the silver in weight of metal worked as well as being many times more valuable. It is unlikely that all the new coins remained in England, since both silver and gold could now be exported without even the formality of a licence. The king himself sent gold to Gascony in 1357 and no doubt money was exported to finance other expeditions in this period.[31] However, a favourable balance of trade meant that there was no net export of bullion to pay for imported commodities. Furthermore, the seizure of the lands of alien priories and hostility to the papacy meant that there was little loss through these channels. Only in 1361 did the Pope obtain a grant of nearly £17,000 and most of this was actually paid to him in French gold, which formed part of the ransom of King John.

By the 1360s gold must have been abundant in England and the nation must have become familiar with its use in the coinage. Why else should the parliament of 1362 have petitioned for the introduction of a gold coin of as small a denomination of ten pence sterling? These facts demand a reconsideration of the role of gold in the country's internal economy. Since a tenpenny gold coin would have been about double the daily earnings of a craftsman clearly it could have played no part in petty trade. Yet gold did not need to enter directly into petty trade for it to have a revolutionary effect on the money supply. It would have been sufficient that it released silver for use at this lower level, and it is very likely that this did happen. In the early fourteenth century with only a silver coinage supplemented by foreign gold of uncertain value a considerable part of the silver money, particularly of official issues, must have been permanently out of circulation, either as savings or while being accumulated to make large payments. The nobles of the 1350s provided a stable currency with an official value which was known to everybody; they could readily be exchanged for silver at a small discount at official exchanges. This meant that the noble was superior to silver as a store of value and for making large payments. If the noble did indeed release silver for other uses then the increase in the velocity of circulation may well have increased the effective silver money supply even if the actual amount of silver per head of population was smaller than in some previous periods. If, in addition, confidence in gold allowed it to circulate at the middle levels of internal trade then an abundant money supply must clearly be regarded as one of the major causes of the inflation of the 1350s.

Although some of the gold which poured into England was spoil of war the fruits of victory were not gathered until fairly late in the period now under consideration. The first instalments of the really important ransoms, those for the neutrality of Burgundy and the release of King John, were paid only in 1360. Furthermore, by no means all of the spoils passed through the English mint. Some of John's ransom went to the Pope, some was expended overseas and some the king hoarded in his chamber for a number of years.[32] Close roll recognisances of the 1360s indicate that private citizens also held large amounts of French gold which had not been reminted. It is suggested, therefore, that a large part, probably the greater part, of the newly minted gold represented a favourable balance of trade, which was established in the first half of the 1350s.

The foundation of England's prosperity remained the wool trade, which embarked on a remarkably buoyant phase during the 1353 season after several years of disrupted trade. From that summer to Michaelmas 1362 exports totalled 327,000 sacks, an average of well over 33,000 sacks per season.

Although prices paid to the growers were low all exports bore a duty of 50s so that the value f.o.b. can hardly have been less than £8 per sack. This produced overseas earnings of about £264,000 a year plus profits, say £300,000 in round figures. It is impossible in this period to make separate calculations for denizen and alien trade. Some two or three years after the boom in the wool trade there was an upsurge in the export of English-made cloth. Exports of woollen cloth averaged 2221 pieces a year in 1351-5 but 8702 pieces in 1355-62. These figures do not include worsted cloth exports which reached an average of 22,969 pieces a year in 1357-60. Thereafter worsted exports declined, but exact figures are not available since Hanseatic exports were no longer recorded. The editors of England's Export Trade chose not to print details of worsted exports, on the grounds that their value was insignificant compared with that of woollens.[33] This reasoning is based on the fact that a piece of worsted paid only one fourteenth of the duty of a piece of woollen cloth. However, negotiations between the English crown and the German Hanse in the late 1350s suggests that worsted was worth at least 10s a piece, while the average value of woollens cannot have been much greater than £2 per piece. As exports of English cloth increased so alien imports of cloth declined, the averages being 4108 pieces in 1351-5 and 3705 in 1355-62, with an acceleration in the rate of decline thereafter. Whether there was any denizen import in this period cannot be determined. It is likely that as the import trade contracted it concentrated more and more on luxury fabrics so that the average value per piece would have risen. Nevertheless it is clear that before 1360 the total value of woollen and worsted exports exceeded that of foreign cloth imported so that England became a net exporter of cloth, although the earnings were small in comparison with those of the wool trade. Exports of commodities other than wool and cloth cannot be quantified but it must be assumed that tin, lead, grain, fish and possibly other items made some contribution to overseas earnings and helped to swell these to a figure in excess of £300,000 a year.

Although imports increased during the 1350s their value cannot have approached the figure which has been set on English overseas earnings. As in previous periods only alien imports are measureable and these must be used as a basis for assumptions about denizen trade. Alien merchandise paying 3d in the pound, consisting largely of imports, increased from an average of £29,099 a year in 1351-4 to £36,643 in 1354-7, £48,362 in 1357-60 and £43,656 in 1360-2. Denizen imports of similar commodities may have equalled, or even exceeded, this level, but they are unlikely to have amounted to anything like double the value of alien imports. This crude upper limit is suggested by comparing alien petty custom revenue with the proceeds of a subsidy of poundage levied on all trade other than wool and wine. In 1371-2 the total value of goods paying poundage was £217,726. From this must be deducted at least £35,000 for denizen and alien imports and exports of cloth, a figure in excess of £87,630 for alien merchandise paying 3d in the pound and some £6,000 for alien wax imports.[34] This leaves about £89,000 for all denizen imports and exports other than wool, wine and cloth. For the sake of argument, therefore, denizens may be assumed to have had an import trade not very dissimilar from that of aliens and for the period now under consideration they may be assigned a value of £43,000, which is the alien average of exports and imports for 1354-62. Additionally aliens must be assigned £3,000 for wax imports. The last commodity which needs to be considered is wine, which was both scarce and dear in England in the 1350s. In 1350-1 total imports amounted to 8730 tuns, of which aliens handled 2169 tuns; the alien average for 1350-62 was 1806 tuns.[35] It will be assumed that wine imports averaged 10,000 tuns a year, with a value of £5 per tun; possibly the amount errs on the low side. In conclusion, therefore, it is suggested that during much of the 1350s and early 1360s English exports were earning more than £300,000 a year overseas and that no more than half of this, possibly less than half, was required to pay for import of commodities. The balance was available for overseas expenditure by the crown or by private persons or for repatriation in the form of specie.

Notwithstanding an abundance of money, in the spring of 1364 the government decreed that henceforth silver and gold might be exported only under licence. In the absence of an official explanation of this action one can only hazard a guess at the reasons which lay behind it. Towards the end of 1362 a ban had been imposed on the export of herrings, cloth and various other items in an attempt to hold down prices in England. Although licences soon began to be issued to enable individuals to evade the ban it is likely that some importers found it more convenient to export money in lieu of goods which were now forbidden to them. The restriction of the export of silver and gold possibly was intended to counter an increase in this traffic, although no attempt was made to stop the outward flow of money entirely. Between May and October 1364 licences were enrolled on the patent roll for the export of sums totalling more than £7649.[36] Most of this money was taken to Poitou and Gascony to finance purchases of wine and salt and it seems likely that the recent trade restrictions had created, or worsened, an adverse balance of trade with these regions. In contrast, although licences were granted for the export of grain, ale, dairy produce and other goods to Flanders there was no need to send money there since the earnings of the wool trade still provided a favourable balance with that country. After October 1364 the general enrolment of licences to export money for trade purposes came to an end, although the implication of this is not obvious. Similarly, one may only record without comment the chronology of enrolments of licences for the export of money for purposes other than trade. Between October 1367 and May 1368 special membranes on the patent roll were reserved for enrolments,[37] but before and after those dates there is apparently no record of this business, at least not in such a readily accessible place. In the period in question lay persons were issued with licences for the export of over £4,700 in cash and over £2,300 in the form of letters of exchange, while monks and clerics exported £350 and over £2,223 in the respective forms. Some very large amounts were exported by nobles and knights going to Prussia, presumably on crusade, while among ecclesiastics the most notable item was a letter for £1,600 carried by a papal nuncio. The inadequacy of the records makes it difficult to speculate about the amounts of money which were legally or illegally exported in the later years of Edward III and the difficulty is compounded by the opening of a mint at Calais in 1363. It is not clear whether coins made at Calais were officially subject to the same restrictions as those made in England. In any event it must have been easier to breach the regulations at Calais, since merchants could pretend that coin taken away from the town was going to England.

Whatever the effect which the restriction of the export of specie may or may not have had upon the total móney supply there can be little doubt that the rate of flow of new gold into England diminished about this time. This is not merely reflected in the combined output of the London and Calais mints but it is also suggested by a consideration of overseas trade. The 1360s saw the beginning of a secular decline in wool exports which continued for the remainder of the fourteenth century. The institution of a wool staple at Calais, which acted as a disincentive to alien exporters, was undoubtedly responsible for some of the loss of trade, although it was by no means the only factor working in this direction. During the life-time of the first staple at Calais, 1363-8, the average export was only about 28,000 sacks a year. It is possible that in the late 1360s and early 1370s some of the reduction in the volume of trade was compensated for by a rise in the value of wool, but prices paid to the growers suggest that any such increment disappeared long before 1380.[38] By 1376-80 exports averaged little more than 20,000 sacks a year and total overseas earnings must have been considerably less than two thirds of the level prevailing twenty years before. The continued growth of exports of English cloth and the virtual ending of imports provided some compensation for the loss of wool revenue, but cannot have made up all the deficit. In 1368-72 woollen cloth exports averaged 13,721 pieces, while alien imports were only 940 pieces a year. For much of the 1370s cloth exports were depressed, although precise figures are not obtainable because of the practice of customs farming. In the early 1380s, however, the upward trend resumed at a remarkable rate, while imports averaged a mere 286 pieces in the years 1377-83.

While export earnings declined it is possible that the value of miscellaneous imports increased, although evidence exists only for the alien share of the trade. The value of alien merchandise paying 3d in the pound, excluding trade at Yarmouth and Ipswich, averaged £55,443 a year in 1363-6, £58,872 in 1366-9 and £69,691 in 1369-72. After the period of customs farming the average value in 1378-81 was £65,676, excluding Yarmouth, Lynn and Exeter, while an almost identical average is obtained by processing all the figures which are available for the period 1376-87. Such little evidence as is available about the state of the wine trade suggests that imports were low throughout the 1370s, although high prices and increased costs ensured that any decrease in the total import bill was by no means commensurate with the decline in the volume of traffic. Taking an overall view of trade there can be little doubt that after 1363 the favourable balance which had been established during the 1350s was steadily eroded, although there seems no reason to suppose that trade came into deficit.

Although merchants probably continued to make a positive contribution to the country's money supply there can be no guarantee that the gain was not entirely frittered away by other sectors of the community. With the renewal of the war in 1368 exports of money by crusading nobles were replaced by potentially more damaging overseas expenditure by the crown. Apart from military expeditions the fortress policy which was adopted in an effort to maintain the English hold on France was very expensive and it is unlikely that the whole cost was recouped from the local populations. The unsuccessful prosecution of this phase of the war meant that there was little booty or ransoms to make good the loss of bullion resulting directly from that war. In 1372 the Pope demanded a subsidy of a tenth from the English church and by 1378 he had managed to collect about £8,000, but anti-papalism in England ensured that losses of revenue in this direction were small in comparison with those of the early fourteenth century.

Any reduction in total money supply during the 1360s and 1370s was counterbalanced to some extent by a decline in population, caused by recurring outbreaks of bubonic plague. It is difficult to believe that there was a shortage of money and the revival of parliamentary interest in the bullion question in 1379 may have been occasioned less by awareness of a real shortage than by information about the drastic reduction in mint activity in recent years. The commons complained that no gold or silver was being brought into the country, while both metals were exported. However, the legislation which was enacted in an effort to reverse this trend was limited to the period which should elapse until the meeting of the next parliament. It was ruled that merchants importing certain luxury commodities must, within six months, bring to the mint one shilling's worth of gold for every pound of their value. Similarly wool merchants were required to render 1s. in the pound within twelve months of export. There is no evidence that the new regulation was enforced against importers but surviving mint receipts indicate that at least £2,515 worth of gold was obtained from wool merchants, from whom the customs officials of London and Boston had taken security at the time of export.[39]

In the parliament which sat from November 1381 to February 1382 there were renewed complaints about the export of specie and a commission of mint officials and goldsmiths was summoned to advise on this and allied monetary matters. The experts were agreed that in order to preserve the nation's stock of precious metals the value of imports must not exceed that of exports, in other words trade must be in balance. They also recommended that controls against the export of money should be tightened, including in their definition of money not merely coin but letters of exchange. The latter advice was accepted and incorporated in a permanent statute. However in their pursuit of the letter of exchange the legislators had been led astray by their detestation of the use made of it to transfer money to Rome. The law proved to be too severe in its application and in the next parliament, October 1382, it was amended to allow the use of the letter of exchange in commercial transactions. A joint petition from the commons and Italian bankers claimed that the letter of exchange was essential to the conduct of the wool trade.

There was no further legislation on monetary policy until the parliament of 1390 which also secured the return of the staple from Calais to England. Then it was enacted that all alien merchants must buy English goods to at least half the value of any merchandise imported. Further, whenever letters of exchange were sent abroad English goods must be bought to their full value. It is suggested that these measures provide a clue to the thinking which resulted in aliens being vested with a monopoly of the export of wool. With the establishment of a compulsory staple at Calais the alien share of the wool trade had declined even more than the overall fall in exports. Although there was no legal impediment to their trading at Calais they could not compete in this market with Englishmen since they were burdened with a higher rate of export duty. Aliens continued, however, to handle a large part of the import trade. They were embarrassed by the lack of a suitable investment for the proceeds resulting from the sale of their goods, since the overseas market for English cloth was not yet sufficient to employ much of their capital. Legally prohibited from exporting bullion aliens could only repatriate their money by means of the letter of exchange about which parliament was still uneasy. The new regulations were a compromise, which allowed aliens to transmit half of the proceeds of the sale of imports as a letter of exchange and half in the form of English products. In order to provide aliens with a suitable export commodity parliament was willing to vest them with a monopoly of wool exports. It is quite certain that parliament expected Englishmen to evade the ban, but it presumably believed that the legal monopoly would enable aliens to increase their share of the trade sufficiently to engage much of the capital generated by the sale of imports.

For English merchants the cure proposed for the country's monetary problem was worse than the disease and the alien monopoly of wool export was swiftly rescinded. The restoration of the denizen trade was accompanied, however, by a new bullion regulation. In December 1391 it was ruled that all merchants, denizen as well as alien, must import one ounce of gold in foreign coin for every sack of wool or 240 fells exported. After Midsummer 1392 the gold was to be taken to the mint at Calais. After parliament dispersed the council, apparently on its own authority, decided that merchants might pay an additional duty in lieu of importing gold, the rate being 13s 4d per sarpler or 480 fells. In fact this sum had to be paid to the customs officials by all exporters as security for importing gold. If, within six months, they produced receipts for gold delivered to the mint the money would be refunded, otherwise it was forfeit. In March 1392 the penalty was reduced to 6s 8d per sarpler and when the Calais mint became the delivery point it was probably abandoned altogether.[40]

By the end of the fourteenth century credit played an important part in the relationship between the wool staplers and their overseas customers. Buyers coming to Calais put down only a proportion of the total price and the balance was paid at a later date in the Low Countries. With the local currency the staplers bought letters of exchange, by means of which they transmitted their earnings to England. Furthermore, some of the money handed over at Calais probably consisted of Flemish imitations of the English noble, which were then introduced into England. It was probably dislike of the provision of credit and fear of the spurious nobles which provoked the parliamentary ordinance of January 1397 that henceforth all merchants must bring to the London mint one ounce of gold in foreign coin for every sack exported. Security was to be given at the customs at the rate of 13s 4d per sarpler. Twelve months later in the Shrewsbury parliament there was a joint petition from native and alien merchants protesting at being made to bring gold to London when there was a mint at Calais. Much was made of the inconvenience caused to provincial merchants, who exported only 10-20 sacks of wool, by having to make an unnecessary journey to London. It was also pointed out that the Duke of Burgundy had banned the exports of bullion from his dominions. The only answer afforded to the protest was that the king would raise the matter with the duke. No remedy was provided until the first parliament of Henry IV when it was ruled that henceforth merchants might take the bullion to the Calais mint. The king also pardoned the merchants for past offences against the bullion regulations and ordered that all outstanding securities be cancelled.

The period 1384 to 1402 has been portrayed by J. H. A. Munro as one in which there was conscious and intense mint competition between England and Burgundy.[41] This he describes as the 'war of the gold nobles'. Whether or not he is correct in his general analysis Munro is mistaken in his conclusion that England lost this war. On the figures which he presents the London mint coined 21,098 marcs de Troyes of gold during this period compared with a combined production of 22,348 marcs de Troyes in the mints of the Burgundian Low Countries. Given the fact that the latter mints were the first to close this is hardly a major defeat. Further, on Munro's own statement most of the 8,554 marcs de Troyes coined in Burgundy in the first two years of the period were recoinages of earlier issues. More seriously, however, Munro failed to discover the figures for coin production at Calais and accepted that this mint was closed from 1384 to 1422. When the Calais figures are added to those of London the total English production of gold considerably exceeded that of Burgundy. The surviving Calais accounts record the coinage of £107,288 in gold, 10,221 marcs de Troyes, while accounts are missing for two important years, when production may easily have reached £50,000, 4,763 marcs de Troyes.[42] It may seem as though England won the 'war of the gold nobles' only at the cost of losing a 'battle' for silver, since in this other metal Burgundy had a minting superiority of twenty two to one during the same period. However, the latter figures undoubtedly exaggerate any advantage enjoyed by Burgundy. Frequent manipulation of the currency probably ensured that many Burgundian coins passed through a mint more than once during the period under consideration. This cannot have happened in England since the silver currency, like the gold, was stable and mint output was a genuine addition to the money supply.

Surviving examples of certificates[43] issued by the London mint during the 1390s prove that the statutory bullion regulation was enforced, at least intermittently, during this period. However, it is impossible to determine the extent to which enforcement was responsible for the increase in mint activity during the last years of the century. It is difficult also to determine what effect current mint output had upon the total money supply. Since military expenditure, probably the main drain upon the nation's bullion stock in recent years, slackened after the making of a truce with France in 1389, it is possible that new production kept the money supply constant or even increased it slightly. Nevertheless, the 1390s may have seen the beginning of the late medieval shortage of silver coin, since there is superficial evidence of an increase in clipping and counterfeiting and there were several complaints about the use of inferior Scots money.[44] A mint indenture of 1394 indicates that the ban on the export of silver and gold was not total, since sums could be exported for personal expenses.[45] Previous to this date all exports may have been forbidden, since an exchange roll covering the years 1382-1393 shows that even relatively small sums were taken abroad in the form of letters of exchange.[46] The roll also records not a few letters involving large sums of money and is a clear indication of how expenditure overseas by clerks and other Englishmen ate into the favourable balance of trade.

TABLE 4

Balance of Trade, 1386-99

				Imports	Exports
			£	£	£
Value of Goods		Alien Merchandise	60 000	50 000	10 000
Subject to		Denizen Merchandise	80 000	60 000	20 000
Poundage	£210 000	Denizen & Alien Cloth	70 000	-	70 000
				110 000	100 000
Wine 17 000 tuns at £5				85 000	
Wool 19 000 sacks at £8 f.o.b.					152 000
				195 000	252 000

There can be no doubt that in the last years of the fourteenth century England continued to enjoy a favourable balance of trade, although the increase in mint activity cannot in itself be taken as evidence that the balance improved during this period. It is, in fact, likely that despite an overall expansion of trade there was comparatively little change in the net balance, since a growth in exports was matched by a growth in imports. From 1386 subsidies of tunnage and poundage were levied almost continuously and information derived from this source[47] can be used to supplement the figures for wool, cloth and alien miscellaneous trade. Table 4, based on all the surviving statistics, offers a very tentative picture of English trade during the period 1386-99. It is intended to demonstrate little more than the fact that England enjoyed a favourable balance and to suggest a rough order of magnitude for that balance. In the wool trade this was a period of stagnation, but with an average export of almost 19,000 sacks a year the trade remained the largest single earner of foreign exchange. In contrast there was remarkable expansion in the cloth trade, with exports exceeding 40,000 pieces in certain years. The net result was that the combined earnings of these two pillars of English trade probably exceeded those of the preceding period. The average value of alien merchandise paying the petty custom, about £60,000 a year, disguises a downward trend during this period. The trend probably reflects a fall in the value of alien imports, although ignorance of price changes makes it dangerous to speculate about fluctations in the volume of trade. The overall value of denizen miscellaneous trade is derived by deducting from £210,000 the average value of goods subject to poundage, £60,000 for alien petty merchandise and a tentative £70,000 for denizen and alien cloth.[48] The resulting figure of £80,000 has been arbitrarily divided into 75 per cent imports and 25 per cent exports. Although the total value of imports of general merchandise may have altered little during this period there was a substantial revival in the wine trade, with imports averaging some 17,000 tuns a year.[49] The price of wine remained high and an increased import bill in this sector dampened the effect of growing earnings in the cloth trade. These figures, then, suggest that during the last years of the fourteenth century English trade remained comfortably in balance and may even have been able to support the overseas expenditure of the non-mercantile sector of the community. If this was the case then there should have been a net inflow of bullion, although this was undoubtedly on a much smaller scale than that of the early years of the century and of the 1350s.

The fourteenth century was probably unique in English medieval history in that massive rises and falls in the national stock of bullion were concentrated into comparatively short periods of time. If this was indeed the case then it would not be strange to find that shock waves were imparted to the country's economy. The monetarists have alleged a direct connection between a growth of the money supply and high prices in the early years of the century and between dwindling money stocks and falling prices in the 1330s.[50] It is difficult to dispute the connection. Equally, it seems impossible to doubt that monetary expansion was a major factor in the very high price level which prevailed in the 1350s and 1360s. It is only in the following period that it becomes patently unwise to make a simple correlation between money supply and price levels. Prices fell, the balance of trade was undoubtedly less favourable than before and the stock of money may have been reduced. Yet the fall in prices seems to have been disproportionate to any reduction in money supply, particularly bearing in mind the likelihood of a continuing fall in total population. One is obliged, therefore, to consider the possibility of some other factor which acted as a depressant to prices in this period.

FOOTNOTES

1. For a brief statement and references to further reading see, W. C. Robinson, "Money, Population and Economic Change in Late Medieval Europe", EcHR, 2nd ser., XII (1959-60), 63-76 and M. M. Postan, "Note", ibid., 77-82. The demographic factor is offered as the 'prime mover' of economic change in D. C. North and R. P. Thomas, The Rise of the Western World (Cambridge, 1973), p. 26.

2. Postan, "Note", 78. H. A. Miskimin, "Monetary Movements and Market Structure - Forces for Contraction in Fourteenth- and Fifteenth-Century England", Journal of Economic History, 24 (1964), 490.

3. All figures for wool exports are based on E. M. Carus-Wilson and O. Coleman, England's Export Trade, 1275-1547 (Oxford, 1963). See also T. H. Lloyd, The English Wool Trade in the Middle Ages (Cambridge, 1977), p. 123.

4. Lloyd, Wool Trade, pp. 99-107.

5. See M. M. Archibald, below.

6. M. Mate, "High Prices in Early Fourteenth-Century England: Causes and Consequences", EcHR, 2nd ser. XXVIII (1975), 5.

7. E122/93/3.

8. Unpublished figures derived from E356/1, 2, 9, 10.

9. Where, as in this case, customs valuations are available the official figures have been given without adding anything for profit from sales within the country. Profit must be considered only in the case of alien imports and denizen exports.

10. E159/90 m 7.

11. E159/83 m 10d.

12. M. K. James, Studies in the Medieval Wine Trade (Oxford, 1971), p. 10.

13. All estimates of papal revenues given in this paper are derived from W. E. Lunt, Financial Relations of the Papacy with England to 1327 (Cambridge, Mass. 1939) and Financial Relations of the Papacy with England, 1327-1534 (Cambridge, Mass. 1962).

14. M. Morgan, The English Lands of the Abbey of Bec (Oxford, 1946), pp. 42, 123.

15. G. L. Harriss, King, Parliament and Public Finance in Medieval England to 1369 (Oxford, 1975), p. 525.

16. CCR, 1302-7, p. 175; 1313-18, p. 448.

17. R. L. Baker, The English Customs Service, 1307-1343 (Philadelphia, 1961), pp. 12-13.

18. For a fuller discussion, Lloyd, Wool Trade, 106-115, 122-4.

19. CCR, 1323-7, p. 156.

20. E122/93/17. E356/2.

21. C. Johnson (ed.), The De Moneta of Nicholas Oresme (London, 1956), pp. 77-8. But see Mayhew and Walker, below, pp. 132-7.

22. Mate, "High Prices", 12-13.

23. E101/297/20.

24. Lloyd, Wool Trade, pp. 183-5.

25. Lloyd, Wool Trade, pp. 193-6.

26. A. M. Watson, "Back to Gold and Silver", EcHR, 2nd ser. XX (1967), 22-7.

27. E159/88 m 135.

28. CCR, 1333-7, p. 575.

29. E. B. Fryde, "Edward III's War Finance, 1337-1341", unpublished D.Phil. Thesis (Oxford, 1947), Appendix C.

30. Based on the fiat value of new coins and takes no account of mint charges.

31. H. J. Hewitt, The Black Prince's Expedition of 1355-57 (Manchester, 1958), p. 141.

32. D. M. Broome, "The Ransom of John I, King of France", Camden Miscellany XIV, Camden Society, ser. 3, 37 (1926).

33. England's Export Trade, p. 199.

34. The poundage figure (from E356/5) is from 1 November to 1 November, while the other figures, which are abnormally high this year, cover the period from Michaelmas to Michaelmas.

35. James, Wine Trade, pp. 34, 98.

36. CPR 1361-4, pp. 492-515, passim; 1364-7, pp. 13-16.

37. CPR 1367-70, pp. 52-9, 126-34.

38. T. H. Lloyd, The Movement of Wool Prices in Medieval England, Economic History Review, Supplement 6, (Cambridge, 1973), p. 20.

39. E364/20.

40. Lloyd, Wool Trade, pp. 242-3.

41. J. H. A. Munro, Wool, Cloth and Gold (Toronto, 1972), pp. 43-63.

42. Lloyd, Wool Trade, p. 241.

43. E122/126/24; 149/35.

44. CPR 1388-92, pp. 28, 414; 1392-6, pp. 372, 491, 524.

45. CCR 1392-6, pp. 381-4.

46. CCR 1392-6, pp. 518-48.

47. E356/5.

48. Miskimin's figure for cloth exports, £120,000, is too high, but if accepted it makes his conclusion of an unfavourable trade balance even more untenable. "Monetary Movements", p. 489.

49. James did not use the enrolled tunnage accounts and, consequently, was unable to comprehend the magnitude of the boom in the wine trade in the late fourteenth century.

50. N. J. Mayhew, "Numismatic Evidence and Falling Prices in the Fourteenth Century", EcHR, 2nd ser. XXVII (1974).

CROCKARDS AND POLLARDS: IMITATION AND THE PROBLEM OF FINENESS IN A SILVER COINAGE[1]

N. J. Mayhew and D. R. Walker

The imitations common in England in the 1290s illustrate a number of important monetary themes. Because crockards and pollards were different from the usual money they sometimes occasion comment in contemporary documents which otherwise take the use of money for granted. We are told explicitly of their influence on prices, and of government measures to control their circulation.[2] The introduction of these foreign pieces into England made necessary a series of inquests revealing in some detail the state of the circulating medium, and culminated in the recoinage of 1300, which, like every recoinage, is important as a kind of crude monetary census. Finally crockards and pollards provide an introduction to the themes of weight and fineness which are central to the understanding of any intrinsic monetary system.

The bibliography of this subject is founded upon Chautard's study[3] of sterling imitations which still provide the basis of most identifications. Essays by Berghaus[4] and Rigold[5] have shown how the areas making imitations changed over the 13th and 14th centuries and how these changes coincided with the activities of English merchants and princes abroad. I shall concentrate on the imitations of the late 13th century. The dating of this series has to be established, as this may help our understanding of the fluctuations of mint output in England and Europe.

First, a general review of imitative types in the late 13th century will help put crockards and pollards in their context. Sterling imitations of Edward I's pence came in a number of types. Pollards were those coins with a single thick cross and pellets on the reverse - which I call the Edward type reverse - and a bare headed facing portrait on the obverse (Pl. I, 14) Crockards were coins of the same type with a garland of roses on the head (Pl. I, 15). Sometimes this Edward reverse appears with a heraldic shield in place of the portrait on the obverse. The heraldic type is also commonly found with a double long cross and pellets on the reverse (Pl. I, 13). This reverse type derives from the earlier long cross pennies of Henry III and the first years of Edward I, and is called the long cross reverse. In as much as the continental sterlings copied the changes in the English reverse, the general chronological sequence for these varying types must be:

1. Heraldic obv. long cross rev.
2. Heraldic obv. Edward rev.
3. Portrait obv. Edward rev.

However, imitations were struck in the Low Countries by a number of princes, and the types produced at different mints may have overlapped chronologically. The position is further complicated by the existence of portrait sterlings with a crown, in more direct imitation of Edward's pence, and of certain crowned sterlings which even went so far as to imitate the English legends. Examples of both these types of crowned sterling are known to have been made before 1300, though these types became much more common in the 14th century.

The principal authors of crockards and pollards were Gui de Dampierre of Flanders and Namur, Jean d'Avesnes of Hainaut, Jean I (and II ?) of Brabant, and Arnold VIII of Looz. In addition the series struck by the bishops and chapter of Cambrai are important for the help they give with the chronology, and Renaud of Guelders is worthy of note as the first prince to strike Edward type sterlings with a crowned bust.

The dating of the crockards and pollards series is difficult since most of the documentary evidence is ambiguous: the records usually speak of sterlings without distinguishing between the old long cross type, the heraldic types, and portrait sterlings.[6] Ghyssens[7] dates the crockards and pollards after 1292, but does not consider the English hoard evidence. Baerten[8] chose an early date of 1282/3-6 but this is based on false dating of the hoard found at Marchienne-au-pont. The evidence in favour of a date early in the 1280s for the introduction of crockards and pollards is as follows.

In 1282 the French issued a monetary ordinance prohibiting the use of various currencies then circulating in northern Europe but specifically excepting sterlings. It is argued that this edict stimulated the production of sterlings on the Continent.[9] In 1283 Gui de Dampierre ordered sterlings to be made at Namur of the same weight and same fineness as the sterlings made the previous year in Brabant.[10] Both these issues can be seen as a response to the French edict of 1282. Both Brabant, and Flanders-Namur, struck crockards and pollards plentifully, and it is seen as unlikely that European mints should cling to the old long cross type three years after it was superseded in England. Ubiert Alion was working for Gui in 1283, and few men could have been better placed to oversee the striking of sterlings since he had served Edward I of England in 1279.[11] There is clear evidence of the early use of the Edwardian reverse at Huy[12] and by Henry de Louvain.[13] Also, more fully deceptive sterling imitations can also be dated to the early 1280s. A fairly common imitation with English legends but reading EDWREANGL etc. which can be assigned to Flanders on the strength of a mule of this type with an Alost reverse,[14] is usually regarded as early because of its approximation to English pence reading REX which were made early at the beginning of the 1279 recoinage. This Alost reverse is only otherwise known with Gui de Dampierre portrait sterlings à tête and with his sterlings with a double headed eagle. Finally the crowned sterlings made by Renaud of Gelders at Arnhem are found in the early English hoards and may have been the coins struck after Rudolf I gave permission to strike sterlings in July 1282[15] - though Renaud did strike long cross types too.

There are, however, reasons why a date in the late 1280s might be preferred. In 1284 a detailed description of the various imitations then causing problems in England was published. This document specifies certain heraldic types, but there is no mention of crockards and pollards and in a document which is otherwise so specific, this would suggest that these coins were not then in circulation in England. Mavis Mate has shown that this same document was reissued in 1289.[16] It may perhaps be argued that crockards and pollards had still not made their appearance by this later date, but it is possible that the document was simply recirculated in 1289 when imitations became troublesome again and that the details of the proclamation were not brought up to date. In 1284, Walter Volcart served as receiver general in Brabant[17] and one may wonder whether the W A L T which occurs on certain Brabant long cross types refers to him and shows that this type, though obsolete in England, was still being struck in Europe. If this could be confirmed, it would negate the evidence from Namur about sterlings there and at Brabant in 1283 and 1282. Moreover, it should be remembered that in the English hoard evidence[18] coins from Hainaut, Flanders and Arnhem are the forerunners, not those of Brabant, which are said to lead the way in 1282.

Thus, the documentary evidence is fairly equivocal. The European hoard evidence, laid out by Ghyssens, is more useful.[19] It shows that portrait sterlings did not generally circulate alongside the earlier long cross types, and that no crockards and pollards occur in European hoards which can be dated with certainty before 1292. The English hoards, Coventry, and Broughton push this date back to about 1290. Unfortunately this date is not as sure as one might wish. Numismatists feel there is work still to be done on the detailed classification of classes V, VI and VII and the chronology at this point becomes a little vague. However, it is probably safe to assume that the comparatively rare class V can be linked to the marked drop in mint output which occurred around 1289. The absence of continental sterlings in the Skegby hoard, which may have been concealed early in class V, may suggest a more precise date for the advent of crockards and pollards in England. However, as Miss Archibald has suggested in her report on the hoard, imitations may have been deliberately excluded from this group of good weight coins.[20]

Negative hoard evidence cannot be conclusive. Nevertheless the information we have is consistent with the introduction of portrait sterlings late in the 1280s and it is with such a date in mind that I intend to proceed.

Dr. Prestwich and Dr. Mate[21] have shown that the importation of foreign silver fell dramatically in 1288, and continued to fall till it levelled out at the low level which became the norm throughout the 1290s, and they have linked this phenomenon with the introduction of crockards and pollards c. 1288, together with the beginnings of French debasement in the 1290s. The suggestion is that merchants chose to take their silver to continental, rather than to English mints, because the pound of silver was stretched to make more coins in Europe. Obviously debasement or weight reduction were expedients which, if pushed too far were self defeating, as really poor coins would find no takers anywhere. Miskimin has observed in France that the largest quantities of silver were struck not at times of debasement but in periods of good money.[22] The massive English coinages of the first decade of the 14th century may reflect distrust of European mints, which had tried debasement. However, so long as the reputation of the coin was generally good - and the quality of English sterling for a long time reflected some respectability on all sterling types -

there would be some room for a slight reduction in weight or fineness which would enable the European mints to offer a more attractive rate for bullion. The reduction of seignorage and mintage charges, that is shaving the profit margins to increase the turnover, would enable the mint to offer the merchant a genuine improvement in terms, but there was never much room for manoeuvering of this type compared with the opportunities provided by manipulation of weight and fineness. If the movement of silver from mint to mint was taking place in this way, it is obviously of great importance for our understanding of the mint output figures and the balance of trade, and would go a long way towards explaining silver famines or gluts at the English mints, when we have no evidence of corresponding alterations in the levels of imports and exports.

It is at this point that we come to the rather serious admission that I do not know the fineness at which crockards and pollards were struck. The rather small Ashmolean collection of imitation sterlings, together with a much larger number of imitations generously lent to us by Peter Woodhead, Ian Stewart, J. J. North, and Spink and Son have been analysed here in Oxford by D. R. Walker. The results appear below (see Appendix 1) and they show, in general terms, three things.

Firstly, the majority (71 out of 90) of continental sterlings were of sterling fineness - i.e. about 92.5% silver.

Secondly, some sterlings were struck at a lower fineness - sometimes about 3/4, or 2/3 or ½. Certain princes, particularly later in the 14th century struck only debased sterlings. However, a number of princes struck sterlings of varying fineness. Consequently, my third conclusion is that we do not have anything like enough analyses to provide a full picture.

On the basis of analyses carried out so far, Gui de Collemède, bishop of Cambrai, Florent V of Holland and Arnold of Looz appear to have only struck sterlings at the correct sterling standard. We have other results for Gui de Dampierre, Jean d'Avesnes, Jean I and II of Brabant, Guillaume of Hainaut and Jean of Louvain which give a confused picture: all struck at the sterling standard, but all of them also issued pieces of reduced fineness.

Sometimes it appears as if different types were struck at different fineness, and this looks to be true of Jean of Louvain's issues. Chautard 135, and 139 were sterling fine, but Chautard 134 var. was only about 86% silver, while Chautard 137 and 137 var. were struck at 74% and 73%. If subsequent results confirm this picture, it might be possible to show a steady reduction in fineness over the period when these coins were struck. Similarly, Guillaume of Hainaut as bishop of Cambrai only struck one type at reduced fineness, marked with a quatrefoil on the bust; his other coins were of sterling fineness. Of the three principal issuers of sterlings, Jean I of Brabant does present a fairly straightforward picture, but the issues of Gui de Dampierre and Jean d'Avesnes seem more complicated. Jean of Brabant's issues were generally sterling fine, except Chautard 97 (with : stops), and a rare sterling from the Antwerp mint. However, we cannot know whether future results will confirm such theories. Moreover, where we have most analyses - for Flanders and Hainaut - it seems that the picture becomes more complicated with every analysis made.

The majority of Gui de Dampierre's pennies were sterling fine, but some show a slight reduction (84% Chautard 6, 11) while others look to have been struck at about 67% which is 2/3rd fine = 8d. Chautard 11 - the rosarius with the reverse legend reading SIGNUM CRUCIS is known at all three standards.

Similarly confusing results were achieved for Jean d'Avesnes. Chautard nos. 23, 24, 26, 27 var., 29, 33, 38, 39, 42 are all known with sterling fineness, but Ch 27, 29 var. and 33 are also known at about 80% fine. I have done some work on the chronology of these types,[23] based on hoard evidence, but unfortunately it is not possible to say that Jean d'Avesnes began to strike at a reduced standard and then stuck to it. Although Chautard nos. 27 and 33 are what I take to be later types of Valenciennes and Mons, Chautard 29 (Mons) comes near the middle of the series. Perhaps these slightly baser series were occasionally made secretly and sold to the public as sterling fine. However, the Hainaut mint accounts for 1298[24] record more or less openly that sterlings were struck at 8d fine, which is a further puzzle, since none of the sterlings of Jean d'Avesnes which we have so far analysed was found to be 8d fine. Had they been baser we could explain it in terms of fraud by the mint officials, but since they are better, one can only imagine that no coins of the particular issue mentioned in the surviving account have yet been analysed. It was, however, a very large issue - 38,000 marks = 6,800,000 coins. The puzzle could be explained if they were using the English Tower system of 10 dwt to the $\frac{1}{2}$ oz:[25] 8d fine would then mean 80%. But this also seems unlikely.

Again and again we are forced to conclude that we need many more analyses, but the picture which emerges so far is one in which the generally reliable fineness of most sterling imitations was punctuated by occasional debasement. Further study of this debasement may indicate that it occurred as rival mints struggled to offer the best price for bullion, or a more haphazard picture may emerge suggesting that debasement was carried out simply for fraudulent profit. The results we have so far, however, do make it clear that enough crockards and pollards were struck at sterling fineness to explain their widespread acceptance as sterlings and to suggest that most of the profit in striking them came from their poor weight rather than from poor fineness.[26]

It is more difficult to establish the weight of crockards and pollards than one might imagine. Examples in museums and private collections can be weighed, but an allowance must be made for the length of time the coins circulated, losing weight through wear and/or clipping. Crockards and pollards from the Galston hoard (1300) might be expected to be a good deal heavier than similar coins from the Montraive hoard concealed in the 1360s. Different hoards of similar dates can also exhibit quite different weight patterns: for example, the Dover hoard consisted of particularly heavy coins probably collected for that reason.[27]

Ghyssens has calculated that Hainaut sterlings would have weighed about 1.3 g when fresh from the mint,[28] and there are plenty of museum examples to support this. A glance through Chautard indicates that weights anywhere between 1.0 g and 1.4 g were common, though examples lighter than this can be found and heavier examples are known but are rare. It would probably be fair to say that crockards and pollards were struck about 10% lighter than English sterlings and this is confirmed by an exchange rate of 22s pollards for 20s sterling.[29]

However, although a random sample of pollards might consistently weigh less than a random sample of sterlings, the weight range of legitimate English sterlings was such that individual crockards and pollards fell well within these limits. Heavy examples of English sterlings were, it seems, quickly removed from circulation, so the currency actually in use had a lower average weight than when it left the mint. Legitimate wear and illegitimate clipping would lower the average weight still further, so that crockards and pollards, although initially struck to lower specifications, fitted into the English monetary system well.

The searches made in the 1290's for light, clipped or foreign money are useful to us for the information they give about the state of the currency. A number of rolls survive, telling us how much bad coin, out of how much legitimate cash, merchants had.[30] The totals of English coins are themselves impressive, sums of £100 and £200 being common; such sums are far larger than the largest adequately recorded hoard. The proportions of clipped and counterfeit or foreign coin held by each merchant varies, but the totals for one such roll (E 401/1784) were as follows:

Total examined	Clipped	Foreign and Counterfeit
£13,136	£264-11-2	£110-0-8

Thus in the early 1290's a good deal of fuss was made about a very small problem. Sometimes the sums examined have a suspiciously rounded look but usually the sums of bad coin found are irregular, and it looks as if the money really was examined. We know that moneyers were specially chosen to scrutinize the coins.[31] Sometimes the weight of all the money was also noted[32] but money of light weight was not usually confiscated. However, at Easter 1291[33] a number of merchants had their money arrested for this reason at Westminster and the Tower. On the strictest interpretation of the law English pence should number 20s 3d to the pound weight. A number of men lost money at 20s 6d to the pound. Three separate pounds were weighed from each man's money, and the worst recorded weight in this document was for the coins of Hugh de Byrchall which stood at 20s 8d for the first two pounds and 20s 10d for the third.

Knowing what we do of wear from the medieval coins found in hoards, almost all coin more than a few years old must have been liable to confiscation. If we consider the pound weight which was made up of 20s 10d tale, this was only about 150 grains light, and 70 coins weighing 20 grains instead of $22\frac{1}{2}$ would explain the deficiency. We must remember that in 1291 when this inquest was made, the new coinage had only seen about 10 years service, but estimating wear at 0.5 grains lost per coin per decade,[34] a pound weight of coin made in 1280 might be expected to have lost 120 grains by 1290. This would put it well into the prohibited weight when the king's officers were in such punitive mood. In fact, confiscation of this type was rare and a number of those who lost money had it restored to them, including the clipped and foreign coin. The lucky men were chiefly those Flanders merchants for whom Gui de Dampierre interceded, and the Italian bankers who often had special treatment from the King. However, some Englishmen who had English coin confiscated on the technical charge of poor weight never saw it again.

All this raises the question of how far the confiscation of light, clipped or foreign money may have been seen as an easy source of income, as well as a means to maintain English monetary standards. After the expulsion of the Jews, such measures will have fallen on other sections of the community, and whether or not they were intended to raise cash, they must certainly have caused considerable resentment. The adequate policing of the money supply, like a recoinage if there was no reduction in weight, was paid for by the holders of cash and required considerable energy and authority on the part of the king and his officers.

In addition to mounting searches, Edward initially hoped that individuals would check the weight of coins and pierce light weight coins.[35] This was a fundamental error. It was not possible that all payments should be weighed, and the weighing of coins by a few only, encouraged clipping and culling of heavy coins and further reduced the average weight. Thorold Rogers believed that all payments were made by weight.[36] This was how he explained the fact that the weight reductions of the 1340s did not provoke a popular outcry or a jump in the level of prices. In fact payment was by tale, and weighing was rare. Weights and balances simply were not plentiful enough to permit universal payment by weight.[37] Moreover, the standardization of weights to a fraction of a grain would have presented problems at a time when weights and measures varied throughout the country. The alternative to weighing all coins was to forbid the weighing of any coin except at the mints and exchanges, but such a radical step in the direction of a token coinage was not practical while the coins still had their intrinsic value. Nevertheless, this was the policy pursued by Gui de Dampierre in an agreement with the cities of Ghent, Ypres and Douai, dated June 11 1299.[38] This document illustrates the policies which a prince might seek to implement. The rates at which domestic coins were to pass were clearly stipulated. Foreign coins were prohibited and were to be pierced; bringing foreign coins into the country was tantamount to counterfeiting. No one was to sell bullion to a foreign mint, and no one was to buy or sell or trade in money. Occasionally merchants were excluded from certain prohibitions, and maximum values were set on French coins apparently current despite the ban on foreign coins. The arrangements seem to show, at one and the same time, both an ideal monetary policy and a realistic policy to be operated when the ideal system failed. On one point, however, they were quite firm: no one was to weigh coin as bullion except at the mint, and no one was to keep scales or weights in their house.

Generally, England was in a much better position than the Low Countries to operate a monetary policy of this kind. Because of the channel, if searches were made regularly at the principal ports, the introduction of foreign coin into England could be fairly effectively discouraged. If these searches were accompanied by a general prohibition of fairly easily recognised types as occurred in 1300, the interlopers could be almost entirely driven out of circulation. However, the coins had to be recognised by their types, rather than by weight. As a result, the 14th century saw the introduction of imitations which copied the English types more exactly but continued to weigh slightly below the usual English weights. Nevertheless, although in the 1290s crockards and pollards were easily recognised, their circulation in England was widespread.

As Dr. Mate has suggested, the toleration of lighter foreign coins in England must be seen in the context of Edward I's preoccupation with his other troubles in the 1290s.[39] Early in the decade attempts were made to restrict their circulation , but these petered out by about 1294. Apart from being unwilling to devote energy to a task which would only cause further discontent at a time when sections of the Establishment were already disaffected, Edward may have hesitated to proscribe the crockards and pollards while the alliance with Gui de Dampierre was so important for the French war. The Government may also have reconciled themselves to their circulation on the grounds that they were of good fineness and reasonable weight. As the decade progressed, the crockards and pollards must have become increasingly irritating. Their fineness was less uniform, and the work which they brought to the Low Countries must have been in stark contrast with the slackness at London and Canterbury. Good English coin was becoming increasingly scarce and the economy was becoming correspondingly dependent on the interlopers. While there was no adequate policing of English ports and no prohibition or adequate discount in the market place, bullion holders continually chose continental mints, and Edward was unable to gather enough English coin to float a recoinage.

It is necessary at this point to pause and ask, "What methods and standards were in use at English mints for the regulation of weight and fineness?" This will take us far from 1300, but the digression will help our understanding of the recoinage of crockards and pollards. Weight controls were relatively simple. A fixed number of pence were to be struck from the pound of metal, and limits of tolerance were laid down for individual coins. Six heavy and six light coins were permitted to exceed these individual limits providing that the pound as a whole made up the right number of coins. As coins circulated they lost weight and the exchequer devised a number of rules for accepting old coins. Such coins might be taken ad scalam - that is, with a predetermined additional charge for probable light weight, or ad pensum, which meant that the payment was made entirely by weight without regard to the theoretical face value of the coins.

The exchequer also devised a system of blanched payments intended to check the alloy of the coin paid to them. Certain royal farms were obliged to pay blanch which meant that a pound of their payment was assayed. The discovered silver content in the assayed sample would be applied to the whole debt, and additional payment required to make good the deficiency. It was nothing less than a means of extorting additional cash from the sheriff.

The Dialogue of the Exchequer,[40] which provides this information, is also interesting for the details it gives us about the Assay which was carried out by means of lead cupellation. Richard Fitznigel makes it clear that the process required considerable expertise which he did not possess, and that the principal danger was that if the silver were left too long in the fire some would be lost, but if it were not left long enough, some of the alloy would remain. The Dialogue is also the first reference we have to 6 dwt of alloy in the pound as a maximum, and also provides an early instance of Government declaring how bad the current coin had become, in order to justify a recoinage.

The figure of 6d permissible alloy in the pound reappears in the documents we have, which tell us of the 1247-8 recoinage.[41] An inquest was held in London in 1248. Twelve citizens of London were to be elected to meet with twelve goldsmiths selected by the mint to assay the new and the old money. In fact 15 citizens turned up with 13 goldsmiths. They found that a pound of the new money contained not more than 6 dwt of silver less than the standard pound, and this was a verdict which met with universal approval. By contrast the old money when assayed was found to be 10 dwt short. As a result, all those exchanging old money for the new superior coin had to pay 10d in the pound for loss in the fire as well as 6d seignorage to the king, making a total deduction of 1s 4d in the pound. Pure silver brought to the mints had a total deduction of only 6d for the king, but 6d of copper was added by the mint to cover their costs.

At the end of the long cross issue in 1279, the permitted level of alloy was still said to be 6 dwt and Philip de Cambio and one of the assayers at the mint were hanged for adding 8½ dwt.[42] However, with Edward's new coinage two separate pieces of evidence speak explicitly of the addition of about 18 dwt of copper to the pound,[43] and a third, undated document speaks of an addition of 16 dwt copper and an allowance of a further 2 dwt copper arising from the loss of silver in the fire.[44]

One may summarise the documentary evidence for the copper content of English sterlings as follows:

1177-9	Dialogue of Exchequer 6 dwt copper permitted
1247-8	Short Cross found to contain 10 dwt copper
	Long Cross found to contain 6 dwt copper
1279	Recent issues found to contain 8 dwt copper, but standard of 6 dwt still in force
1279-80	Recoinage 18 dwt copper added to the pound of pure silver. This is the famous 'sterling standard' of 92.5%.

One might have hoped that the analyses of the coins themsleves would have confirmed the documentary evidence. They do not. A number of analyses of English Medieval coins are in print. The R.N.S. special publication Methods of Chemical and Metallurgical Investigation of Ancient Coinage[45] is an indispensible starting point. For the period now under consideration the results of Harris,[46] Forbes and Dalladay,[47] and Gordus and Yvon[48] all indicate that English sterlings were consistently at, or slightly above, 'sterling' fineness of 92.5%. No sterlings with only 6 dwt of alloy added have yet been found, and there is no evidence of significant debasement in the 1279-80 recoinage.

However, the numbers of analyses so far published is small, and the comparison of results achieved by different methods is difficult. Accordingly, we have analysed a whole series of short cross, long cross and Edward pennies, and print the results here (See Appendix 2). We particularly want to check the statements made in the documents about the quantities of alloy present, and the relative fineness of cross and crosslet and short cross, short cross and long cross, and long cross and Edward's coins. The results indicate:

(1) No coins fall below 'sterling standard', not even Philip de Cambio's, although his coin was of a lower average fineness than the others.

(2) Short cross up to, and including class V look best, but the best group and the worst differ by only 1.5% - less than 4 dwt.

(3) The analyses do not confirm the claims of the mint about the quality of the new compared with the old money - in fact the oldest money analysed was the best. There may, however, have been a slight tendency for the latest issues in each series to fall off a little - perhaps by 1 dwt.

How then is the documentary evidence to be explained?

The documents for this subject are difficult. Among the pitfalls of medieval mint terminology is the fact that pure silver can be described as 10d fine and as 12d fine according to whether the Tower or the Troy ounce is used.[49] But perhaps the most serious pitfall is too literal an interpretation of medieval remarks about 'pure silver'. 'Pure' meant different things in different places.[50] Apart from the desirability of retaining some alloy in coinage silver to harden the metal a little, refining metal to absolute purity would have involved an inevitable and unacceptable loss of silver, given medieval techniques. Methods and skill varied from place to place. In London, the purest silver was refined in Guthren's Lane. At the mint, in 1279, silver of lesser fineness passed as 'pure'. In France, argent de roi (942) differed from Montpelier or Marseilles silver (984 - effectively as pure as possible) which had the highest reputation in England. In fact, Montpelier silver was said in England to contain only 1d or 2d alloy,[57] but, at 63/64 fine, this underestimated the amount of alloy present, and illustrates how far Montpelier skills surpassed those of the Mint.

In short, at the English mints and exchanges it was all done by rule of thumb until 1279. Silver was refined according to custom and then 6 dwt of copper was added, but the resulting metal contained more than 6 dwt of copper since the customary methods of assaying had not removed all the copper from what they chose to call 'pure' silver.

William of Turnemire took charge of Edward's recoinage of 1279-80 and established a more explicit and accurate statement of the standard at which the money was to be made. He came from Marseilles, where refining techniques were good, and insisted on using the best English standard - Guthren's Lane - rather than the traditional mint notion of 'pure' silver as the starting point for his coinage. To this he added 18 dwt of copper, and ended up with money of the same standard as that struck by his predecessors, who had not refined so well and who had added only 6 dwt of alloy. William de Turnemire had every reason to seek an explicit statement about the approved alloy. Philip de Cambio and William de Harlewyn had forfeited their lives by adding $8\frac{1}{2}$ dwt of copper instead of 6 dwt to 'pure' silver. For anyone knowing, as William de Turnemire must have known, that all the English coins made for well over a century contained more than the lethal $8\frac{1}{2}$ dwt of copper, customary notions of 'pure' silver must have been disquieting.

Our analyses have shown that Philip's coins may have contained less silver than usual, but nevertheless they never fell below the 'official' level of 92.5%. It is also worth noting that his standard trial plate, preserved in the Mint, bearing his die, was fractionally lower than his coins, at 92.1% AR.[52] It seems to have been usual to strike coin slightly better than the minimum standard. The bullion holders paid for this safety margin, since the mint and the exchanges regularly underestimated the value of the coin they bought. It is significant that the record of Philip's hearing states that his coin was compared with an old trial plate of King Henry; comparison with his own trial plate would have acquitted him.

This rule of thumb approach to assaying may explain the references to 6 dwt of copper in thirteenth century sterlings, and also throw light on the untimely death of Philip de Cambio and William de Harlewyn. However, it cannot explain the findings of the jury in 1248 that the new long cross coin had 4 dwt less alloy in it than the old short cross, or justify the additional charge of 1½d on recoining English money in 1279-80 "because, compared with the King's new standard, the old money was said to be so much worse".[53] Tales about the poor quality of coin in circulation which necessitated a recoinage were common, and loss of weight through wear and clipping will have given substance to these tales. There was no truth in the rumours that the earlier coins were of poor quality, yet it was a regular feature of every repair of the coinage that the existing coin was said to be debased.

The Dialogue of the Exchequer refers to the badness of money 1177-9 [54] though Allen has shown that the coins were not as bad as the rumours and the exchange rates might indicate.[55] Accordingly, large profits must have been made on the exchange. Similarly, the inquest of 1248 has all the hallmarks of a public relations exercise. The exchange had everything to gain from the pretence that their coins were better than they were, as the rates for converting the old into the new money could then be correspondingly high. It was also in their interest to spread the rumour that the old coin was below standard, not only to reduce the price they had to pay for it, but also to discourage the public from continuing to accept it. The execution of Philip de Cambio will have served to discredit the long cross coinage of 1279 when it was time for its withdrawal, and the myth of a new improved coinage was again current.

Finally, and at last we can return to the crockards and pollards, the pattern repeats itself with the 1300 recoinage when the continental imitations were made out to be much worse than they really were. In every case, the existing coin was disparaged, both to force its recoinage and to reduce the rates which the exchange had to pay for it.[56]

At the turn of the century the political crisis eased, and Edward felt able to order a recoinage, paid for by the unfortunate holders of the bad money, when its value was halved, and partly financed in the short term by the Italian bankers who reaped some of the profit. It is worth noting that those who received crockards and pollards at ½d face value and then exchanged them at the mints by weight will have made a substantial profit, even allowing for any deficiency in fineness.

It has been suggested that crockards and pollards were taken at the mint at a halfpenny, and not by weight.[57] Moreover, orders forbidding men to melt crockards and pollards and take the bullion to the mint suggest that some men saw an advantage in having their money treated as bullion rather than coin at the mints, which implies that the coins were taken at ½d each, and the bullion by weight.[58] However, usual mint practice, the mint accounts, and cases from the Liber Quotidianus all indicate that all coin was taken by weight and not by tale.[59] The order that crockards and pollards should be charged the seignorage due on English coin, rather than the lower rate for foreign coin, confirms that crockards and pollards were to be taken as bullion.[60] Under these circumstances it seems that the order that men should not melt down their own crockards and pollards was motivated by a desire to make it harder for men to establish the true value of their coin, and also by the feeling that any melting of coin outside the mints would, at best, remove much needed coin from circulation, and at worst would be a prelude to clipping, culling and downright forgery - the activities normally associated with the melting or 'forging' of coins outside the mints.

The Liber Quotidianus also shows that it was the assessment of the fineness of the silver, as well as the weight, which finally fixed the price at which the mint brought each lot of bullion. This assessment of fineness often seems to have involved fraud. Any man who held crockards and pollards when their value was halved would lose money. However, if he took them to the exchange and received a fair valuation, his losses, including recoinage, should not have reached anything like 50%. Furthermore, if a man received crockards and pollards at ½d. and then had them recoined by weight, with a fair assessment of their fineness, he should have been able to make a significant profit. One case in the Liber Quotidianus illustrates this: the wardrobe received £121 8s 8d pollards by tale, valued at £60 14s 4d. They were accepted at the exchange at £109 5s 3d by weight, and the stiff charge of 5s in the pound was levied to cover the costs of exchange and to make the silver up to sterling fineness. After this deduction, the wardrobe was left with £81 18s 11½d weight, making £82 19s 5d tale. Since they had only given £60 14s 4d for the coin in the first place, they declared a profit of £22 5s 1d.[61] The exchange must also have made a substantial profit with an allowance of 25% to cover the costs and make good any deficiency in fineness. We have seen that some crockards and pollards were very base, but in a mixed selection it seems unlikely, though not impossible, that so large a deduction could be justified.

Nevertheless, the wardrobe made a profit since they had only taken the crockards and pollards at half their face value. They were not always so fortunate; they held some pollards at the time of their devaluation (£174 16s 0d cut to £87 8s 0d)[62] and lost heavily, and on one occasion accepted as little as £40 sterling for £100 pollards from the Spini in London.[63] Usually they did better: £326 3s 11½d pollards was recoined with full allowance for charges, poor weight and fineness, and yielded £266 10s 6d - a loss of only 16%.[64]

The variation in value of the pollards in the wardrobe might be explained in terms of the varied weight and fineness of the coins themselves. However, on one occasion the fraud, either at the exchange or at the wardrobe, is so great that one is inclined to suspect cheating on other occasions. £1000 of pollards were said to weigh £893, but to have a fineness of only £432 10s 7d. In the light of what we know of the fineness of crockards and pollards, such an assay is frankly incredible. Moreover, according to the wardrobe official, the exchange deducted a further £11 3s 3d as a charge for the assay, and levied a further sum of £20 8s 7½d for poor fineness. Thus £406 1s 11d sterling was paid on £1000 pollards, but the wardrobe regarded it as a loss of only £93 18s 7½d, since they had only valued the pollards at £500 in the first place. Either the exchanged deceived the wardrobe, or the wardrobe deceived the king, or both.[65]

With profits of this sort to be made at the exchanges, it is not surprising that the Friscobaldi were so willing to serve there. Similarly, the profits to be had by buying crockards and pollards at ½d each and selling them to the exchanges, providing a full allowance for their fineness could be had, would explain why so many societies of Italian bankers were willing to pay for a licence to deal in these coins.[66]

Thus there were three stages in the demonetisation of crockards and pollards:

(1) May 1299 - statute of Stepney prohibited the further import of crockards and pollards, but made no restrictions on their use if already in England.

(2) Christmas 1299 - their value was halved overnight.

(3) Easter 1300 - complete demonetisation - which in fact involved an increased valuation for those willing to take on the exchanges.

However, most holders of crockards and pollards, especially the small fry, were glad to get them off their hands. Between Christmas and Easter, many men refused to accept them at any price, despite a law obliging everyone to accept them at ½d. After this experience, many men, without any means of testing the fineness of the coins, would have counted themselves lucky to get ½d for them.

But for those capable of establishing their true value and extracting it from the mint, the 1300 recoinage provided an opportunity for considerable enrichment. This may help to explain the efficiency of the recoinage. The hoards of the fourteenth century show that although some crockards and pollards slipped through the net, the thousands of pounds of crockards and pollards in circulation in the 1290s were removed surprisingly easily. Those who knew the value of the coins, above all the Italian bankers, bought up the crockards and pollards and then took them to the mints and exchanges as they saw very clearly that it was in their interest to do so.

The recoinage of crockards and pollards illustrates how far the English monetary system was subject to the problems which arose from the difference between the intrinsic and the face value of coins in circulation. The weight, and particularly the fineness, of the coins was difficult to establish, and those who knew them could generally make a profit at the expense of those who did not. The emphasis which I have placed on the metal content of medieval money may also serve to remind us that despite the use of barter, credit and tallies, this was above all a time when money was metal, and the supply of metal was at times irregular.

ACKNOWLEDGEMENTS

The analyses recorded in these two appendices were made using x-ray flourescence spectrometry.[67] The Research Laboratory for Archaeology and the History of Art in the University of Oxford, under the direction of Professor E. T. Hall, provided the necessary facilities. Without their assistance this project would not have been possible.

APPENDIX 1

ANALYSES OF CROCKARDS AND POLLARDS[68]

Gui de Dampierre

		Ag %	Pb %	
Chautard 1	Ashmolean	92.25	2.50	
	"	91.00	1.75	
	"	92.75	1.00	
	Woodhead	92.75	1.00	
	"	92.75	0.25	
	"	94.00	0.25	
Chautard 5 (5 pointed star on rev.)	"	67.00	1.75	
Chautard 6	North	93.00	0.75	
	Ashmolean	84.00	2.50	
	Woodhead	93.00	trace	
	"	93.00	1.00	
Chautard 7	"	68.50	1.50	
Chautard 8	North	94.50	0.75	
	"	90.50	2.00	) ex Broughton
Chautard 10	"	93.25	0.75	) hoard
	Ashmolean	92.25	1.00	
	Woodhead	93.00	1.00	
Chautard 11 (Rosarius, Signum Crucis)	North	65.60	2.00	
	Ashmolean	91.75	1.00	
	Woodhead	69.50	2.25	
	"	84.00	1.50	
	"	63.75	1.75	
	"	67.50	1.75	
Chautard 47	"	92.00	0.50	
Chautard 50	"	92.25	0.50	
	"	93.25	1.25	
Chautard 55	"	94.00	trace	

Total 27, of which 19 at or above 90% 2 at 84%, 6 at c. 66%.

Jean of Brabant

		%	Pb%	
Chautard 88	Ashmolean	91.75	1.00	
	"	93.00	0.50	
	Woodhead	91.25	1.00	
Chautard 89	Ashmolean	93.50	0.20	
	Woodhead	94.00	0.25	
	"	93.25	0.75	
Chautard 91	"	92.25	0.50	
Chautard 93	"	94.00	0.50	
	Ashmolean	90.25	1.00	
	"	92.50	0.75	
Chautard 95	North	93.25	0.75	
Chautard 95-7	Ashmolean	53.00		8% Sn, 2% Fe
Chautard 97	Woodhead	72.00	2.25	
Chautard 101	Spinks	94.00	-	
	Woodhead	93.50	1.75	
Chautard - Maestricht	Ashmolean	91.75	2.00	
Chautard - Antwerp	Woodhead	62.50	1.00	

Total 17, of which 14 at or above 90%   1 at 72%, 1 at 62%, 1 at 58%.

Jean d' Avesnes

Chautard 23	North	93.25	0.75
	Woodhead	93.75	0.25
	"	94.00	0.25
Chautard 24	"	93.75	0.25
	"	92.00	1.00
	"	92.25	1.50
Chautard 26	"	94.25	1.00
Chautard 27	"	91.75	1.25
	"	81.50	0.50
	Ashmolean	79.00	1.00
Chautard 28	Woodhead	93.50	0.50
Chautard 29	"	93.25	0.75
	"	92.50	trace
	North	93.75	0.75
	Ashmolean	92.25	0.75
	Stewart	93.00	0.50
	Woodhead	77.00	0.75
Chautard 33	"	92.50	0.25
	"	79.50	1.00
	Ashmolean	93.50	0.50
	"	93.00	-
Chautard 38	Woodhead	93.00	0.75
	"	92.50	1.00
Chautard 39	"	92.00	2.00
Chautard 42	"	92.00	1.25

Total 25, of which 21 at or above 90%   4 around 80%.

Jean of Louvain

		%	Pb%
Chautard 134 with rose on bust	Woodhead	86.25	1.50
Chautard 135	"	93.00	1.00
Chautard 139	"	92.00	1.00
Chautard 137	"	74.00	2.50
	"	73.00	3.00

Total 5, of which 2 at or above 90% 1 at 86%, 2 at about 74%.

Gui de Collemède: Cambrai 1296-1306

Chautard 216	Ashmolean	91.50	1.25
	Woodhead	89.00	-

Arnold VIII of Looz

Chautard 143	Woodhead	92.50	-
Chautard 144	Ashmolean	90.00	1.50
Chautard 146/7 mule	Woodhead	91.00	1.00
Chautard 147	"	93.75	0.25
	"	92.50	1.75
	Ashmolean	92.00	1.75
	"	93.25	0.75
	"	89.00	2.50

Total 8, of which 7 at or above 90% 1 at 89%.

Guillaume de Hainaut: Cambrai 1292-6

Chautard 209-14	Stewart	93.25	0.50
Chautard 210	Woodhead	92.50	1.50
Chautard 214	"	93.75	trace
Chautard - quatrefoil on breast	"	78.00	1.50

Total 4, of which 3 at or above 90% 1 at 78%.

Florent V of Holland

Chautard 459	Woodhead	92.50	1.00
	Stewart	94.00	0.50

Renaud of Gueldres

Chautard 463	Ashmolean	92.25	1.00

" Enigmatic"

Chautard 80	Ashmolean	91.50	2.75

Totals 90 coins with an average fineness over 85% of which 71 approximate to the sterling standard, 19 are of varying fineness, averaging 72.94%

APPENDIX 2

ANALYSES OF ENGLISH COINS IN THE ASHMOLEAN COLLECTION[69]

Short Cross

Moneyer	Class	Syll. No.	Ag%	Pb%
Aimer	Ib	529	94.25	0.25
Alain	Ib	530	95.00	0.25
Alward	Ib	532	94.50	0.25
Davi	Ib	534	94.25	0.25
Davi	Ib	535	94.00	0.50
Davi	Ib	536	93.75	0.25
Davi	Ic	537	94.50	0.25
Davi	Ic	538	94.50	0.25
Fulk	IVa	544	94.00	0.75
Fulk	IVa	545	93.50	0.50
Fulk	IVb	546	94.50	0.25
Fulk	Va	547	94.25	0.25
Fulk	Vb-i/Va	548	93.75	0.50
Fulk	Vb-ii	549	93.75	0.25
Abel	Vc	507	93.50	0.50
Abel	Vc	508	93.50	0.50
Abel	Vc	509	93.75	0.50
Abel	VIa-i	516	93.00	0.50
Abel	VIa-i	517	94.00	0.50
Abel	VIa-iii	519	94.25	0.50
Abel	VIb	520	92.75	0.75
Abel	VIc	521	93.00	0.75
Abel	VIc	522	93.25	0.50
Abel	VIIa	523	92.50	1.00
Adam	VII	527	94.00	0.25
Adam	VII	528	92.75	1.00
Elis	VII	539	92.50	1.00
Elis	VII	540	93.25	0.75
Elis	VII	541	93.75	0.25

Long Cross

Moneyer	Class	Syll. No.	Ag%	Pb%
Anon	I	847	94.00	0.75
Nicole	I/II	864	93.00	0.50
Nicole	II	865	94.00	0.25
Nicole	II	866	93.50	0.50
Nicole	II	867	93.25	0.75
Nicole	II	868	94.00	0.50

Moneyer	Class	Syll. No.	Ag%	Pb%
Henri	IIIa	850	93.75	0.50
Henri	IIIb	851	94.00	0.50
Henri	IIIb	852	93.50	0.50
Henri	IV	856	94.25	0.25
Davi	Va	848	94.25	0.25
Davi	Vf	849	94.00	0.50
Renaud	Vg	886	93.25	0.50
Renaud	Vg	887	92.50	0.75
Renaud	Vg	888	92.75	0.75
Renaud	Vh	892	93.50	0.25
Ricard	Vg	899	93.50	-
Robert	Vg	902	93.50	0.75
Walter	Vg	904	93.50	0.50
Walter	Vg	905	95.00	0.25
Philip	VII	883	93.00	0.50
Philip	VII	884	93.00	0.50
Philip	VII	885	92.50	0.50
Philip	Trial Plate	-	92.10	0.81
				Copper 6.19

Edward

Class	Ag%	Pb%
Ia	93.75	0.50
Ic	93.50	0.25
I-II	93.25	0.50
IIa	93.50	0.25
IIb	93.75	0.25

NOTES

1. The text and argument of this paper are the work of Nicholas Mayhew and any errors of interpretation must be attributed to him. However, it is heavily dependent on the metal analyses carried out by D.R. Walker, and has benefitted greatly from his advice throughout. It is offered here as a joint paper.

2. M. Prestwich " Edward I' s Monetary Policies and Their Consequences" EcHR 2nd ser. XXII (1969), 406-416, and M. Mate " Monetary Policies in England, 1272-1307" BNJ XLI (1972), 34-79, provide a full introduction to the documentary evidence for crockards and pollards.

3. J. Chautard Imitations des Monnaies au Type Esterlin (Nancy 1871).

4. P. Berghaus " Der Periode der Sterlings" Hamb. Beitr. zur Numismatik I (1947), 34-53.

5. S.E. Rigold " The Trial of the Easterlings" BNJ XXVI (1949-51), 31-55.

6. C. Richebé Les Monnaies Féodales D'Artois (Paris 1963), pp. 121-3.

7. J. Ghyssens " Essai de Datation des Premiers Esterlins de Brabant" Annales du Congrès de Liège de la Féderation Archéologique et Historique de Belgique II (Liège 1971), 567-572.

8. J. Baerten " Un esterlin inédit d' Arnould V, comte de Looz 1279-1323" Cercle d' Etudes Numismatique: Bulletin Dec 1965, 54.

9. R. Chalon Recherches sur les Monnaies des Comtes de Hainaut (Brussels 1848), pp. 36-7.

10. Ibid. p. 37.

11. N.J. Mayhew " Imitative Sterlings in the Aberdeen and Montrave Hoards" NC 7th ser. XVI (1976), 85-97.

12. C. Piot Notice sur un dépôt de monnaies découvert à Grand-Halleux (Académie Royale de Belgique Brussels 1847).

13. Chautard no. 133.

14. N.J. Mayhew " Imitative Sterlings" op. cit.

15. W. Jesse Quellenbuch zur Munz-und Geldgeschichte des Mittelalters (Halle-Saale, 1924), pp. 49-50.

16. M. Mate, op. cit., 57 and notes 1 and 8.

17. A. De Witte Histoire Monétaire des Comtes de Louvain, Ducs de Brabant et Marquis du Saint Empire Romain (Antwerp 1894), I, p. 70.

18. For the Broughton hoard see J.J. North in BNJ XXV (1966), 120-7. For the Coventry hoard see D.F. Allen in BNJ XXXIII (1940), 279-80. The earliest English hoard with coins of Brabant must be dated after 1292 as it contains a sterling of Guillaume de Hainaut, bishop of Cambrai. See M.M. Archibald "The King's Lynn Hoard" CH I (1975), 93.

19. J. Ghyssens "Datation des Esterlings" op. cit., 571-2.

20. M.M. Archibald "The Skegby, Notts., 1967 Hoard" BNJ XL (1971), 49-50.

21. M. Prestwich op. cit., 409. M. Mate op. cit., 61.

22. H.A. Miskimin Money Prices and Foreign Exchange in Fourteenth Century France (New Haven 1963), p. 92.

23. N.J. Mayhew "La Chronologie des Esterlins de Jean d'Avesnes" RN 6th ser. XVII (1975), 172-81.

24. J. Ghyssens "La Monnaie de Hainaut sous Jean d'Avesnes" RBN CXIX (1973), 78.

25. The De Moneta of Nicholas Oresme and English Mint Documents ed. C. Johnson (London 1956), p. 72, hereafter, English Mint Docs.

26. It might be thought that hoarders and modern collectors would have shown a preference for coins with higher silver contents. If this were so, the coins which have survived for us to analyse would not be representative. However, in practice, it is not possible to select coins of higher or lower silver content on sight; again and again coins which looked poor turned out to be sterling fine, and vice versa.

27. M. Dolley, "The Dover Hoard, the first English hoard with groats of Edward I" BNJ XXVIII (1955-7), 147-68.

28. J. Ghyssens "La Monnaie de Hainaut" op. cit., 79.

29. M. Prestwich, op. cit., 412.

30. P.R.O. King's Remembrancer, Accounts Various E101/288/22, Lord Treasurer's Remembrancer, Receipt Rolls E401/1784.

31. P.R.O. E101/288/26.

32. P.R.O. E101/288/22.

33. P.R.O. E401/1784.

34. M. Dolley and W. Seaby in Seaby's Coin and Medal Bulletin (1968), 166 Note 25.

35. R. Ruding Annals of the Coinage of Great Britain (London 1840), I, p. 198.

36. J.E. Thorold Rogers A History of Agriculture and Prices in England (Oxford 1866) I, pp. 75-6.

37. N.J. Mayhew "A Tumbrel at the Ashmolean Museum" The Antiquaries Journal LV (1975), 394-6. Weighing of gold was probably more common.

38. W. Jesse, op.cit., 190-2.

39. M. Mate, op. cit., 63.

40. The Course of the Exchequer ed. C. Johnson (London 1950), pp. 36-40.

41. "Assay of the New Money 1248" in English Mint Docs., pp. 53-5.

42. E101/301/1.

43. English Mint Docs., pp. 68 and 87. The undated "Treatise on the new money" can be assigned to the period August 1286 - November 1287 because of the rates for mintage and seignorage mentioned.

44. English Mint Docs., p. 82.

45. Methods of Chemical and Metallurgical Investigation of Ancient Coinage eds. E. T. Hall and D. M. Metcalf (R. N. S. Special Publication No. 8, London 1972).

46. E. J. Harris in Seaby's Coin and Medal Bulletin 1961, 389-90 and 1962, 5-7.

47. J. S. Forbes and D. B. Dalladay BNJ XXX (1960), 86.

48. A. A. Gordus and J. Yvon BNJ XXXIX (1970), 37.

49. English Mint Docs. p. 72 and 74.

50. L. Blancard Essai sur les Monnaies de Charles 1er Comte de Provence (Paris 1868), 36.

51. English Mint Docs., p. 40.

52. J. H. Watson Ancient Trial Plates (London 1962), 43.

53. English Mint Docs., p. 68.

54. The Course of the Exchequer, p. 39.

55. D. F. Allen A Catalogue of English Coins in the British Museum: The Cross-and-Crosslets ("Tealby") Type of Henry II (London 1951), p. xlii.

56. Occasionally the high fineness of crockards and pollards was admitted by the royal authorities, but only when they wished to pay royal debts with them. See Prestwich above, p. 55 note 29.

57. Sir John Craig The Mint (Cambridge 1953), p. 55.

58. M. Mate, op. cit., 66.

59. For confirmation that crockards and pollards were taken at the mint by weight see C. G. Crump and C. Johnson "Tables of Bullion Coined under Edward I, II, III" NC 4th ser. XIII (1913), 201, Liber Quotidianus Contrarotulatoris Garderobae Anno Regni Regis Edwardi Primi Vicesimo Octavo (London, Society of Antiquaries 1787), and M. Prestwich, op. cit., 412.

60. CCR 1296-1302, 347.

61. Liber Quotidianus, 5.

62. Ibid., 52-3.

63.1 Ibid., 60.

64. Ibid., 67-8.

65. Ibid., 57.

66. M. Mate, op.cit., 69.

67. See F. Schweitzer "Analysis of Ancient Coins using a Point Source X-ray Spectrometer: A Critical Review" in Methods of Chemical and Metallurgical Investigation of Ancient Coinage, 153.

68. References to Chautard op.cit. This work is by no means comprehensive and variants are listed under the Chautard type which they most resemble.

69. Syll = D. M. Metcalf Syllage of Coins of the British Isles 12: Ashmolean Museum Part II English Coins 1066-1279.

EVIDENCE ON THE POSSESSION OF "TREASURE" FROM THE LAY SUBSIDY ROLLS

J. F. Hadwin

During the course of the August 1976 Colloquium Dr. Michael Metcalf asserted that England came to be "awash with silver" in the thirteenth century.[1] On the hypothesis of a generally favourable trade balance[2] and on the evidence of the Mint records[3] and of prices[4] such a verdict may seem quite justified. Much imported silver obviously remained - if in reminted form - in the money supply while some may have been turned into plate. As for coin, even on the assumptions of a high "wastage rate"[5] and a high population,[6] the average *per capita* holding of currency for the first year of the fourteenth century would have been as high as about two shillings,[7] rising perhaps to three shillings by 1310 before dropping to two shillings or under in the 1340s. Two shillings might represent the wages of an unskilled man for about a fortnight; by a curious coincidence present figures of *per capita* currency in circulation are also roughly equivalent to two weeks' average earnings.[8]

It is one thing to calculate such averages, however, and quite another to prove a wide dispersion of the possession or use of plate or money. No doubt much of the coin that we might regard as technically "in circulation" was in the hands of the better off, some of it tied up in hoards. Throughout the 1290s a great deal was on its way to and from the royal coffers, while in this decade some of it must be regarded as "lost" through export to pay for campaigning overseas.[9] Inventories of possessions at death, reports of thefts and similar evidence will tell us about the quantities of treature belonging to the rich and provide useful information on the forms in which silver or gold plate was held[10] but do nothing to indicate how wide a spectrum of the population ever owned such valuables. Manorial records sometimes provide us with clues,[11] but these are mainly in the form of monetary obligations and we cannot be certain about the pool of resources from which these might be met; full inventories of peasant possessions are rather rare. There is only one group of sources that might allow us to form a somewhat clearer picture of the social spread of the possession of precious metals - the detailed local rolls compiled for the lay subsidies on movables.[12]

Such subsidies were levied frequently from the late thirteenth century and until 1334 were based on new inventories compiled for every subsidy.[13] From 1334 a specified sum was levied on each township and its inhabitants were left to make their own arrangements as to how it might be raised, with very little governmental advice or restriction.[14] Until that date the chief taxers arranged for local sub-taxers to value the goods of their fellows and of this total a certain fraction was to be paid to the crown. Often the fraction was higher on Ancient Demesne and in boroughs and cities. Though the 1301 subsidy was to be paid on all types of movables every other levy exempted certain goods from assessment and also usually specified a taxable minimum below which a person should not be taxed. This limit often varied with the fraction required, in 1295 11/- being the limit below which no one was to be taxed for the eleventh and 7/- the limit for the seventh. There were also some customary exemptions of which we have no direct proof but which appear to have included food for household consumption, simple furniture and the smaller livestock.[15]

Precious metals do not often feature among the goods listed. "Treasure", which to the government but not to the assessors seems to have meant "money", was specifically exempted in 1294 and 1295 but equally specifically included in 1296 in the instructions for rural valuations.[16] After this time it was simply omitted from mention. We might expect several references to sums of money in the later local rolls but in fact there are very few in the tiny fraction surviving from the thousands of these documents that must have been compiled. It would in particular seem that cash had simply become one of the customary exemptions for rural districts. For the economic history of the period such a practice is most important, since lords who leased their demesne for money rents would thereby in practice be escaping from some of the obligations of taxation.[17] From this viewpoint the instructions of 1296 appear a despairing attempt to prevent such a convenient consequence; such evidence as we have suggests that the attempt was unsuccessful. The rural assessment rolls give the impression of being composed therefore in an economy innocent of actual contact with money.

The valuation of plate in rural areas brings us to further exemptions. The very earliest instructions tell assessors to ignore its possession - at least by the top social ranks.[18] From 1290 we get something more specific: for gentlemen and above jewels, clothing and vessels of gold, silver and brass were exempt, but not other articles of these metals.[19] Again, however, the reality seems different, for we find no mention in the rural records of silver or gold, either for gentlemen or for their social inferiors, though brass goods do appear. As in the case of food for domestic consumption it would seem that older rules were being tacitly applied.[20] Nevertheless one should not be too sweeping in what must be a verdict based on a "sample" of evidence that would satisfy no statistician, while both money and plate might be included in broad descriptions, for example such Buckinghamshire entries for 1332 as "Waltere le Barkere had in all 15/-". Nevertheless it must be concluded that the surviving rural rolls are of little assistance in our quest.

The frustrations met in a study of the urban rolls are somewhat different. In the first place there are fewer of them. No boroughs appear in the Yorkshire local rolls for 1297[21] nor the Buckinghamshire ones of 1332;[22] among printed rolls the only one containing a borough together with rural lists is that for 1297 in Bedfordshire, where the county town was of course paying the same fraction as its villages; however, the only definite items of precious metal are four silver spoons.[23] The urban lists for larger boroughs are much more informative. Unfortunately I know of only five such documents, two being for the same borough, though it is possible that some others may be reposing unnoticed in private or municipal archives.[24] These five, however, can yield a significant amount of information. Of them, four relate to years in which borough exemptions applied. These were drawn up in terms rather different from those for rural areas and from 1291 excluded only one cup, ring and clasp of precious metal for every taxpayer. Money was taxed except in Colchester in 1295 when the specific exemption of "treasure" for rural areas may have been interpreted by the taxers as covering towns as well. In that year the taxable minimum for boroughs stood at 7/-; in 1283, when the Ipswich rolls were compiled, it was 6/8d; for 1313, when we have the Shrewsbury return, it was 10/-, while for 1319, for which we have two brief rolls for York it was 6/8d again. In only one of these documents, therefore, are we fortunate enough to have a return that shows no taxable minimum, in theory or practice, and no specified exemptions - the Colchester assessment for 1301.[25] It is to this we must first turn, before looking at the more slender evidence from the other towns.

There are obvious dangers in using an analysis of a single return to indicate general social dispersion of the possession of money or plate; the commercial life of a borough might of course make it more familiar with both. Colchester paid in 1301 only just over 2% of its county's assessment and under a thousandth of the nation's total.[26] How typical might it have been and what trust may we place in its records?

The initial impressions given by the Colchester lists for 1301 are of considerable thoroughness. Clearly many of the instructions are being applied; no "taxable minimum" has been used and the lowest payment is a mere penny-farthing. Though there are no small animals and little furniture, the assessments of the value of agricultural stock are much closer to the price averages with which we are familiar than is usually the case. Items of precious metal abound and 59 taxpayers of the 389 are credited with possession of cash.

A comparison with the 1295 return for the same borough seems to confirm the reliability of that for 1301 - though this might be a dangerous conclusion since both of course might simply be revealing the same distortions. Both returns seem to cover an identical area, often a problem with taxation accounts; despite the failure of the 1301 return to mention the four associated hamlets of Miland, Grinsted, Westdonilaunde and Lexedene we find that names noted in these hamlets in 1295 nevertheless appear in the 1301 list sufficiently often to give us some confidence on this matter.[27] The 1301 return's 389 names contrast with only 243 on that for 1295 but a deduction from the 1301 list of all those valued at under 7/- (the 1295 taxable minimum) would leave a total of about 250. This was, of course, not the only point at which the exemptions of the assessment differed in the two years, but is a helpful guide. Naturally the 1301 valuation is considerably higher (£518 as against £310) but since the fraction required was less than a half of that asked in 1295 the apparent assessment for the earlier year was substantially more (c. £44-6-4$\frac{3}{4}$ as against a stated £34-12-7d).

Both assessments may seem to be rather low in comparison with what might be expected from a town of this size, and it is true that there is something very strange about Colchester's taxation valuations when these are contrasted with her 1377 taxpaying population.[28] Nevertheless the relatively

TABLE 1

Gold and Silver in Colchester, 1301

	Number	Total Value	Range of Values
Articles described as silver			
rings	4 (5)	1s-6d	2d to 6d
clasps	70 (73)	£2-10-0½d[31]	2½d to 2s (plus one at 4s)
cups	6	£1-1-8d	3s to 5s
spoons	36	£1-10-6d	8d to 1s-4d (most at 9d or 1s)

(additionally; 1 silver clasp and a silver ring jointly at 2s; two references to a silver clasp and a ring (no adjective) jointly at 1s 6d in each case)

	Number	Total Value	Range of Values
Articles described as gold			
rings	13	12s-0d	8d to 1s; most at 1s
clasp	1	3s-0d	- - -

	Number	Total Value	Range of Values
Articles possibly containing precious metals			
rings	9	6s-1d	3d to 1s
clasps	24	15s-3d	4d to 1s
cups	17	£1-8-8d	1s 2d to 2s

(additionally: a possible two rings - see above)

	Number	Total Value	Range of Values
Money			
Persons listed	59	£16-8-6½d	6d to 30s (6 above 10s; 26 under 3s)

Persons listed as possessing silver or gold articles:	84	
Persons possessing such articles and money:	21	
Persons possessing cash and no other silver/gold:	38	
Persons possessing silver or gold articles or money:	121	(= 31% of the taxpayers)
Additional persons with articles possibly of silver or gold:	25	
Total persons in last two groups:	147	(= 38% of the taxpayers)
Total persons taxed:	389	

low subsidy figures might be explained for these years by the incidence of other royal exactions. Essex was subject to twelve separate orders for purveyance within twelve years from 1296 to 1307 and nine during Edward II's reign;[29] during 1301 there were two, both stated to be met from the proceeds of the fifteenth, and preceding the date of its first payment. It is also possible that Colchester's textile industry, which features less in the assessment than one might have imagined, was one of the major sufferers from Flemish competition at this particular time.[30]

The value of the 1301 returns for evidence of the possession of plate is well illustrated by comparison with the 1295 Colchester assessment, where a mere seven of the 243 taxpayers were listed as possessing taxable silver or gold articles, yielding a total of only four silver cups (plus two of mazer) and twenty-four silver spoons. If one were to recalculate the 1301 assessments on the basis of the 1295 exemptions only twenty persons would appear as owning gold or silver goods (instead of 84) and sixteen of these would be listed merely on account of their silver spoons. The Ipswich, Shrewsbury and York assessments of course included money, so a recalculation of the 1301 Colchester figures on the basis of exemptions applying when each of these towns was taxed would show a larger number (of up to fifty in addition to the twenty who would have paid on their goods). The highest number who would appear as possessing either cash or articles of silver or gold, based on any of these exemption-limited years would thus be 70, compared with the actual 122 who definitely owned such goods.

The assessors clearly approached their task quite systematically, possibly after being instructed to look for certain classes of goods in a particular order, since all the early entries fit the same pattern. They first deal with any money;[32] then comes a group of valuables prefaced by "in thesauro:"[33] and occasionally we even find "in thesauro: nihil". As the listing progresses, however, there are a few signs of either individual or group carelessness. Some entries seem suspiciously similar. Items mentioning money - or clasps[34] - or mazer cups - often appear in "bunches": an unusually high proportion of entries on a page will include them and then comes a dearth for the next few columns. The same is true of patterned valuation: four of the eight entries for money that record sums that are not divisible by 6d are in the first dozen for people assessed on coin. The Ipswich references to money seem to follow a similar grouping, while one of the York parishes contains an inordinate number of silver spoons. Possibly the discovery of one item made the assessors more sensitive to its possible presence when they moved on to the next taxpayer; since the process of valuation must have taken some time it would not be inconceivable that they should sometimes forget to ask if certain property were held. Nevertheless it would be dangerous to hunt too long for "patterns" of valuation, especially as the groupings might merely represent the assessment of different streets inhabited chiefly by taxpayers of particular social classes. Overall, the impression of quite considerable thoroughness seems justified.

But how accurate might be the valuations of these articles? Since there are so few references to any form of "treasure" in other tax rolls it is hard to judge from these. If, however, there is any justification for an analogy with agricultural valuations then there could be room for some confidence. Rickword quotes Thorold Rogers on grain prices, showing his figures to be very similar to those listed in Colchester, while Willard's extensive list of places where the prices in Rogers were much higher than those of the tax valuations excludes this borough.[35] A comparison with the best current set of national prices for the late thirteenth and early fourteenth centuries suggests a high degree of reliability in the 1301 assessments,[36] while the considerable increase in the number of animals assessed in the Colchester returns for this year[37] again supports this conclusion.

One suspects that assessors often found non-agricultural goods hard to value,[38] and this may be a major reason for the apparent under-valuation of boroughs throughout the history of the lay subsidies, a feature that may also be connected with the higher fractions of their goods they were usually required to pay in taxes. Certainly some of the valuations of silver and gold articles in the Colchester return seem remarkably low; this could imply either that many of these goods contained only a small proportion of precious metal or that the valuations were being done on something like a "second-hand" basis. It is rather hard to believe that a wearable silver ring could contain as little as two pennyworth of silver of any high degree of fineness and harder, perhaps, to believe this of an 8d ring of gold.

With respect to money holdings, the figures are well below what we might have expected from the estimates of coin in circulation. Instead of something like two shillings for every man, woman and child, we get the following:

TABLE 2

Holdings of Coin

Average listed holding (59 persons)	6s $6\frac{3}{4}$d
Average holding of all taxpayers (389)	10d
Average holding per head of 1377 estimated population (4432 - Russell)	$\frac{3}{4}$ to 1d

Something seems seriously amiss here, but before an answer can be suggested it would seem best to examine the social dispersion of such holdings, and that of "treasure" in the broader sense. We must obviously be especially careful about the possessions of the poorest taxpayers, since such lists simply do not appear in any other urban records. In fact 33% (128) of Colchester's taxpayers owned property valued at less than 10/-, the most common minimum tax limit applied. Of these only 27 owned any property of the types listed above in Table 1. There we saw that 38% of all taxpayers were assessed on some item of "treasure"; for the poorest third the proportion is only 21%. Of the 27, two held both clasps and money, fourteen only clasps, ten only money, and one a mazer cup. If we drop the taxable minimum to 7/-, as in 1295, we should have only 15 fewer persons assessed on these valuables than were actually assessed in 1301, five having clasps alone, eight sums of money, one both, and Henry Vynch with his mazer cup again.

No rings, silver spoons, silver cups or any articles of gold were listed for anyone assessed at below 10/-, but too much should not be made of this fact since we reach the "poorest" owner of a silver ring at 11/- and a gold one at 13/2d, the same figure at which we find our first silver spoon. Only with silver cups do we have to wait until we reach the really substantial level of 53/7d before encountering one of these items.

Coin itself seems at first to be fairly evenly distributed among those taxed on "treasure", though 18% of all taxpayers assessed at above 10s and just under 10% of those assessed below this figure were listed as possessing any. Of the 146 persons classed as possibly holding some silver or gold we have seen that 59 (40%) held money. Of the 26 persons valued at under 10/- but with some such "valuables", twelve (46%) held money. Of the 33 (among the 146) with total assessments of over 50/- 13 had money (39%). At the upper end of this group, however, only one of the seven assessed at over £5 was credited with possessing coin; the richest of these holders of "treasure" was Henry Pakeman the tanner, assessed at £9-17-10d; he paid on table linen as well as on four silver spoons (he had paid on eleven in 1295) but was not assessed on money at all. This seems strange, but the evidence suggests that perhaps coin was assessed only if it were held in substantial quantities <u>or</u> if the taxpayer had little else. The second of these conclusions cannot be tested in the other towns but the first seems endorsed by the evidence of the Ipswich and Shrewsbury returns. In the former, nearly all the coin is held in multiples of half a mark or five shillings; in Shrewsbury the smallest sums are half a mark and the next a whole mark.

We cannot unfortunately go into the same degree of detail in analysing the returns from urban centres other than Colchester. In York the entries are too few and one of the parishes concerned seems to have been especially rich. In Ipswich, as in many of the rural rolls, one finds much use of portmanteau phrases such as "domestic utensils", "aliis bonis", "in omnibus" and grouped categories like "in pecunia et pannis", while rings and clasps may lurk behind the references to "jocalia" (jewels). The Shrewsbury return is more precise, but a combination of vagueness in some areas ("jocalia") with paucity of "treasure" entries limits its value for our purpose. The similarities between these last two assessments, separated by 200 miles and thirty years, are nevertheless considerable, and it may seem plausible to suggest that the other borough returns, now lost, probably approximated more to these than to the very meticulous compilation for Colchester in 1301; indeed the 1295 assessment for that borough itself perhaps resembles this distant pair more than its own records of six years later. Such analysis as seems relevant from the Ipswich and Shrewsbury returns appears in Table 3. The exemption limits were slightly different in the two years concerned; in 1283 (Ipswich) the phrase for the urban exemptions states that they should be, for "burgesses and merchants", those applied in the time of the king's ancestors - not an especially helpful instruction since different practices were common for different subsidies of Henry III; nevertheless a general 6/8d lower taxable

TABLE 3

"Treasure" in Ipswich and Shrewsbury

	Ipswich (1283)	Shrewsbury (1313)
Number of entries	276	189
Entries for all forms of "treasure" - including money	68 (25%)	25 (13%)
Entries for money	39 (14%)	10 (5%)
Entries for Cups	12	20
Entries for Spoons	4	9
Entries for Clasps	-	2
Entries for Jewels (Jocalia)	33	8

Notes to Table:

Entries: 19 of the Ipswich ones and 4 of those for Shrewsbury appear merely on account of the possession of "jocalia" in the "Entries for treasure" row.

Money: "in denariis" throughout the Shrewsbury return and occasionally in the Ipswich one; "in pecunia" usually in Ipswich. The Ipswich money total valuation is something over £71 but some entries are damaged and others link money with debts, cloth, jewels, etc. The Shrewsbury money total is £24-7-8d.

Cups: Almost all the Ipswich entries are "in cyffis" without specifying either quantity or material. The Shrewsbury ones are for seven silver and thirteen of mazer.

Spoons: As for cups, the Ipswich entries give no quantities, being simply "in cocklear' ". In Shrewsbury only one entry has this form and as most spoons there were valued at a shilling it seems reasonable to divide this assessment by that figure. This yields a total of 80 spoons.

Clasps: Both of silver.

Jewels: With wide-ranging valuations; many of the Ipswich entries link these with other goods.

No identifiable articles are said to be of gold in either return but that for Ipswich lists "silver and gold jewels" once and there is one reference there also to "in auro 10/-".

limit was strictly adhered to; in 1313 (Shrewsbury) the urban exemptions were those listed above (p 154) with a 10/- taxable minimum.

Ipswich and Shrewsbury both had far larger 1334 valuations than Colchester (Ipswich at £645, Shrewsbury at £800, Colchester at £261); on the other hand the 1377 poll tax shows Colchester well ahead, with 2,955 taxpayers as against Shrewsbury's 2,082 and the 1,507 of Ipswich.[39] Whether or not Shrewsbury and Ipswich deserve the high places they occupy in the estimates of wealth (1334) *per capita* (1377) there is no doubt that their burgesses were credited with greater holdings of "treasure" than those of Colchester, where the highest assessment for persons with such goods was under £10, and the largest sum of money mentioned 30/-. Ipswich contained eight men with more cash, the highest sum being the £20 of Rogel Blundel, whose total valuation was of £37-14s, while Hugo Golding, who had 20 marks of money and £3 worth of jewels was valued at £163.[40] Shrewsbury had three men who held 40/- "in denariis" and one with £6; all were assessed at £10 and over in all, while John of Ludlow, with £9 in coin, was the richest taxpayer with a valuation of £22-10s. In neither case, however, can we be sure that the rolls are complete. The Ipswich roll is damaged at the foot and entries are crowded into the left-hand side, leaving us unsure whether much of the damage occurred before completion, whether more taxpayers were noted in the missing area or whether this space was filled with the usual concluding total. The Shrewsbury roll simply comes to an end without the total - an unusual but not unique conclusion.[41] We cannot therefore be certain that the evidence we have covers all of the taxpayers of these towns. As for the poorest, the application of the tax minimum hides them from our observation, and even with the richer inhabitants the numbers paying on any clearly identifiable form of "treasure" are too few for much to be learnt from them, save perhaps that the *Colchester* record for 1301 is probably the fullest that can ever be used to try to answer questions about the social dispersion of holdings of "treasure" in this period.[42]

This search for clues from the Subsidy Rolls about the size and extent of holdings of plate and coin has not produced any startling results, but it could, perhaps, have dispelled some illusions. England may not quite have been "awash with silver" in the late thirteenth century, but she had enough to provide many of Colchester's poorer inhabitants with small articles of the metal and thus, in a sense, to keep a "reservoir" in readiness for the day when a straitened money supply might cause the Mint price to rise. There were bigger contributors to the stock of silver than Golda ate Helle, whose sixpenny clasp was a third of her wealth, but to it she, like many others, added rather more than her widow's mite.

NOTES

1. See D. M. Metcalf, above p. 6. The present study was compiled after the Colloquium in response to a number of requests that such a survey should be undertaken.

2. Assumed, possibly erroneously, by C. G. Crump and A. Hughes, "The English Currency under Edward I", *Economic Journal*, V, (1895). For short- and medium-term fluctuations see M. C. Prestwich, *War, Politics and Finance under Edward I* (1972), the same author's "Edward I's Monetary Policies and their Consequences", *EcHR*, 2nd series, XXII (1969), T. H. Lloyd, *The Movement of Wool Prices in Medieval England*, Economic History Review Supplement No. 6, (1973), pp. 14-18, and the papers by these scholars in the current collection.

3. C. E. Blunt and J. D. Brand, "Mint Output of Henry III", *BNJ*, XXXIX (1970), 61-6; C. G. Crump and C. Johnson, "Tables of Bullion coined under Edward I, II and III", *NC*, 4th series XIII (1913), 200-245. A summary of the latter appears in the Appendix to Sir J. Craig, *The Mint* (1953), p. 410 drawn from Crump and Johnson. For more recent detail see Mavis Mate, "Monetary Policies in England, 1272-1307", *BNJ*, XLI (1972), 34-79.

4. D. L. Farmer, "Some Grain Price Movements in Thirteenth-century England", *EcHR*, 2nd series, X (1957), 207-220, and "Some Livestock Price Movements in Thirteenth-century England", *ibid.*, 2nd series, XXII (1969), 1-16.

5. N. J. Mayhew, "Numismatic Evidence and Falling Prices in the Fourteenth Century", *ibid.*, 2nd series, XXVII (1974), 1-15, especially Fig. 1 on p. 9. Mr. Mayhew's estimates of currency give a little over £$\frac{1}{2}$M *c.* 1300 and *c.* £1M by 1310.

6. M. Postan, *Cambridge Economic History of Europe*, I, 2nd ed. (1966) pp. 561-2, suggests a little over 6M for the early years of the fourteenth century. That this may be too high is accepted by J. Z. Titow, *English Rural Society, 1200-1350* (1969), p. 71; it would imply a population density for the whole country as great as that estimated for the overcrowded Fenland villages by H. E. Hallam, *Settlement and Society: A Study of the Early Agrarian History of South Lincolnshire* (1965). The smallest estimate for early fourteenth century population is *c.* $3\frac{3}{4}$ M by J. C. Russell, *British Medieval Population* (1949), but this seems implausibly low. The lowest estimates of population and wastage rates for coin would suggest currency *per capita* was twice the figures cited in the text.

7. On the basis of the $1\frac{1}{2}$d to 2d a day averages in Beveridge's "Wages in the Winchester Manors", EcHR, VII (1936). J. Z. Titow has heavily criticized these calculations (op.cit. p. 46); his own preference is for a lower average of 1d to $1\frac{1}{2}$d (ibid. p. 47); the publication of further evidence from Dr. Titow is anticipated shortly, casting doubt on more of Beveridge's calculations. If Beveridge was in error it follows that the much-used wage indices compiled by Professor E. Phelps-Brown and Miss S. V. Hopkins must be treated with great care for this period.

8. Current figures from Central Statistical Office, Abstract of Statistics, annual (1975) and quarterly volumes. 1974 currency in circulation was almost exactly equivalent to a fortnight's average male manufacturing wage; in 1975 it was equal to about $1\frac{2}{3}$ weeks' wages. Needless to say, current total money supply today is much higher than the £100 per person (approx.) currency in circulation.

9. "A reasonable estimate would be that as a result of the war some £350,000 was exported from England in the period 1294-8"; Prestwich, "Edward I's Monetary Policies", loc.cit. 411.

10. For example, the detailed inventory cited by Brown (see note 21), pp. xx-xxiii, including silver candlesticks and saucers; a theft including 100 gold rings and 50 gold brooches (? firmacula), worth £20; CPR, 1292-1301, p. 547 (March 1301).

11. M. Postan and J. Z. Titow, "Heriots and Prices on Winchester Manors", EcHR, 2nd series, XI (1959), 392-417, argued that an increasing proportion of money heriots among total heriots betokened decreasing living standards because only tenants without heriot animals paid money heriots. Though with much manorial evidence we cannot be certain that the statement of a debt in money terms implies its intended settlement in cash, the phrases in pecunia, in argento, and in denariis are used often enough in manorial documents to suggest that less explicit references to money probably also often mean coin.

12. Only the "local" rolls, which give details of the property valued, are of assistance in the present quest; these were not normally sent to the Exchequer. Names of all taxpayers and their total assessments were recorded on "County" rolls, but even these were not kept at the Exchequer regularly until after 1323. For a thorough examination of most matters concerned with this subject see J. F. Willard, Parliamentary Taxes on Personal Property, 1290 to 1334, (1934).

13. From Edward I's accession the subsidies levied were as follows (where two fractions are listed, the former applied to the "rural" areas, the latter to boroughs and Ancient Demesne):

1275	1/15th	1297	1/9th
1283	1/30th	1301	1/15th
1290	1/15th	1306	1/30th & 1/20th
1294	1/10th & 1/6th	1307	1/20th & 1/15th
1295	1/11th & 1/7th	1309	1/25th
1296	1/12th & 1/8th	1313	1/20th & 1/15th

1315	1/20th & 1/15th	1322	1/10th & 1/6th
1316	1/16th & 1/15th	1327	1/20th
1319	1/18th & 1/12th	1332	1/15th & 1/10th
		1334	1/15th & 1/10th (nominal)

The sums assessed are listed on a county basis from the Pipe Rolls and later from the Enrolled Accounts by J. F. Willard in EHR vols. 28 (1913), 29 (1914), and 30 (1915) for the reigns of Edward I, II and III respectively. Willard omitted the 1309 and 1319 figures because they had already been published by Sir James Ramsay, in ibid., 24 (1909). Unfortunately Ramsay's 1319 list contains several errors of transcription; a corrected table for this year should shortly be published.

14. The arrangements in 1334 are described in an excellent introduction and editorial notes by R. E. Glasscock, The Lay Subsidy of 1334 (1975).

15. On exemptions see Willard, Parliamentary Taxes, chapters 4, 5 and 6. The clergy were always exempt from parliamentary taxation on their spiritualities and from 1307 regularly exempt from payment on temporalities acquired before 1291. Taxes on these possessions henceforth could be raised only by consent of Convocation, save that villeins on clerical estates paid normally as laymen. All clerical temporalities were assessed in the lay subsidy of 1290 but in 1294 the clergy and their villeins were exempt because of the high sums voted in Convocation; this remained the position in 1295 but the 1297 arrangements were similar to those outlined above for 1307 and after. In 1301 all temporalities were again assessed and the assessors clearly followed this instruction. In 1306 a more ambiguous order was eventually interpreted in the same spirit.

16. In 1294 and 1295 the exempting clause for rural taxpayers read "treasure, armour, riding horses, jewels and clothing of knights, gentlemen and their wives, and their vessels of gold, silver and brass," implying, presumably, that "treasure" excluded plate. The 1301 Colchester return, however, prefaces most of its entries for coin with "in pecunia num'ata"; separately, afterwards, comes "in thesauro:" followed by references to cups, rings and clasps, thus clearly implying a different meaning for the term. It is possible that tax-assessors themselves were unclear but "in thesauro" surely cannot mean "in the treasure chest", as it was taken by S. Dowell, History of Taxation and Taxes, I (1884) p. 254, since it is used of even the poorest. On this point see Willard, Parliamentary Taxes, pp. 77-81; the instructions to chief taxers from 1275 are printed in Sir F. Palgrave, Parliamentary Writs, I (1827).

17. In his most valuable study of the burden of taxation on the lower classes J. R. Maddicott, The English Peasantry & the Demands of the Crown, 1294-1341, Past and Present, Supplement no. 1 (1975), p. 7, slightly exaggerates the lords' position. They were not assessed merely on the produce of their demesne manors but should have paid on their rental income, be it in money or kind, according to what they had in hand on

the "named day" of the assessment (usually Michaelmas). Chief taxers were often reminded from 1307 that rents should not escape taxation (Willard, Parliamentary Taxes, p. 78); such reminders were omitted after 1319 but thanks to the errors of the Surrey sub-taxers in 1332, who valued villein property without allowing for rent, we know that the rules remained unchanged. Nevertheless Dr. Maddicott is almost certainly correct when he states that "all those whose livelihoods came primarily from rents escaped lightly" (loc.cit). Professor Miller reaches the same conclusion on the basis of the surviving assessments, and the county rolls reinforce the lessons to be learnt from the local ones. A "preference for rents", however dangerous it might be in view of these instructions, would therefore seem justified by their lack of implementation: E. Miller, "War, Taxation and the English Economy in the late Thirteenth and early Fourteenth centuries" in J. M. Winter (ed.) War and Economic Development (1975), p. 16. (I am most grateful to Dr. A. R. Bridbury for pointing out to me these inconsistencies.)

18. The exempting clause in 1237 began "exceptis argento et auro ...."; W. Stubbs, Select Charters to 1307, 9th ed. (1909) p. 358.

19. Willard, Parliamentary Taxes, p. 78.

20. Ibid., pp. 84-5.

21. W. Brown (ed.) "Yorkshire Lay Subsidy: Being a Ninth Collected in the Reign of Edward I (1297)" in Yorkshire Archaeological Society, Record Series, XVI (1894).

22. A. C. Chibnall, "Early Taxation Returns: Taxation of Personal Property in 1332 and later", Buckinghamshire Record Society 14 (1966). Despite its title this volume also transcribes the surviving 1327 rolls for this county.

23. A. T. Gaydon, "The Taxation of 1297", Bedfordshire Historical Record Society, 39, (1959). The four spoons belonged to one man, John Cubler.

24. Three are printed, those relating to Colchester in 1295 and 1301, in Rotuli Parliamentorum I, pp. 228-238 and 243-265. The others are as follows:

- Ipswich (1283) Public Record Office E179/242/40 and 242/42. These are the earliest urban lists and the second longest. The neglect of them is quite extraordinary since they were printed long ago by Edgar Powell; Proceedings of the Suffolk Institute of Archaeology and Natural History, XII (1906), pp. 137-157. These records (which may be incomplete) give details for 276 persons. The (incomplete) total valuation is well over £1,800.

Shrewsbury (1313). This roll is still in its place of origin, in the Salop County Record Office (SBR/156), and is mostly quite legible. H. Owen and J. B. Blakeway, A History of Shrewsbury (1825), cite some entries from it (pp. 152-4) and mention that it contains 189 persons assessed at a total of £398-1-2d, paying £26-1-8 3/4d to the fifteenth. The sum seems rather low and the roll may be incomplete, as the borough itself paid £28-15-9d (on 131 taxpayers) to the twentieth in 1327, implying taxable wealth of over £591, and £80 to the tenth of 1334, suggesting a doubling of its assessable movables since 1313; nevertheless the 1313 roll may well be complete. Comparisons of the taxpaying population support this, while the modest sum paid by the whole country at the higher rate in this year (£41) suggests that if any part is missing it probably contains few people and those not particularly rich. W. G. D. Fletcher, The Shropshire Lay Subsidy Roll of 1327 (1907) and Glasscock, op.cit. p. 257. (I must record my gratitude to Mrs. M. Halford, Salop County Archivist, for swiftly providing a photocopy of the 1313 roll and for elucidating some of its less clear passages.)

York (1319). Lists for three parishes survive. P.R.O. E179/242/75 contains a membrane with 18 names for the parish of St. Martin in Sonning Street. The early entries are clear but the later ones are indecipherable. E179/242/95 purports to cover the parishes of St. Helen's, Stonegate and St. Wilfrid but only the first and last are named in the text. 25 persons are listed in St. Helen's, assessed at £30-9-6d and 19 in St. Wilfrid's, at £4-9-7d. Though several of the York entries are very detailed (Willard quotes some from the latter document in Parliamentary Taxes, p. 76) a number are simply valued "in bonis" or "in omnibus bonis". The more decipherable of these 62 entries nevertheless show articles of precious metal, nearly all the legible ones on the first document mentioning silver spoons. Since York's population was probably over twice that of Colchester and as the city paid £171 to the Twelfth of 1319 compared with Colchester's £35 to the fifteenth of 1301 it is clear that these two documents might represent only a small proportion of the city's taxpayers. [Two rolls also exist for the borough of Bridport in 1319 and 1322, listing 67 and 80 persons respectively. Neither includes any coin or identifiably silver or golden articles and the details appear more "rural" than "urban". The richest burgess in the former year was valued at only £4-8s and in 1322 the largest taxpayers have no specific goods listed against their names; Historical Manuscripts Commission, sixth Report (1877), pp. 491-2.]

25. Rot. Parl. pp. 243-65. This year should have produced evidence of rural "treasure" as well but none of the five surviving local rolls - four of them for Kent - reveals any; P.R.O. E179/123/4, 5, 6 and 9. The roll for Shillington (Beds.) is printed as an Appendix in Gaydon, op.cit.

26. Calculated from Willard's tables (see above, note 13). Using the printed returns for Colchester in 1295 and 1301, extracting Colchester's payment from the enrolled accounts for 1315 (P.R.O. E359/14, where Colchester was the only place in Essex paying the higher fraction) and the figures printed by Glasscock (op.cit. p. 88) we get the following:

	Colchester		Essex	
	Assessment	Valuation	Assessment	Valuation
1295	£44-6-4$\frac{3}{4}$d (?)	£310	£1918	£20998
1301	£34-12-7d	£518	£1604	£24060
1315	£30-2-3$\frac{3}{4}$d	£452	£1340	£26650
1334	£26-2-9d	£261	£1235	£18277

	Ratios	
	Assessments	Valuations
1295	2.3%	1.48%
1301	2.16%	2.15%
1315	2.25%	1.7%
1334	2.12%	1.43%

(The greater stability of payments as opposed to valuations is common to other areas under investigation.) The 1295 assessment is much higher than the sum shown to be paid by Essex to the seventh of 1295, which is just over £25. The difference probably results from the cancellation of payments from some of those named, notably the clergy (see above, note 15). It is most unfortunate that the originals of the two Colchester documents are now missing; Rickword believed they had been extracted soon after publication (see next note).

27. Notes by George Rickword in Transactions of the Essex Archaeological Society, New Series, IX (1903) pp. 126-154. Neglect of this helpful analysis of the Colchester rolls seems attested by the fact that the relevant pages in the London University Library copy were still found uncut. Several of the calculations that follow derive from this work.

28. Colchester's poll tax-payers in 1377 numbered 2,955; from this total J. Cox Russell deduced a population of 4,432 (op.cit. p. 143). Either figure represents 5.8% of the comparable figures for the county of Essex (ibid. p. 132); this contrasts very sharply with the ratios shown above in note 26 for taxation. Colchester occupies tenth place in the 1377 borough population list given by Russell; it held a place in the top nine of Russell's 1086 valuation list and equal eleventh in its number of burgesses reported at that date (ibid. p. 48). In his own more cautious estimates of 1086 population Professor Darby places Colchester among the top sixteen; in H. C. Darby (ed.) A New Historical Geography of England (1973) p. 71. When we move to the next general taxation figures, those for the aids given to Henry II, however, Colchester has dropped to 27th place in a list that excludes London; R. A. Donkin in ibid. p. 134. It does not even merit a position in Dr. Glasscock's table of the 37 most highly valued towns for 1334 (ibid. p. 184) and even if we take town payments and not valuations as our criterion Colchester could not lie higher than 30th. In the new 1524-5 subsidies, however, Colchester was back in tenth place again; J. Sheail, The Regional Distribution of Wealth in England as indicated in the Lay Subsidy Returns of 1524-5, University of London Ph. D. thesis

(1968) p. 119. Part of the answer to the contrasting medieval taxation and population figures may lie in the castle, since Willard mentioned that he had been unable to find any instances of property being assessed to the lay subsidy in a castle (Parliamentary Taxes, p. 80 n. 3). Calculations of wealth (1334) *per capita* (1377) suggest however that most boroughs may have been undervalued compared with rural areas, though their average payments were roughly similar; nevertheless, even in such a list, Colchester occupies 37th place with a valuation *per capita* of only a third of the borough mean. (I hope shortly to complete an extended study of this problem.)

29. Prestwich, War, Politics and Finance, pp. 153-4 and Maddicott, *op. cit.* p. 17. Essex shares first place with Lincolnshire for the incidence of purveyance 1294-1327. The 1295 subsidy, following three years of bad harvests (Farmer, "Some Grain Prices", p. 212) also coincided with the levying of the *maltote* on wool.

30. E. Miller, "The Fortunes of the English Textile Industry in the Thirteenth Century", EcHR, 2nd series, XVIII (1965) pp. 64-82. Wool and cloth are found much more commonly in the Ipswich and Shrewsbury assessments.

31. There are three entries for silver clasps where the valuation ends in a fraction (two at 2½d; 1 at 3½d). The only other valuations in fractions are 11½d in coin and a handful of entries for bushels of grain where the valuation per quarter was given in whole pence.

32. The phrase used here in the printed record for introducing coin is "in pec(unia) numata", with a tilde over the "m". Dowell (*op.cit.* p. 254) took this to mean that the full word was "nummata" (i.e. minted), as would probably be the case if the original had this appearance. Unfortunately, the conventions that applied to the printing of some works in "Record Type" meant that almost any MS abbreviation mark coming other than at the end of a word was liable to be thus represented and we cannot be sure that the original was not "numerata" - which would lead the phrase merely to mean "ready money". Twice, indeed, the text actually has "numerata" in full after "pecunia". Powell took the ab-abbreviation to be of "numerata" in his transcription of the Ipswich return (see below). If Dowell was right, however, it is just possible that special attention was being drawn to distinctions within the general class of "money". Two of the Colchester entries in fact have merely an unqualified "pecunia"; both refer to small sums (12d and 6d); this might just possibly be an implicit acceptance as "money" of what other writers have taken to be counters or tokens. This may be going too far, but a further point of interest concerns the four entries "in pecunia (num'ata) pro(or ad) mercand' ". The amounts concerned are moderate (all 5/- to 7/-) but among the owners we find "John Hust, nauta". Could the additional words imply foreign coin? More interesting still is Robert Lyndraper's "in *argento* ad mercand' " - but here speculation must end. It is of course possible that these unusual entries are merely the result of haste or carelessness by the sub-taxers;

certainly their position in the text gives no ground for suspicion but it would be most helpful to have the originals to check for such matters as possible changes of hand. Only the first entry for coin in Ipswich has the "num'ata"; the Shrewsbury references to coin are all "in denariis".

33. Often the only article listed after "in thesauro" is not specifically stated to be of precious metal, e.g. "Edmund Tinctor: in thesauro 1 firmacul', 4d". The inclusion of cups of mazer (usually maple-wood) in this category may be explicable by the fact that such vessels were often silver-mounted.

34. "Firmacula" are translated in some texts as "brooches" (as in *CPR*) and in others as "buckles" (as by Willard). The Latin, like its French counterpart, has a more comprehensive meaning for almost any ornamental fastening, however, and might more exactly be rendered by the term "clasp". Bronze examples of the sorts of item involved are listed and illustrated in the *Medieval Catalogue of the London Museum* (H.M.S.O.)(reprinted 1967) pp. 264-79. It must be presumed that such items in silver would only rarely be lost and never thrown away.

35. Rickword, *op.cit.*; Willard, *Parliamentary Taxes*, pp. 140-1. Both take their prices from J. E. Thorold Rogers, *History of Agriculture and Prices*, I (1866). Little difference is made if one takes the prices given by Dr. Farmer who, nevertheless, is quite rightly critical of Rogers's methods ("Some Grain Price Movements", p. 207). Willard also commented upon the "surprising" fall in the number of taxpayers assessed in several counties (*Parl. Taxes* pp. 178-9), a feature that became more pronounced by 1332.

36. One must of course use great care when comparing prices derived from one group of areas with those used in valuations of others; nevertheless the results are of interest. Wheat was valued at Colchester (in the 1295-6 winter, when the assessments were made) at 6/8d a quarter, rye at 5/-, barley 4/- and oats 2/-. Dr. Farmer's 1295 sale prices are nearly 50% higher overall at 9/2¾d, 6/9¾d, 6/3d and 3/0½d respectively ("Some Grain Price Movements", p. 212). The 1301 Colchester valuations were 4/-, 3/-, 3/- and 1/8d for the same grains on average; here Farmer's prices are only some 20% higher, being 4/10¾d, 3/9½d, 3/4¾d and 1/10¾d respectively. (The Kentish valuations were broadly similar to those of Colchester; see references cited in note 20, above). Comparisons of animal valuations are more difficult because of the greater variation in terms used to describe livestock in manorial documents compared with the narrower vocabulary of the taxers. Here, however, oxen, valued at 6/8d in 1295 (Farmer's sales price 10/-) appear in 1301 at 10/- (when Farmer's sale price reached only 9/4½d). Cows were 5/- in the valuations of both years while Farmer's sale price rose slightly (6/7¾d to 7/0¼d). Sheep, on the other hand, where Farmer's prices are virtually unchanged (muttons at 1/1¼d in 1295 and 1/1½d in 1301) rose in valuation from 8d to 1/-. (Farmer, "Some Livestock Price Movements", p. 5.)

The reason for the increase in the ratio between valuation prices and Farmer's could be the events that occurred between the grant of the 1301 subsidy in January and its collection, which did not begin until nearly a year later. In between we have two orders for purveyance affecting Essex, one on March 1st, involving 500 quarters of wheat, 500 of oats and 200 of malt (CPR, 1292-1301, p. 578), and the other on October 13th, for 600 quarters of wheat, 500 of barley and malt and 1,000 of oats (ibid., pp. 608-9). Both were ordered to be paid for from the proceeds of the subsidy; one feels therefore that the appointment of Walter de Cloun in November to expedite the collection of the tax in Essex was not entirely unwelcome (ibid. 1301-7, p. 7). Nevertheless the first instalment of the Essex payment was not due until shortly before Christmas and the remaining two instalments were to be paid just after Easter and Midsummer 1302 (ibid. 1292-1301 p. 613). Meanwhile a substantial group of crown creditors in Essex would be impatiently awaiting the subsidy; in such circumstances it might be hard to justify for tax purposes a valuation lower than the purveyance price negotiated. The similarity of the Kentish and Colchester valuations is not fatal to this explanation since the four Kentish rolls are from the North of the country. (On the problems of purveyance and its burden see Maddicott, op.cit. pp. 25-34).

37. Rickword, loc.cit. Because of the lack of a lower taxable limit one might expect a rise in the totals of livestock. This seems confirmed since the total of animals increases from 761 to 1,861, while 269 of the 389 persons assessed are credited with the possession of at least one beast. The greatest rise is for sheep which appear in 1295 as 305 animals owned by 22 persons; in 1301 the total is 1,129 owned by 133. On a priori grounds one might expect a rise in grain totals also, especially after the excellent 1301 harvest; in fact there is a fall of 8%, while the number of entries mentioning such holdings increases only from 178 to 191. This is not the place to speculate on possible reasons for such a phenomenon but purveyance might well be among the solutions.

38. Where we have records for substantial settlements that were not taxation boroughs, as in the West Riding and Bedfordshire returns for 1297 or the Buckinghamshire ones for 1332 we find brief notes of trade or industrial possessions under such phrases as "in merchandise", "in utensils", "in utensils for tanning", etc. This habit has also been noted above for some of the borough lists. If one takes lack of detailed description as indicative of the assessor's ignorance (or indifference) then it seems likely that valuations of such goods would often be almost "self-assessed", and only the jealousy of competitors might act as a check on this practice. A "fair" valuation might also in such circumstances have been the second-hand value of the property - in some cases virtually a scrap value. This may help to explain some of the generally "low" urban valuations mentioned above in note 28. This suggests similarities with which modern valuation practice is to assess "stock" at cost or market value, whichever is the lower. (I am most grateful to Mr. J. D. Brand for clarifying some of these comparisons with current practice.)

39. Glasscock, op.cit., pp. 88, 257 and 294; Russell, op.cit., p. 142.

40. In Ipswich and Shrewsbury debts owed to the taxpayer were included in his property and thus accounted taxable. I know of no other instances of this practice in surviving local rolls for these subsidies but it parallels the procedure used for assessing villein rents (see note 17). The Tudor subsidies certainly treated debts as taxable; R. S. Schofield, "Parliamentary Lay Taxation, 1485-1547", unpublished Cambridge Ph. D. thesis, 1963.

41. The 1327 Shrewsbury subsidy has its concluding total only after the listing of the associated separately taxed liberties and these are missing in 1313 (see note 24). In some County rolls concluding totals are omitted altogether as in the townships of the Hundred of Farnham (Surrey) in 1332.

42. There is also the problem of the coins used in payment of the taxation. The instructions for a subsidy that was actually raised only once expand on the matter - and then it is somewhat ambiguously. This is in the orders for the levying of the ninth of 1297, of which the relevant passage runs "E que les cheifs Taxours preignent la monee le Roy par counte sanz peisser tiele come court en Roiaume", borrowed almost exactly from the instructions for the abortive eighth and fifth of the same year (Rot. Parl. I pp. 239 and 241; also in Parliamentary Writs, I, pp. 62-3). The sentence is translated by J. A. C. Vincent as "The chief taxers shall take the king's money as current in the realm by tale and not by weight"; (Lancashire Lay Subsidies, I, (1893), p. 314). This is unexceptionable; "tiele" must refer to the feminine "monee" and not to the verb preceding it. But why are the final five words there at all? They seem to be perhaps an afterthought, reinforcing the instruction to take the money "par counte"; the earlier orders for the eighth and fifth, however, had "priser" and not "peisser" - the more general "valuing" rather than specifically "weighing". This may have been an error, of course, but the whole passage seems somewhat ambiguous and could just possibly in either form mean that any money, including "pollards" and "crockards", would do. Since the previous subsidies of the 1290s had each shown a declining yield the phrase, never found elsewhere, may have been a sign of desperation. (I am very grateful to Dr. M. C. Prestwich for drawing my attention to this passage, and to my wife, Mrs. M. Hadwin, for her assistance with the elucidation of its possible shades of meaning.) It is possible that the two versions of this passage derive from Chancery clerks' separate attempts to make sense of the Exchequer original (E159/70 m.117), where the key verb appears to have been written "paisier". "Peser" rather than "priser" would seem nearer to what was presumably intended.

WASTAGE FROM CURRENCY: LONG-CROSS AND THE RECOINAGE OF 1279

Marion M. Archibald

In recent studies of the price changes in the later Middle Ages there has been an increasing appreciation of the evidence which numismatic sources can provide. The interpretation of this evidence however is not always so straight-forward as it may appear nor are the results obtained from it capable of the precision sometimes assigned to them. The object of this paper is to consider the evidence for the total amount of the English Long-Cross issue lost to currency before it was superseded by the sterling type after 1279 and in so doing to discuss some of the difficulties encountered in using this sort of numismatic evidence.

Since the official records of the bullion struck into coin at the London and Canterbury mints are complete for both the Long-Cross issue and for the sterling period under review[1] it might seem a matter of simple subtraction to arrive at a precise figure, for these two pre-eminent mints at least, for the total amount of lost Long-Cross coins thus:[2]

Total output of London and Canterbury in Long-Cross	£1 378 000
Total 'English' silver recoined at London and Canterbury 1279-1290	£ 428 874
∴ Total amount of London and Canterbury Long-Cross lost	£ 949 126

Disregarding for the moment the assumptions involved in the choice of 1290 as the date at which the recoinage ceased at both mints and in regarding all bullion designated as 'English' in the mint records as deriving exclusively from obsolete English Long-Cross coins, this subtraction is valid only if the recoinage figure to 1290 represents, in volume if not in name, all the coins struck at London and Canterbury during the Long-Cross period which had survived in England to 1279. In fact it does not for, as will be shown, by the end of the Long-Cross coinage almost five out of every six coins issued had been struck at London or Canterbury whereas only somewhat fewer than two out of every three of them were recoined there. In other words although a considerable number of Long-Cross coins struck at the provincial mints[3] were recoined at London and Canterbury, a far greater number of London and Canterbury Long-Cross coins were recoined at the provincial mints. In this respect therefore the figure of £949 126 over-represents the amount of Long-Cross coins struck at London and Canterbury lost to currency by 1279. It also means that despite the limitations of the statistical methods available, it is necessary to base the calculation of the Long-Cross coins lost on the total output for the Long-Cross coinage as a whole and the amount of the recoinage issues at all mints.

Mint records comparable to those for London and Canterbury are lacking for the provincial mints but it is possible to estimate their combined production by noting the proportion of provincial coins to those of London and Canterbury in hoards and then by using the known output of the latter to calculate the former. To obtain completely reliable results the hoards would require to be plentiful, large, self-evidently homogeneous and buried at a suitable date. These ideal conditions are never fulfilled and so it is most important, before using hoard statistics, to consider the distortions which may be present and, if it is not possible to quantify them exactly, to form some idea of their scale and the likely extent of their influence on the final result. There are sufficient Long-Cross hoards extant to show that the currency at this time was in broad general terms consistent throughout the country but on present evidence it is not possible to say how rapidly new coins from distant mints established themselves in sufficient numbers to conform, if ever, to a theoretical 'norm'. (The difficulty of quantifying this and other aspects of the 'velocity of circulation' would seem to limit the usefulness of the formulae in which it is incorporated.) Local conditions and circumstances peculiar to the original owner or to the source of his coins which there is little hope of assessing - also influence the content of hoards. For such reasons hoards may end 'weakly' that is with an abnormally low number of the latest issues present or 'strongly' that is with an abnormally high number of the latest issues present.[4] In the case of a Long-Cross hoard of the post-recoinage phase, a 'weak' ending would mean that the provincial mints would be over-represented in the coinage as a whole and a 'strong' one that they would be under-represented.

Another distorting factor is local bias in the form of a higher than normal presence of coins struck at the nearest functioning mint or mints. This is likely to affect to the greatest extent the most recent issues present and so it is often better to exclude the latest classes in a hoard and to base any calculations on its earlier portion. However a hidden 'savings' element which includes a large number of earlier coins abstracted from currency when a long-closed local mint was still in operation can, if it goes undetected, mislead even more disastrously.[5] This bias need not even be local to the find-spot since groups of coins could pass from hand to hand virtually intact and a hoard from, say, Bristol could have within it an element in which London is over-represented because somewhere along the line a payment was made by a London merchant who had access to larger than normal quantities of coins from his local mint. When a sufficient number of suitably large hoards from a particular period are known it is often possible to recognize the various sorts of bias but in less favourable circumstances it is not always clear which of those distorting factors, or combinations of them, are involved especially if only one or two hoards are available. How these problems affect the particular Long-Cross hoards which must be used in calculating the total output will be discussed in detail later.

It is also necessary to consider the question of wastage from the currency and whether it is likely to have fallen evenly across the entire coinage. London, closely followed by Canterbury and Bury got off to a prompt start at the beginning of the Long-Cross coinage and had produced many thousands of pounds worth of coin before all the other mints were under way a year later. Theoretically therefore the early issues of London and Canterbury had had a longer time in circulation in which to be subject to wastage than the bulk of the products of the provincial recoinage mints. It is also possible that the disappearance of coins could have been a particularly significant factor at the start of a recoinage if hoards of obsolete coin were unearthed for conversion into new coin and immediate reburial. Unfortunately there is little evidence on which to base an assessment of these matters, but as the output of London and Canterbury during this phase was small when considered as part of their total production during the whole Long-Cross period the effect of any bias of this sort on the overall figures is likely to be negligible. Another possibility is that the newly-struck coins of London and Canterbury may have been more vulnerable to immediate export than the issues of the provincial mints. The latter were opened essentially for the purpose of recoining the local currency and closed when this had been completed. London and Canterbury on the other hand maintained their production at a high level in the post-recoinage phase. Although the mint records do not, as in the post-1279 period, distinguish the bullion coming to the mint from 'English' and 'foreign' sources, it is clear that the high output can have been kept up in the Long-Cross as in the sterling period only by the striking of large quantities of foreign silver. The very fact that regulations existed forbidding the export of English coin showed that it was attempted on a scale which worried the authorities. The evidence is again not conclusive but the Slype hoard from West Flanders comprizes the usual mixture of mints and types current in England and the Brussels hoard[6] although it has never been fully studied appears to contain a similar typical range of English coins. At least there is no evidence to demonstrate a clear London and Canterbury bias in Continental finds. It will therefore be assumed that the incidence of wastage fell on the products of the two groups of mints in direct proportion to their output and may therefore be disregarded in the calculation of the total Long-Cross output. If the bias were in fact significant the effect would be to decrease the size of the Long-Cross issue as a whole and so the amount lost before 1279. Unless it were much greater than there is reason to believe however the sum involved would be only a few thousand pounds.

There are in fact six Long-Cross hoards whose contents have been published in sufficient detail and which are of statistically viable size for the present purpose. They are set out in Table 1. Unfortunately most of these six hoards were deposited about the middle of the Long-Cross period and all of them by c. 1270 at the latest, some eight years before the end of the issue. This is a serious drawback since the relative output of the two groups of mints was not consistent throughout the coinage. It began with the recoinage of the previous Short-Cross coins from 1247-50 and during this three-year period the total national output was shared about equally between London and Canterbury on the one hand and the provincial mints on the other. The provincial mints then closed with the exception of the ecclesiastical privilege mints of Bury and Durham which maintained a fairly exiguous existence thereafter.[7] The London and Canterbury mints remained open for a further twenty-eight years and, as the bullion figures demonstrate, maintained their output at a high level until nearly the end of the coinage.[8] The closer to the end of the period therefore, the higher the proportion of the currency composed of coins struck at London and Canterbury. The share of these two mints is

TABLE 1

Hoard	Date of discovery	Date of deposition	Number of English coins	Reference
Colchester (Essex)	1969	1256	11 297	Unpublished. Details in British Museum.
Hornchurch (Essex)	1938	1260 +	408	*BNJ* XXIII (1940), 274-9.
Palmer's Green (London)	1911	1262 +	208	*NC* 1912, 70-97.
Slype (Belgium)	1914	*c.* 1265	1 312	*NC* 1914, 256-9.
Steppingly (Beds.)	1912	*c.* 1270	333	*NC* 1914, 60-76.
Coventry (Warks.)	1958	*c.* 1270	225	NC 1958, 109-22.

TABLE 2

COINS OF LONG-CROSS CLASSES I-III IN HOARDS DEPOSITED 1256-*c.* 1270

Hoard	Date of deposition	London and Canterbury		Provincial mints	
Colchester	1256	3068	52.6%	2767	47.4%
Hornchurch	1260 +	81	49.7%	82	50.3%
Palmer's Green	1262 +	28	60.9%	18	39.1%
Slype	*c.* 1265	260	49.3%	267	50.7%
Steppingley	*c.* 1270	59	49.6%	60	50.4%
Coventry	*c.* 1270	31	64.6%	17	35.4%
		52.3%	54.4%	47.7%	45.6%

further increased by the wastage of earlier coins which, by affecting pari passu the equal numbers of coins struck at both groups of mints during the recoinage up to 1250, further proportionally reduces the survivors of the provincial issues. The percentages of coins from the two groups of mints present in the six hoards deposited between 1256 and 1270 cannot therefore be used as they stand to represent their true positions in the currency of 1270. In them, London and Canterbury are under-represented and any calculation based on their contents would serve to exaggerate the size of the Long-Cross coinage as a whole and consequently the amount lost by 1279.

These difficulties can in large measure be overcome by considering the hoard evidence in two chronological periods within each of which the currency pattern was relatively homogeneous: the first or recoinage phase from the beginning of the coinage in 1247 to the closure of the provincial mints in 1250 and the second or post-recoinage phase from 1250 until the end of the coinage in 1279. For the first period the evidence will be from groups of coins deposited up to twenty, but not less than six, years after the date of issue of the latest coins so considerably increasing the chances of the anomalies discussed above having had an opportunity to be ironed out by the processes of circulation. For the second, this method might appear to present serious difficulties in that, because of the early closing date of the available hoards, the output to the end of the issue in November 1278 must be calculated on the basis of six hoards which were deposited between eight and twenty-two years earlier. While the predictably few coins surviving in modern collections from the last years of the coinage[9] are little help in assessing the relative output of the two groups of mints at that time, it is clear that they were of the same order as in the earlier years of this phase. If there was a change it is likely to have been that the already tiny output of the provincial mints declined still further but a cut-back of a half for these final years would make only a few thousand pounds of difference to the total. The proportions present in the six hoards may therefore be used to represent those to the end of the coinage in 1279.

The last point to be considered before the calculations can proceed is where to draw the line which will coincide with the closure of the provincial mints in 1250, firstly in the bullion returns of the London and Canterbury mints and secondly in the sequence of the actual coins as classified by modern numismatists.[10] Since the present calculations are concerned with the output during this phase of the Long-Cross coinage as a whole the sources of the bullion and questions of how much, if any, of the obsolete Short-Cross issue remained to be recoined in 1250 are irrelevant. Although some areas of uncertainty remain, the line is fairly easy to draw. The evidence of the latest classes struck at the provincial mints and the limiting dates for their closure make it possible to equate the end of class III with the last issues of the provincial mints and also with the mint accounting period ending in July 1250 at London and Canterbury.

In Table 2 are set out the numbers and percentage representatives of both groups of mints in the first recoinage phase of the Long-Cross coinage classes I-III from the six hoards.

Totalling the individual coins of each of the two groups of mints and taking a percentage gives the result 52.3% struck at London and Canterbury and 47.7% struck at the provincial mints. These figures are however very strongly influenced by those of the Colchester hoard which accounts for 5835 out of the total of 6738 coins being considered. If, to counterbalance the influence of Colchester and give each of the hoards the same statistical weight regardless of size the percentage representations of the two groups in each hoard are added up and expressed as a percentage the result is 54.4% struck at London and Canterbury and 45.6% struck at the provincial mints. This method of calculation however gives undue weight to the very high results of 60.9% and 64.6% for London and Canterbury derived from the two smallest and statistically least reliable hoards, Palmer's Green and Coventry, containing only 46 and 48 relevant coins respectively. Whatever the reasons are for these high figures they clearly stand out as abnormal when three of the six hoards are almost identically balanced on the 50%/50% mark and Colchester is only a few points away on 52.6%/47.4%. The figure of 54.5% for London and Canterbury derived from the percentage method is therefore likely to be too high and may be safely disregarded.[11] Even the Colchester figure of 52.6% may be on the high side for while Colchester is by far the biggest hoard and ought to be statistically the most reliable, it is also the earliest and may have been deposited before the distortions of local bias etc. had had sufficient time to be 'normalized' by circulation. The mints of London and Bury were both local to Colchester and although this hoard's final element was certainly biased towards Bury this need not necessarily have been so in its earlier portion where a London bias is a possibility. In calculating the total output for this period of the Long-Cross coinage therefore it seems better to use the 52% figure obtained from the actual coins present and, in view of the possible upward influence of Colchester, to work it out also on the basis of the 50% figure derived from the percentage figures omitting Palmer's Green and Coventry. The precise amount of bullion struck into coin at London and Canterbury from November 1247 to July 1250 was £287 470 hence:

		£
52% of Long-Cross Nov. 1247-July 1250 at London and Canterbury	=	287 470
∴ 48% of Long-Cross Nov. 1247-July 1250 at the provincial mints	=	265 357
∴ Total output of Long-Cross Nov. 1247-July 1250 at all mints	=	552 827

OR

50% of Long-Cross Nov. 1247-July 1250 at London and Canterbury	=	287 470
∴ 50% of Long-Cross Nov. 1247-July 1250 at the provincial mints	=	287 470
∴ Total output of Long-Cross Nov. 1247-July 1250 at all mints	=	574 940

Turning to the second, post-recoinage, phase of the Long-Cross coinage, the numbers and percentage representatives are set out in Table 3.

TABLE 3

COINS OF LONG-CROSS CLASSES IV AND V IN HOARDS DEPOSITED 1256-c. 1270

Hoard	Date of deposition	London and Canterbury		Provincial mints	
Colchester	1256	5171	94.7%	291	5.3%
Hornchurch	1260 +	240	98.0%	5	2.0%
Palmer's Green	1262 +	154	95.1%	8	4.9%
Slype	c. 1265	760	96.8%	25	3.2%
Steppingley	c. 1270	205	95.8%	9	4.2%
Coventry	c. 1270	173	97.7%	4	2.3%
		95.2%	96.3%	4.9%	3.7%

Totalling as before the individual coins and taking a percentage gives 95.2% struck at London and Canterbury and 4.9% struck at the provincial mints. There is much greater homogeneity in the figures this time and the percentage representation in the six hoards for London and Canterbury varies only between 94.7% and 98.0% and for the provincial mints between 2.0% and 5.3%. The averages are 96.3% and 3.7%. The figure for the provincial mints in Colchester is the highest and since this hoard accounts for the overwhelming majority of the coins being considered and Bury is local to the find-spot,[12] the ratio of 95%/5% is perhaps biased in favour of the provincial mints. Also bearing in mind the possibility discussed above that the six hoards by closing early may slightly over-represent the provincial mints as they would have been in hoards ending in 1279, figures of 97%/3% may be nearer the mark. The total output for this phase of the Long-Cross coinage will therefore be calculated on the basis of both the 95%/5% and 97%/3% figures. The precise amount of bullion struck into coin at London and Canterbury between July 1250 and November 1278 was £1 096 530 hence:

		£
95% of Long-Cross July 1250-Nov. 1278 at London and Canterbury	=	1 096 530
∴ 5% of Long-Cross July 1250-Nov. 1278 at the provincial mints	=	57 712
∴ Total output of Long-Cross July 1250-Nov. 1278 at all mints	=	1 154 242

OR

97% of Long-Cross July 1250-Nov. 1278 at London and Canterbury	=	1 096 530
∴ 3% of Long-Cross July 1250-Nov. 1278 at the provincial mints	=	33 913
∴ Total output of Long-Cross July 1250-Nov. 1278 at all mints	=	1 130 443

The total amount of the Long-Cross coinage as a whole can now be calculated, based on the precise figures of the bullion in the mint accounts for London and Canterbury and the figures computed above for the provincial mints thus:

1247-50		1250-78			1247-50		1250-78		
52%/48%	&	95%/5%	=	£1 707 069	50%/50%	&	95%/5%	=	£1 729 182
52%/48%	&	97%/3%	=	£1 683 270	50%/50%	&	97%/3%	=	£1 705 383

The minimum figure for the total output is therefore £1 683 270 and the maximum figure £1 729 182.[13] The difference between the two figures is £45 912 or about 3%. If a middle figure of £1 700 000 is taken it will, on the basis of the available evidence, be correct within about ± 1.5%. Such precision cannot be claimed in absolute terms for these figures however since several factors which would have influenced the totals have not been quantifiable. Their individual effect, as has been demonstrated, is likely to have been small and in aggregate their largely complementary biases will cancel one another out. It is unlikely to be far from the truth to say that in round terms the Long-Cross coinage amounted to some one and three-quarter million pounds.

For the Long-Cross period, the bullion figures in the mint accounts could be totalled as they stood to supply the precise output at London and Canterbury and so provide a secure basis for the calculation of the amount produced in the Long-Cross coinage as a whole. The information in the mint records cannot however be used in the same straight-forward way to arrive at the total amount of Long-Cross coins restruck. The sources of the bullion reaching both mints after 1279 are identified as 'English' or 'foreign' in the accounts but since English silver continues to appear almost without a break to the end of the period when this distinction is made, it is not possible simply to equate English silver with Long-Cross coin. It is necessary to decide when the re-coinage came to an end and when the major constituent of this bullion ceased to be Long-Cross coin.

The provincial mints which had come into operation one after the other in 1280 had already closed in the summer of 1281 and had rendered their accounts by September or October of the same year. Although some people in Lincoln complained that they were left with old money for recoining after their local mint had ceased to function,[14] there is no other evidence that the provincial mints had been closed before the great majority of the old coins in local currency had been restruck. As in the Long-Cross period, the ecclesiastical privilege mints of Bury and Durham continued in operation at a low level of output but the Archbishop's mint at York which had been revived for the re-coinage, closed along with the royal provincial mints in 1281. Canterbury opened in January 1280 and within ten months had received £27 050 of English silver. The purchases of English silver decline sharply to only £2 874 in the next seven months and still further in the years following. At London the peak of English silver purchases was reached in the summer of 1280 when nearly £16 000 a month was reaching the mint. Purchases then fell off rapidly until in September 1281 they were down to a level of between £1 000 and £2 000 a month and they then decline slowly but steadily for the next decade. It therefore appears from the evidence at all mints that the bulk of the old Long-Cross coins had been restruck by September 1281. Some certainly remained to be recoined and if the figures to this date were taken as the exclusive basis for calculation they would give a result which under-estimated the amount of Long-Cross recoined and so over-estimated the amount lost to currency before 1279.

Mr. Mayhew in his calculations however regarded all the English silver received at the mints up to July 1290 as deriving from Long-Cross coins.[15] Very large sums in English silver were purchased by the mints between September 1281 and July 1290: £7,050 at Canterbury and £89 920, or c. £70 000 if the Brabantine silver included with the English in the account of 1285-6 is omitted,[16] at London. When these sums are compared with the total English purchases from the beginning of the recoinage to July 1290, £39 767 at Canterbury and c. £368 000 (£388 325 uncorrected) at London, the figure for 1281-90 represents about 18% of the total in each case. On this basis 18% of the Long-Cross coins current in 1279 were not restruck until after 1281, a year after they had been demonetized. This seems a surprisingly high amount but independent evidence against which to check it is difficult to find. The sources of silver are not differentiated in the accounts for the Long-Cross period and so it is not possible to say how much if any of the large quantities of bullion struck at London and Canterbury following the closure of the recoinage mints in 1250 was from old Short-Cross coins. Hoards are of very little use since the old money would have been discriminated against for this purpose during the recoinage period but for what it is worth the few early sterling hoards known do not contain Long-Cross coins.[17] The next comprehensive recoinage did not take place until 1696 but despite the distance in time the conditions, in so far as they influence the matters under discussion, were not dissimilar. A total of £6 831 510 was produced between 1696 and 1698 but from then until 1701 'when the Great Recoinage was entirely over' only a further £191 521 was struck.[18] This latter amount represents about 3% of the total recoinage. Even allowing for possible variations in the circumstances of the two recoinages, it would therefore appear that to suggest that 18% of the currency in 1279 still had to be restruck after 1281 is likely to be an over-estimate. If however the recoinage had stopped before 1290, it is necessary to offer some explanation for the large amounts of English silver still reaching the mints in the later '80s. Sheet silver made from melted cullings, clippings and illegally imported foreign coins no doubt could account for some of it and the reduced mint charges after February 1281 which brought so much foreign silver to the mints may also have tempted Englishmen to take along their hoarded bullion to be converted into the more useful and negotiable coin. This trend would have been strengthened by the growing reputation of the new currency and the fact that merchants who were having difficulty in getting enough silver to convert into coin for commercial purposes were probably willing to pay a good price for plate. The close connection between plate and coin and the ease with which the one could be converted into the other are important aspects of the problem but difficult to assess. The national stock of coin was not the same as the national stock of bullion and it would be interesting to know if historians can provide information about the private holdings of bullion in the form of sheet silver or domestic plate at this period. The figures for English silver purchased at London pick up again after 1291, that is even before the recoinage of Continental sterlings began in 1299. At so late a date <u>this</u> silver can hardly be old Long-Cross coins so perhaps a comparable amount of two or three hundred pounds per annum or, if the arguments above are valid, considerably more of the English silver was not composed of Long-Cross coins.

All these explanations are speculative and so it appears to be impossible to reach a definite conclusion about when the recoinage of Long-Cross issues came to an end: September 1281 is too early and yet July 1290 seems rather late. There must in any case have been some English silver from sources other than coin struck even during the recoinage phase and also some overlap is inevitable in its final stages. The total amount of Long-Cross coins recoined after 1279 will therefore be calculated using the output to September 1281 and the output to July 1290 in the belief that the true figure will lie somewhere within those limits.

It is then necessary as before to determine which of the classes[19] of the actual coins coincide with the closures of the two mint-accounting periods being used. Since the last of the coins struck at the provincial mints belong to late class III the output to September 1281 can be equated with classes I-III. Drawing a line to denote the issues to July 1290 is more difficult but

TABLE 4

HOARDS CLOSING IN CLASS V c. 1290

Hoard	Date of discovery	Number of English coins	Reference
Skegby (Lincs.)	1967	406	BNJ XL (1971), 44-56.
Broughton (Hants.)	1964	255	BNJ XXXV (1966), 120-7.
Coventry (Warks.)	1937	123	BNJ XXIII (1940), 279-80.
King's Lynn (Norfolk)	1972	29	CH I (1975), 93, No. 363.

TABLE 5

COINS OF STERLING CLASSES I-III AND I-V IN HOARDS DEPOSITED *c*. 1290

Hoard	Classes I-III				Classes I-V			
	London and Canterbury		Provincial Mints		London and Canterbury		Provincial Mints	
Skegby	213	61.6%	133	38.4%	267	65.8%	139	34.2%
Broughton	93	58.5%	66	41.5%	186	72.9%	69	27.1%
Coventry	51	63.8%	29	36.2%	93	76.0%	30	24.0%
King's Lynn	9	50.0%	9	50.0%	19	65.5%	10	34.5%
	61%	58%	39%	41%	70%	70%	30%	30%

if class V did continue a little beyond that date its issue was a comparatively small one and the inclusion of the coins of its latest phase will not seriously distort the results.

There are no suitable hoards closing in class III which can be used as the basis of calculation but there are four well documented hoards closing in class V which at first sight appear to be ideal for this purpose. Their details are set out in Tables 4 and 5. These results appear fairly consistent and homogeneous but they should be compared with those obtained from the representatives of classes I-III and I-V in a number of later hoards set out in Tables 6 and 7. Since the present investigations concern only the earlier parts of these hoards the Renfrew and Bootham hoards may safely be used despite the fact that their overall representations are in some respects anomalous.

In the four hoards deposited c. 1290 the percentage representatives for London and Canterbury both in classes I-III and in classes I-V are considerably lower than the corresponding figures derived from the hoards concealed in the early fourteenth century. It might have been expected that a method which requires using hoards down to and including their closing class would be open to bias in that coins from distant mints would not have had time to establish themselves fully in currency but it also appears that even by 1290 the classes struck before 1281 had not yet become fully integrated. Turning to the hoards deposited in the early fourteenth century, differential wastage between earlier and later classes is not a relevant factor in classes I-III because loss would be directly proportional to the numbers of coins of each of the two groups of mints in circulation. Once normal representation had been achieved, the proportional relationship between the two groups would remain constant. (There would be a slight bias present because all the mints did not start striking at the same date, but the influence of this on the figures would be minimal.) In classes I-V however, the majority of the coins from the provincial mints having been struck in the earlier period up to 1281, there will be a slight bias in the results which will marginally under-represent the provincial mints. This bias must be relatively small and certainly would not account for the difference of some 6-9% between the two sets of figures. Although there are difficulties in using either group of hoards the dangers of bias are greater with those deposited in c. 1290 and therefore the later group of hoards will be used for the main body of the calculations.

Even within this group there are anomalies. The 'Scottish' hoard is so far outside the range of the figures derived from the other hoards that it may be discounted. Whittonstall too is abnormal in the high representation of the provincial mints. This hoard is overall heavily biased in favour of its local mint of Durham and is also one of the earlier hoards in the group so its evidence may also be discounted for the present purpose. Most of the available hoards for the Edwardian period come from Scotland and the north of England where there might possibly, but not necessarily, be a bias in favour of the northern mints of Durham and York. It is significant that the two hoards from outside that area, Neath and especially Boyton, give a high figure for the London and Canterbury group in classes I-V. In view of these

TABLE 6

LATER STERLING HOARDS

Hoard	Date of discovery	Date of deposition	Number of relevant English coins	Reference
Middridge (Co. Durham)	1974	1310 +	2 187	CH II (1976), 115, No. 453.
Whittonstall (Co. Durham)	1958	c. 1311	263	Arch. Ael. 1963, 65-83.
Boyton (Wilts.)	1935	c. 1324	771	NC 1936, 115-55.
Neath (W. Glam.) 2 hoards	1956	c. 1326	36	BNJ XXVIII (1956-7) 294-9 and 555-9.
Knaresborough (N. Yorks.)	1805	c. 1328	196	BNJ XXXII (1963), 117-26.
Loch Doon (Kirkcudbright.)	1966	early 1330s	368	BNJ XXXVIII (1969), 31-49.
Renfrew	1963	c. 1321	376	BNJ XXXV (1966), 128-47
'Scottish'	? 19th century	c. 1345	160	BNJ XXVIII (1955), 196-201.
Bootham (York)	1953	1325 +	385	BNJ XXVII (1954), 281-93.

TABLE 7

COINS OF STERLING CLASSES I-III AND I-V IN EARLY 14th CENTURY HOARDS

Hoard	Classes I-III London and Canterbury		Classes I-III Provincial Mints		Classes I-V London and Canterbury		Classes I-V Provincial Mints	
Middridge	905	63.1%	503	36.9%	1 624	74.3%	563	25.7%
Whittonstall	92	57.9%	67	42.1%	187	71.1%	76	28.9%
Boyton	298	66.1%	153	33.9%	608	78.9%	163	21.1%
Neath	13	68.4%	6	31.6%	30	83.3%	6	16.7%
Knaresborough	85	69.7%	37	30.3%	156	79.6%	40	20.4%
Loch Doon	142	67.0%	70	33.0%	289	78.5%	79	21.5%
Renfrew	163	64.7%	89	35.3%	279	74.2%	97	25.8%
'Scottish'	81	89.0%	10	11.0%	150	93.8%	10	6.2%
Bootham	168	68.0%	79	32.0%	295	76.6%	90	23.4%
	65%	68%	35%	32%	76%	79%	24%	21%
Omitting Wh'stall & 'Scottish'	65%	67%	35%	33%	76%	78%	24%	22%

figures the calculations will include those based on an 80%/20% ratio. To save overburdening this paper still further with arithmetic, the method will be demonstrated for the classes I-V, 1290 figures, 76%/24% and the results for the other ratios and for the class III, 1281 figures, will be given at the end.

		£
76% of classes I-V, output to July 1290 at London and Canterbury	=	891 218
∴24% of classes II-V, output to July 1290 at the provincial mints	=	281 437
∴100% of classes I-V, output to July 1290 at all mints	=	1 172 655

The above figures however take no account of any possible foreign silver which may have been coined at the provincial mints, and are valid only if no foreign silver was coined there. If it was, then the figure for the output at the provincial mints from English silver i.e. old Long-Cross coins will be over-represented in the above figures. It is impossible to know whether the proportion of foreign silver coined at the provincial mints was the same as at London and Canterbury together. Since Canterbury coined an increasing proportion of foreign silver after 1281 the London plus Canterbury ratio of foreign silver to English must represent the maximum likely ratio for foreign silver at the provincial mints and once again the true figure must lie somewhere between this and the uncorrected figure above. About 20% of the output at London and Canterbury to 1290 was from foreign silver. Using this figure for the proportion of foreign silver coined at the provincial mints gives a total of £56 287 which must be subtracted from their total output to obtain the amount of Long-Cross coin restruck.

Another factor not so far considered is the currency of Anglo-Irish and Scottish coins in England during the Long-Cross period. These coins were struck to the same standard as the issues from English mints and circulated freely. There were between 6 and 7% of Scottish and Anglo-Irish coins in the Colchester hoard deposited in 1256. Since however the bulk of these coins were struck during the early Long-Cross period their proportional representation in English hoards must decline steadily towards the end of the coinage. A maximum figure of 5% for their combined presence in the English currency of 1279 is therefore probably nearer the mark. A sum of £35 476 must be subtracted from the total output from English silver to obtain the amount of Long-Cross coins restruck.

There are still several factors which influence the figures which remain to be considered. The output from English silver has been set against the representation of pennies in the hoards but no account has been taken of the groats, halfpence and farthings also produced from this silver. The groats were produced only at London but the amount is not differentiated in the mint accounts where they are included with the pence. Although therefore there is no documentary evidence for the scale of production it does not appear from surviving specimens that it can have been other than a small proportion of the total amount recorded for 'pence'. Their influence on the results is likely to be insignificant. For the halfpennies and farthings struck at London the mint accounts do give exact figures. While neither of the lower denominations were struck at Canterbury both halfpence and farthings were produced at provincial mints. Because hoarders generally prefer the highest denomination available to them, halfpence and farthings are rarely found in any quantity in hoards and therefore it is not possible to provide figures of the ratio of production at the two groups of mints. If however it is assumed to have been in proportion to the output of pence this is unlikely to be far wrong. Even if it was not, the influence of such a bias on the final figures will be very small.

The total amount of Long-Cross lost to currency before 1279 can now be computed thus:

<u>No foreign silver at provincial mints</u>

Total recoinage classes at all mints to 1290	= £1 172 655
Less foreign silver struck at London and Canterbury only	= £ 463 126
	£ 709 529
Less Anglo-Irish and Scottish Long-Cross	= £ 35 476
Total Long-Cross coins restruck at all mints	= £ 674 053

Total Long-Cross output at all mints	= £1 707 069
Less total Long-Cross coins restruck at all mints	= £ 674 053
Total Long-Cross coins lost from currency to 1279	= £1 033 016

The amount of Long-Cross coins lost to currency to 1279 computed on the basis of this and the other ratios discussed are as follows:

<u>Computation based on Classes I-V, Bullion Output to July 1290</u>

No foreign silver at the provincial mints, 76%/24%	£1 033 016
No foreign silver at the provincial mints, 80%/20%	£1 153 582
20% foreign silver at the provincial mints, 76%/24%	£1 086 489
20% foreign silver at the provincial mints, 80%/20%	£1 153 162

For comparison the following are the results using the 70%/30% ratio obtained from the four hoards which close in 1290 and which were suggested above to be much less reliable.

No foreign silver at the provincial mints, 70%/30%	£ 883 574
20% foreign silver at the provincial mints, 70%/30%	£ 956 145

<u>Computation based on Classes I-III, Bullion Output to September 1281</u>

No foreign silver at the provincial mints, 65%/35%	£1 226 054
20% foreign silver at the provincial mints, 65%/35%	£1 245 934

All the above figures are based on the total output of £1 707 069 for the Long-Cross coinage which was the nearest to the middle figure between the extremes of £1 688 270 and £1 729 182 obtained from other methods. The 55%/45% ratio for the Long-Cross output which was considered less reliable above would give a total output for the Long-Cross of £1 653 115. Using the extremes of these other figures would mean subtracting £43 958 from all the above totals or adding £22 113 to them.

The lowest of these figures then becomes £839 616 and the highest £1 268 047. If the 70%/30% figures are ignored because they are likely to under-represent the London and Canterbury group then the limits become £989 058 and £1 268 047. If the class I-III figures are thought to exclude appreciable quantities of the total amount of Long-Cross restruck, the upper limit will be somewhere between the classes I-V upper limit of £1 175 695 and £1 248 167. The object of all this exact computation is not to suggest a precise figure for the amount of Long-Cross coins lost to currency before 1279 but to demonstrate that however it is calculated, and making all the allowances that the evidence permits, the total is assessible within fairly narrow limits. It cannot be less than about a million pounds and is probably about another £100 000 more. The meaning of this colossal sum is beyond the scope of this paper but in considering the scale of the loss it should be borne in mind how quickly coins disappeared at other periods. Pepys for example records that when the Commonwealth issues came to be recoined after 1660 no less than a third had vanished and that after a maximum of only eleven years in circulation.

NOTES

1. For the Long-Cross coinage to November 1272: C. E. Blunt and J. D. Brand, Mint output of Henry III, BNJ XXXIX (1970), 61-6. For the Long-Cross coinage November 1272-November 1278 and for the sterling coinage after 1279: C. G. Crump and C. Johnson, Tables of bullion coined under Edward I, II and III, NC 1913, 200-45; see also Mavis Mate, Monetary policies in England 1272-1307, BNJ XLI (1972), Appendix, 75-9.

2. This was the method adopted by N. J. Mayhew in his pioneer paper, Numismatic evidence and falling prices in the fourteenth century, *Econ. Hist. Rev.* 2nd ser. XXVII (1974), 1-15. These figures have been corrected to include the £177 724 of foreign silver struck at Canterbury which Mr. Mayhew realized later had been omitted from his calculation. His correction appears as note 2, BNJ XLIV (1974), 69.

3. For the sake of clarity all the mints in operation other than London and Canterbury are referred to throughout this paper as the 'provincial mints' although a distinction ought more properly to be made between the royal provincial mints and the ecclesiastical privilege mints of Bury St. Edmunds and Durham.

4. For this and other aspects of hoard-interpretation see J. P. C. Kent, Interpreting coin finds, and M. M. Archibald, English medieval coins as dating evidence, in *Coins and the Archaeologist*, ed. J. Casey and R. Reece, *British Archaeological Reports*, 4 1974, 184-200 and 234-71.

5. A possible instance of such local bias is discussed by M. M. Archibald, The Skegby, Notts., 1967 hoard, BNJ, XL (1971), 44-56. For the distorting effect of a more general 'savings' element in a later hoard

see P. Woodhead and I. Stewart, The Renfrew treasure trove, 1963, BNJ XXXV (1966), 128-54.

6. The Brussels hoard was found in 1908 and contained about 150 000 coins of which about 80 000 were British. The hoard was deposited c. 1265. It has never been published in full but for details of the background to discovery and sale of the contents see B. H. I. H. Stewart, The Brussels hoard: Mr. Baldwin's arrangement of the Scottish coins, BNJ XXIX (1958), 91-7.

7. L. A. Lawrence, The Long-Cross Coinage of Henry III and Edward I, BNJ X (1914), 57-60.

8. During the 1260s London became predominant and Canterbury dwindled until it closed in June 1274, to re-open briefly in April 1278 for the production of only £803 in the final seven months of the coinage.

9. Coins struck late in a coinage had less time in circulation to be lost or hoarded than earlier issues. Even those which had been hoarded had a greater chance of being recovered by their original owners wishing to convert them into the new money. Hoards from the last years of a coinage are rare except where there are abnormal economic or political reasons to account for them. Although hoards of Long-Cross are not uncommon, none concealed in the period 1270-79 can be produced for the present purpose.

10. These classes were created by modern numismatists and the details by which they are identified were not necessarily of significance to the mint or exchequer officials in the thirteenth century. While it is possible to date some classes narrowly, others can be dated only within fairly broad limits. The classification used today is that by L. A. Lawrence, The Long-Cross coinage, BNJ IX (1912), 145-79, X (1913), 69-93 and XI (1914), 101-19.

11. Results based on these percentage representations will however be given for comparison when the figures for the total output are computed later.

12. It will be seen later that in the post-recoinage phase of the Long-Cross coinage this hoard displays a possible bias towards the local mint of Bury. What is certain however is that the final portion of the hoard added to it at least twelve years after the close of the first portion being used for these calculations, was comprised solely of coins of the Bury mint: as they were recovered, 1918 die-duplicate coins of class VI.

13. On the basis of the 55%/45% ratio considered above to be less satisfactory the result for the total output of the Long-Cross coinage is £1 653 115 - the lowest figure of all.

14. Mavis Mate, Monetary policies in England, BNJ XLI (1972), 54.

15. op. cit. in note 2.

16. Between May 1285 and August 1286 £29 106 of English silver was received at the London mint but the accounts record that the Brabantine silver is included with the English. When it is noted that the receipts of English silver at this time are descending in a steady line and that the average monthly output during the previous accounting period had been £597 and in the following one £471 about £20 000 of the 1285-6 figure is likely to have been Brabantine. If this £20 000 is subtracted it would give a monthly average for the period of £607.

17. A few stray Long-Cross coins do occasionally turn up in sterling-period hoards e.g. in Bootham.

18. Sir John Craig, The Mint, 193.

19. H. B. Earl Fox and J. Shirley-Fox, Numismatic history of the reigns of Edward I, II and III, BNJ VI-X (1910-14).

www.ingramcontent.com/pod-product-compliance
Lightning Source LLC
LaVergne TN
LVHW071210210926
848482LV00015B/768